TinkerActive
WORKBOOKS

SECOND GRADE · MATH · AGES 7–8

by Enil Sidat

illustrated by Les McClaine

educational consulting by Lindsay Frevert

Odd Dot · New York

Place Value

Count by tens and write the missing labels on the bags.

Count by hundreds and write the missing labels on the crates.

Write the correct digit in each place on the shelf.

hundreds	tens	ones

356 NAILS

hundreds	tens	ones

687 WASHERS

hundreds	tens	ones

299 NUTS

hundreds	tens	ones

100 SCREWS

hundreds	tens	ones

10 WRENCHES

hundreds	tens	ones

1 HAMMER

Write the total amount of gears.

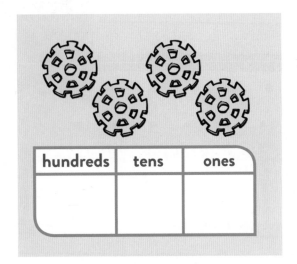

hundreds	tens	ones

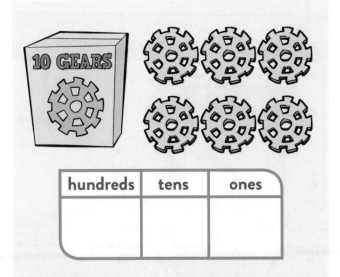

hundreds	tens	ones

hundreds	tens	ones

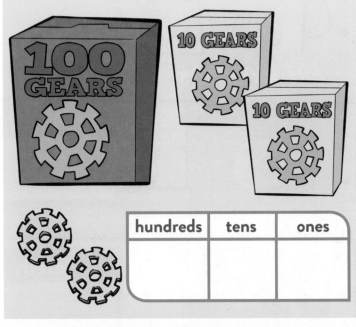

hundreds	tens	ones

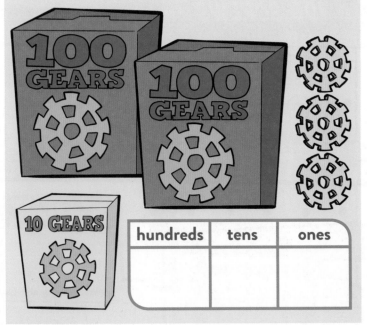

hundreds	tens	ones

Read the place values aloud. Then write the number.

MATH
1

Place Value

3 IN THE TENS PLACE

5 IN THE ONES PLACE

4 IN THE HUNDREDS PLACE

8 IN THE HUNDREDS PLACE

7 IN THE TENS PLACE

0 IN THE ONES PLACE

4 IN THE ONES PLACE

0 IN THE TENS PLACE

1 IN THE HUNDREDS PLACE

1 IN THE TENS PLACE

6 IN THE HUNDREDS PLACE

5 IN THE ONES PLACE

Write an A on Amelia's car. She's on a space with a 7 in the tens place.

Draw flames on Brian's car. He is on a space with an 8 in the hundreds place.

		20	30	40	50
10					
110	120	130	140	150
210	220	230	240	250
310		330	340	350
	320			
410	420	430	440	450
510	520	530	540	550
610	620	630		650
			640	
710	720	730	740	750
810	820	830	840	850
910	920	930	940	950

Draw an oil spill in the space behind Callie's car. She is on a space with a 2 in the tens place.

Dimitri swerved to miss a turtle! He's on a space with a 4 in the tens place. Draw a turtle on the space in front of him.

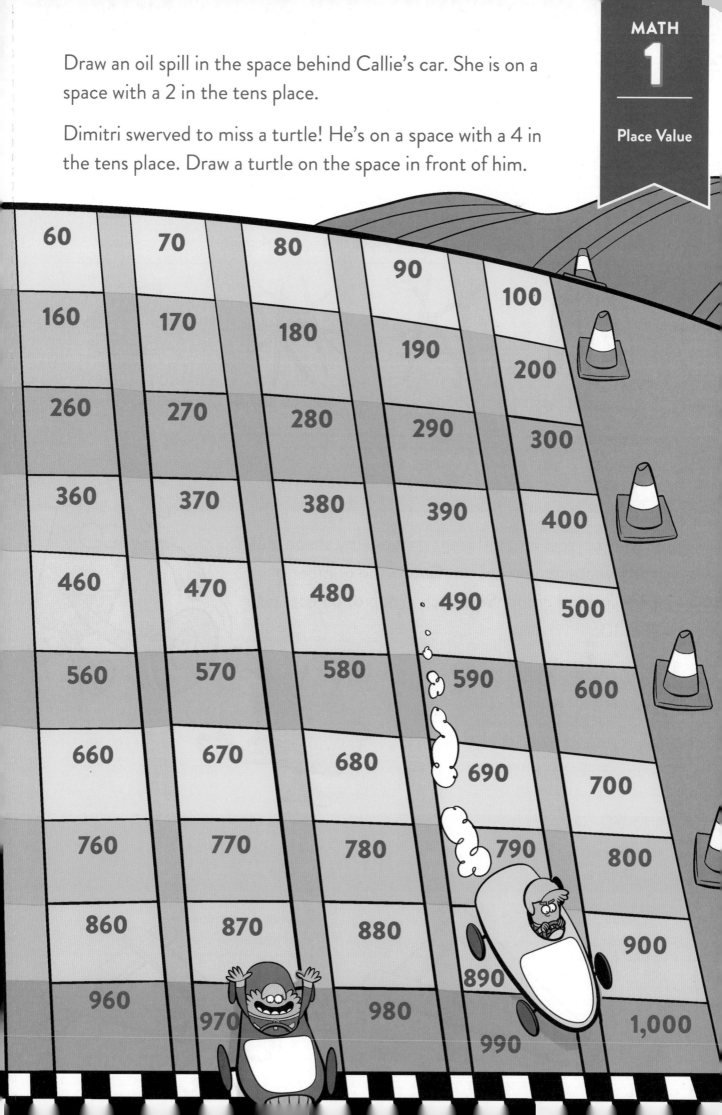

LET'S START!

GATHER THESE TOOLS AND MATERIALS.

 4 bottle caps

 4 buttons

 15 paper clips

 4 coins

 Glue

 10 craft sticks

15 straws

 20 toothpicks

 30 pieces of dried tube pasta

LET'S TINKER!

Put your objects into different groups—by shape, color, size, or whatever you decide. **Count** the number of objects in each group. **Sort** each group of objects into sets of 10.

How many groups of ten can you make? How many objects are left over?

Put all your sets of 10 together. Do you make it to 100?

LET'S MAKE: CRAFT STICK RACER!

1. Glue 3 craft sticks together to form a frame.

2. Glue 2 segments of a straw to the frame.

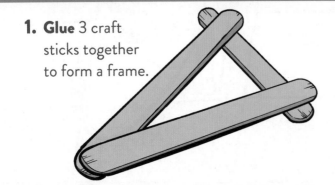

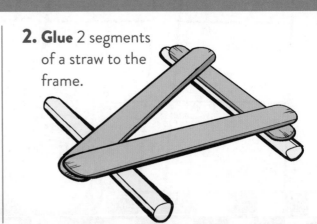

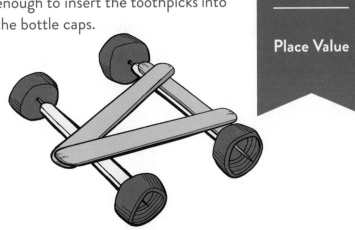

3. Place a toothpick through each straw. (If necessary, you can tape toothpicks together to make them longer.)

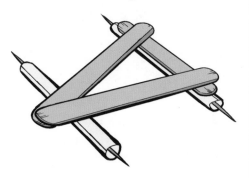

4. With an adult's help, **poke** a hole big enough to insert the toothpicks into the bottle caps.

Test your racer. Can it roll for 10 seconds? 20 seconds? For how many groups of 10 seconds can you get it to roll?

LET'S ENGINEER!

Last year, Enid raced in the MotMot Grand Prix and came in second place. This year, she's determined to win.

How can Enid modify her racer so she can go faster and come in first place?

Set a starting line and a finish line. **Get** your racer from the Let's Make activity and time how long it takes to get from start to finish before making any changes to the racer. Now **look** at your materials and think about how you built your racer—what changes might make a faster racer?

Modify your racer to make it go faster. **Time** your racer again. Was it faster? Slower? If so, why?

PROJECT 1: DONE!
Get your sticker!

Skip Counting to 1,000

Skip the stones by following the instructions below.

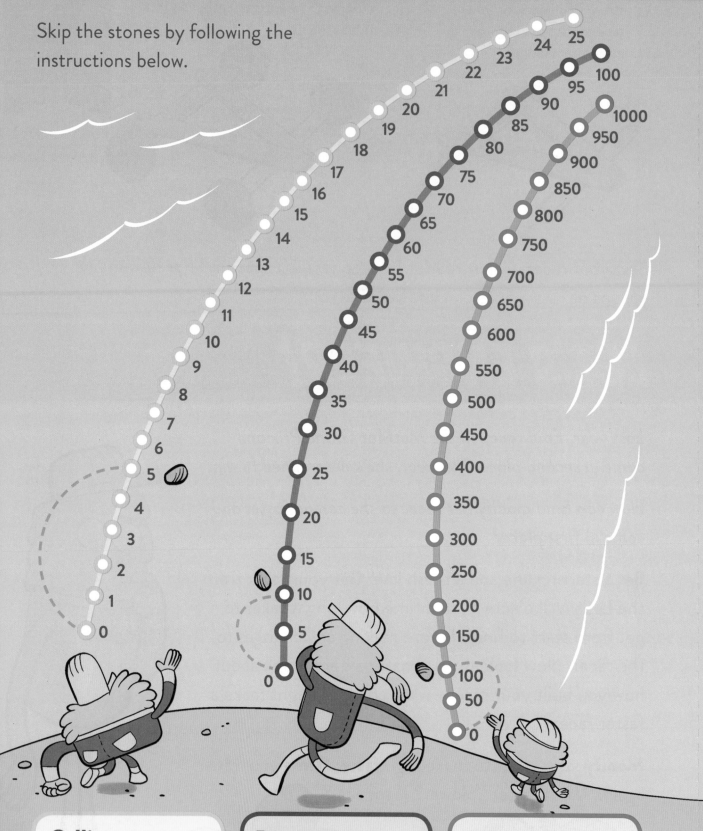

Callie wants to skip her stone by **fives**. Draw how her stone bounces.

Dimitri wants to skip his stone by **tens**. Draw how his stone bounces.

Enid wants to skip her stone by **hundreds**. Draw how her stone bounces.

Frank has a remote control stone that skips forever. Count by
fives and fill in the missing numbers where the stone bounces.

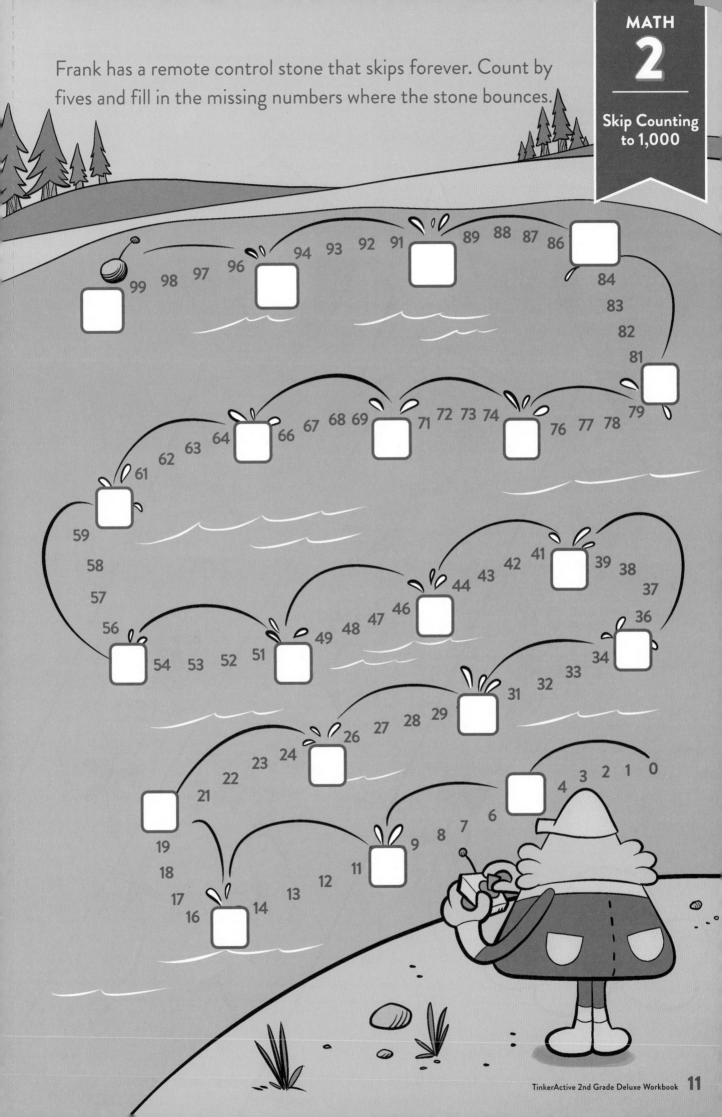

Write the next number in the pattern. Read each answer aloud.

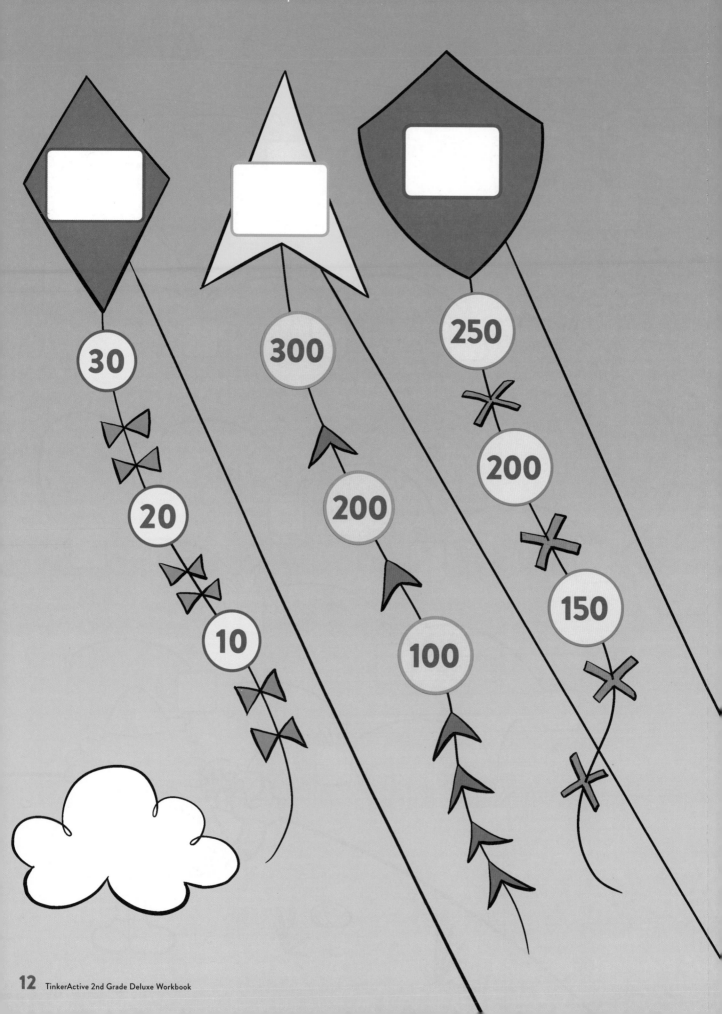

30
20
10

300
200
100

250
200
150

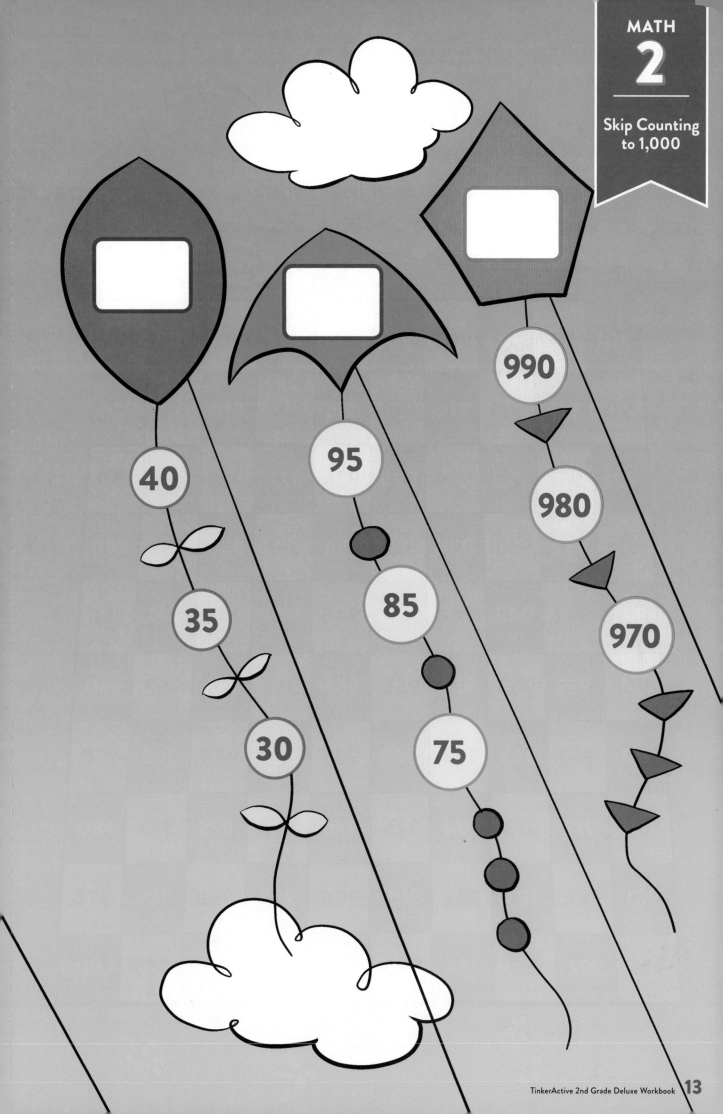

40

35

30

95

85

75

990

980

970

Starting at 905, count by fives aloud and draw a circle around each number you say.

Next, starting at 910, count by tens aloud and draw a square around each number you say.

Last, starting at 950, count by fifties aloud and draw a triangle around each number you say.

901	902	903	904	905	906	907	908	909	910
911	912	913	914	915	916	917	918	919	920
921	922	923	924	925	926	927	928	929	930
931	932	933	934	935	936	937	938	939	940
941	942	943	944	945	946	947	948	949	950
951	952	953	954	955	956	957	958	959	960
961	962	963	964	965	966	967	968	969	970
971	972	973	974	975	976	977	978	979	980
981	982	983	984	985	986	987	988	989	990
991	992	993	994	995	996	997	998	999	1,000

Put your fingers on 50, 100, and 150. Then count by fifties and move a finger to the next number. (Hint: Your next move is to put a finger on 200.) Try to keep two fingers on the page at all times and skip count to 1,000.

30 small stones

30 pennies

40 pieces of dried beans, pasta, cereal, or nuts

Rice

Permanent markers

3 empty plastic bottles

3 balloons

LET'S TINKER!

Sort the stones, pennies, dried beans, and rice grains into groups of 10.

Line up each group at the edge of a sink full of water and flick each object so it skips. Do all your materials skip? What if you position them differently? How many skips can you make with each type of object?

LET'S MAKE: MOTMOT RAFT!

1. Ask an adult to cut a plastic bottle into the shape below.

2. **Decorate** your raft using the markers.
(MotMots love to put their faces on
everything.)

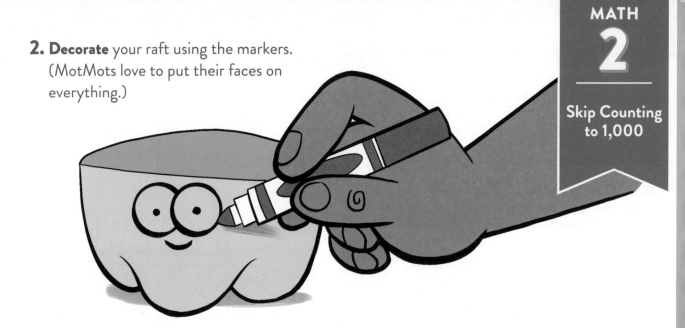

3. **Put** your raft into a sink full of water and place objects in the raft. How many
groups of 10 objects can you fill your raft with before it sinks?

LET'S ENGINEER!

The MotMots want to put more objects into the raft—way more!
100! But they don't want to spend all day counting up to 100.

How can the MotMots quickly count 100 objects? And will the raft
still float?

Find a way to count 100 objects quickly. **Test** your raft with groups
of 10—how many can you fit into your raft before it sinks?

Now **modify** the raft so it holds more objects. How many objects
can your raft carry?

PROJECT 2: DONE!
Get your sticker!

Comparing Numbers

Dimitri and Enid made a game called Less Than, Greater Than, Mot, Mot, Mot! Play it by yourself, or with a friend. Follow the directions, and when you reach each item, shout "MOT! MOT! MOT!"

Look around you. Can you touch something **SOFT** by taking less than three steps? Race to it and shout, "MOT, MOT, MOT!"

Now touch something **SHINY** in less than 2 hops.

Can you touch something **STRIPED** in greater than 9 skips?

Touch something **BIGGER** than you in less than 5 backward steps.

Can you touch something **BLUE** in greater than 12 side steps?

Read each word problem. Then fill in the sentences and circle the >, <, or =.

Brian and Callie went to the cheese shop. Callie put 13 wedge-shaped cheeses into her basket. Brian took 20 wedges.

| Brian has ____ wedges of cheese. | **>** **<** **=** | Callie has ____ wedges of cheese. |

Next, Brian saw a carton of 300 gooey cheeses. It smelled like feet, so he gave it to Callie. He took 125 gooey cheeses for himself.

| Brian has ____ gooey cheeses. | **>** **<** **=** | Callie has ____ gooey cheeses. |

Then Callie added her favorite pouch of 50 mini wheels to her basket. And Brian picked up 50 mini wheels.

| Brian has ____ mini wheels. | **>** **<** **=** | Callie has ____ mini wheels. |

At the last moment, Callie went back and got 3 bags of shredded cheese. Brian doesn't like shredded cheese, so he didn't get any.

| Brian has ____ bags of shredded cheese. | **>** **<** **=** | Callie has ____ bags of shredded cheese. |

Frank's pet alligator is hungry! Which containers have more food?

Compare the number on each container. Then write **>**, **<**, or **=** in each space.

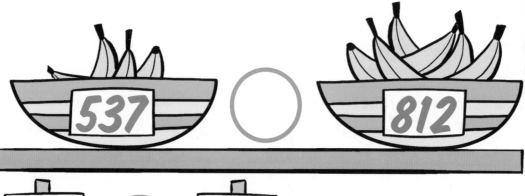

537 ◯ 812

981 ◯ 981

619 ◯ 632

501 ◯ 491

113 ◯ 113

Solve each problem.

Brian has **342** raisins. Amelia has **212**. Who has more? Write the comparison as a number sentence.

[ ]
____ ____

Callie has **102** sunflower seeds, and Frank has **931** sunflower seeds. Who has more? Write the comparison as a number sentence.

[ ]
____ ____

Enid has **113** raisins. Dimitri has **212** raisins. Who has more? Write the comparison as a number sentence.

[ ]
____ ____

Compare Amelia and Dimitri. Who has more raisins? Write the comparison as a number sentence.

[ ]
____ ____

Compare the number of chairs in your house to the number of doors. Which is more?

Color the squares according to the key to reveal Frank's favorite animal.

89	64	29	42	83	73	6	30	84	43	49	72	13	23	12	50
21	27	125	131	14	71	63	22	61	58	176	101	85	155	101	40
34	141	160	28	41	103	170	101	156	74	180	100	177	164		35
72	101	150	70	126	182	178	149	136	161	171	165	179		20	11
86	134	142	151	173	137	127	162	167	172	148	135		87	75	67
15	76	152	168	129	157	174	175	158	133	169	185				10
68	78	54	159	104	138	101	154	108	139	109	186	163	146	105	9
53	77	47	88	145	153	65	69	38	142	156	48	18	8	33	66
37	59	39	81	101	143	87	4	31	132	187	51	32	17	1	36
97	7	46	26	60	88	25	5	25	52	44	82	24	16	3	19

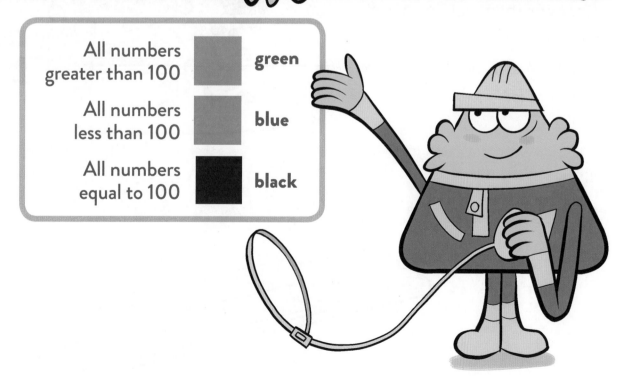

All numbers greater than 100	green
All numbers less than 100	blue
All numbers equal to 100	black

LET'S START!

2 paper cups

10–50 small food items like: pieces of cereal, baby carrots, nuts, etc.

10–50 small items like: coins, buttons, hairpins, etc.

6 craft sticks

Glue

1 toilet paper roll

Tape

LET'S TINKER!

Fill a cup with your food items. **Fill** another cup with your other small items. Which cup is holding more items?

Before counting, **look** inside, hold one cup in each hand, and use different ways to investigate. Then **take** a guess. Which has more? Are they equal?

Last, **pour** them out and count. Were you right? If so, why do you think that is? If not, why do you think that is?

LET'S MAKE: MINI SEESAW!

1. Glue the craft sticks together to form a long platform like so:

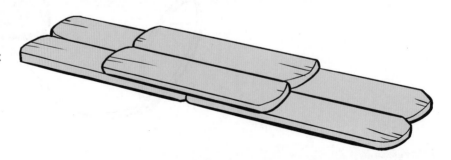

2. Glue the platform to the middle of the toilet paper roll.

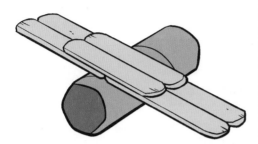

3. Glue a cup to each side of the platform.

4. Tape both ends of the toilet paper roll to the table.

5. Make two groups of random items. First **guess** which group will weigh more. Then **test** it with your seesaw. Does your seesaw stay level? Why or why not?

LET'S ENGINEER!

It's snack time! Brian and Callie are chomping on carrots. Brian got 20 carrots and Callie got only 10 carrots. But everyone should get the same amount of snacks.

How can Brian and Callie make their snacks equal?

Put 20 snacks in one cup on the seesaw and 10 snacks in the other. How can you make the groups equal?

PROJECT 3: DONE!
Get your sticker!

Even & Odd

Callie and Brian are making chocolate bars. Color the squares in the chocolate mold to represent each number. Then circle whether the number is even or odd.

6 — Odd / (Even)

5 — Odd / Even

11 — Odd / Even

10 — Odd / Even

12 — Odd / Even

9 — Odd / Even

Follow the directions to reveal Brian's favorite filling for chocolates.

Color the squares with even numbers between 10 and 30 **red**.
Color the squares with odd numbers between 30 and 50 **green**.
Color the squares with even numbers between 51 and 60 **black**.

19	34	55	11	23	38	57	35	47	31
17	59	34	36	52	56	49	33	41	25
23	36	15	40	58	37	43	45	36	44
13	21	42	29	54	23	46	32	17	11
55	25	19	12	24	26	18	21	15	40
17	15	16	20	28	17	22	14	19	57
59	44	26	16	12	20	34	22	25	29
36	32	24	18	14	26	38	28	34	42
11	53	14	20	24	16	18	12	13	53
42	21	48	22	26	18	18	38	32	15

A number whose last digit is 0, 2, 4, 6, or 8 is even. All other numbers are odd.

Look at the chocolates and write the matching number sentence.
Then solve the problem and circle whether the answer is even or odd.

$\underline{4}$ + $\underline{4}$ = $\underline{8}$ (Even) / Odd

__ + __ + __ = __   Even / Odd

__ + __ + __ + __ = __   Even / Odd

__ + __ + __ + __ + __ + __ = __   Even / Odd

Draw a line from each number sentence to its array. Then find the total and circle whether the answer is odd or even.

4 + 4 + 4 = _____

Even / Odd

3 + 3 + 3 = _____

Even / Odd

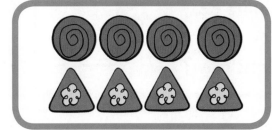

4 + 4 + 4 + 4 = _____

Even / Odd

2 + 2 + 2 = _____

Even / Odd

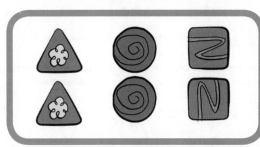

4 + 4 = _____

Even / Odd

Answer each question and circle whether the answer is even or odd. Then draw a chocolate animal sculpture on the next page according to your answer.

		Even	Odd
How many months till your birthday?			
How many chairs do you see right now?			
What is your age plus 7?			
How many steps are between your kitchen and the bathroom?			
What is the number of kids in your class plus 4?			
How many red objects can you count around you now?			

LET'S START!

5 handfuls of semisweet chocolate chips

1 cup milk

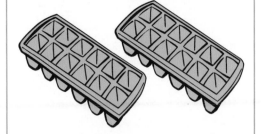

2 cups plain yogurt

Measuring cup

Mixing bowl and spoon

2 ice cube trays

40 craft sticks

LET'S TINKER!

Grab a handful of chocolate chips. **Count** how many you can hold. Is it an even or odd number?

Now **arrange** the chocolate chips in groups of two to check!

LET'S MAKE: ICE POPS!

1. With the help of an adult, **mix** 1 cup yogurt with $\frac{1}{2}$ cup milk.

2. Melt 2 handfuls of chocolate chips in the microwave.

3. Combine the melted chocolate into the yogurt-milk mixture.

4. Pour the mixture into an ice cube tray.

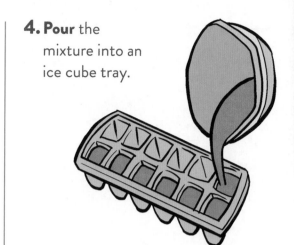

5. Poke craft sticks into each compartment. **Freeze** for at least 6 hours.

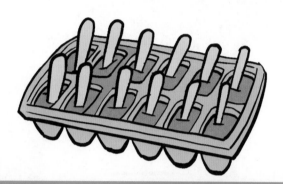

LET'S ENGINEER!

Frank likes chocolate ice pops. But he likes chocolate-chip chocolate ice pops even better. He has some leftover chocolate chips and wants to drop them into his pops evenly.

How can Frank make sure he puts the same amount of chocolate chips in each ice pop?

Follow the directions for ice pops again. Before you put the tray in the freezer, **drop** the same amount of leftover chocolate chips in each ice pop. Did you drop an even amount or an odd amount of chocolate chips into each one?

PROJECT 4: DONE!
Get your sticker!

Addition & Subtraction

You can solve a subtraction problem by thinking of the related addition problem.

Solve each set of problems.

$$\begin{array}{r} 7 \\ -\ 3 \\ \hline \boxed{} \end{array}$$

$$\begin{array}{r} 3 \\ +\ \boxed{} \\ \hline 7 \end{array}$$

$$\begin{array}{r} 14 \\ -\ 6 \\ \hline \boxed{} \end{array}$$

$$\begin{array}{r} 6 \\ +\ \boxed{} \\ \hline 14 \end{array}$$

$$\begin{array}{r} 15 \\ -\ 9 \\ \hline \boxed{} \end{array}$$

$$\begin{array}{r} 9 \\ +\ \boxed{} \\ \hline 15 \end{array}$$

Use the treehouse chart below to solve the problems on the next page. Put your finger on the first number and then add or subtract by moving your finger by tens and then by ones. Fill in the sentences and write your answer.

1	2	3	4	5	6	7	8	9	10
11	12	13	14	15	16	17	18	19	20
21	22	23	24	25	26	27	28	29	30
31	32	33	34	35	36	37	38	39	40
41	42	43	44	45	46	47	48	49	50
51	52	53	54	55	56	57	58	59	60
61	62	63	64	65	66	67	68	69	70
71	72	73	74	75	76	77	78	79	80
81	82	83	84	85	86	87	88	89	90
91	92	93	94	95	96	97	98	99	100

43 + 17 = 60

- Start at 43.
- Jump _10_ spaces forward.
- Then move _7_ more spaces forward.

74 – 19 = ☐

- Start at 74.
- Jump _____ spaces backward.
- Then move _____ more spaces backward.

25 + 28 = ☐

- Start at 25.
- Jump _____ spaces forward.
- Then move _____ more spaces forward.

93 – 19 = ☐

- Start at 93.
- Jump _____ spaces backward.
- Then move _____ more spaces backward.

18 + 53 = ☐

- Start at 18.
- Jump _____ spaces forward.
- Then move _____ more spaces forward.

55 – 26 = ☐

- Start at 55.
- Jump _____ spaces backward.
- Then move _____ more spaces backward.

46 + 16 = ☐

- Start at 46.
- Jump _____ spaces forward.
- Then move _____ more spaces forward.

84 – 77 = ☐

- Start at 84.
- Jump _____ spaces backward.
- Then move _____ more spaces backward.

Cut out the rooms in the tree house. Arrange each in the grid so every row and column adds up to 15.

1	2	3
4	5	6
7	8	9

5	1	9	15
3	8	4	15
7	6	2	15
15	15	15	

2			15
			15
	3	8	15
15	15	15	

7			15
			15
3	4		15
15	15	15	

Arrange the rooms so each row or column adds up to the number outside the grid.

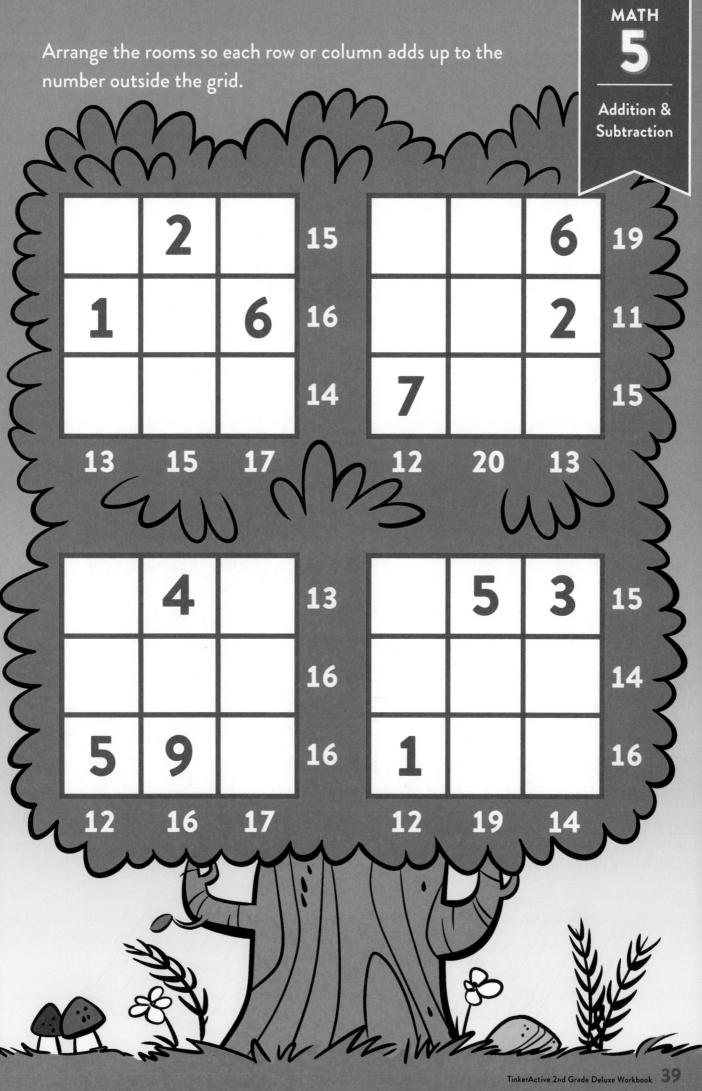

Grid 1

	2		15
1		6	16
			14
13	15	17	

Grid 2

		6	19
		2	11
7			15
12	20	13	

Grid 3

	4		13
			16
5	9		16
12	16	17	

Grid 4

	5	3	15
			14
1			16
12	19	14	

LET'S START!

GATHER THESE TOOLS AND MATERIALS.

1 small cup

40 coins

30 or more craft sticks

20 straws

Paper

10 clothespins or binder clips

Masking tape

Glue

LET'S TINKER!

Place the cup on a table. **Toss** your coins one by one into the cup from a few feet away until you are out of coins. How many coins did you get into the cup? **Count** the number of coins that landed in the cup. Now, without counting, **determine** how many coins missed the cup.

LET'S MAKE: TREE HOUSE!

1. Lay 10–12 craft sticks in a row.

2. Glue 3 sticks across to make the platform of your tree house.

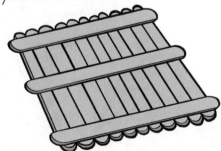

3. Using the rest of your craft sticks, **build** walls.

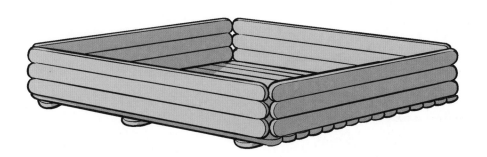

How many craft sticks did you use for each part of the tree house? **Add** the craft sticks used for the floor and walls together. How many did you use in all?

LET'S ENGINEER!

Enid wants to build a table to put in her tree house. She wants to make sure it can hold a bucket of cookies for her and all her friends.

How can Enid build a table that will hold all her cookies?

Using your materials, **build** a table that can support a cup of coins. Put your cup on top and start adding coins. How many coins can it hold up before breaking?

PROJECT 5: DONE!
Get your sticker!

Addition Using Place Value

Look at each addition sentence. Then look at each number as an array. Circle any groups of 10 blocks in the ones place, and circle any groups of 10 blocks in the tens place. Then solve.

21 + 14 = <u>35</u>

	Tens	Ones
21	■■	■
+14	■	■■■■

37 + 22 = ____

	Tens	Ones
37	■■■	■■■■■ ■■
+22	■■	■■

74 + 16 = ____

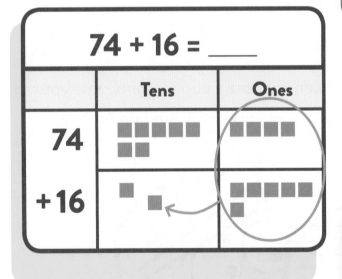

	Tens	Ones
74	■■■■ ■■	■■■■
+16	■ ■	■■■■ ■

32 + 18 = ____

	Tens	Ones
32	■■■	■■
+18	■	■■■■ ■■■

86 + 25 + 18 = _____

	Hundreds	Tens	Ones
86		■■■■■ ■■■	■■■■■ ■
25		■■	■■■■■
+18		■	■■■■ ■■

63 + 58 + 12 = _____

	Hundreds	Tens	Ones
63		■■■■■ ■	■■■
58		■■■■■	■■■■■ ■■■
+12		■	■■

Look at each addition sentence. Then color the blocks in the tens columns and ones columns for each number. Then add.

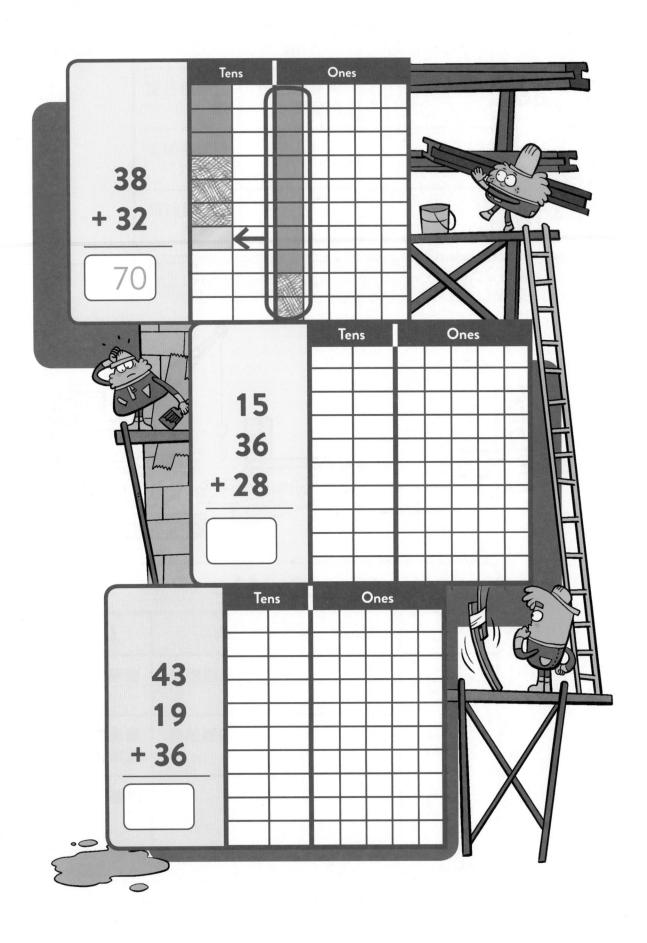

38
+ 32
_____
70

15
36
+ 28
_____

43
19
+ 36
_____

	Tens		Ones	

27
48
+ 16

	Tens		Ones	

13
29
+ 47

	Tens		Ones	

48
36
+ 15

Draw blocks in the place value chart to represent each number in the number sentence. Then add. Circle and carry bundles of tens or hundreds when necessary.

65 + 75 = 140	Hundreds	Tens	Ones

74 + 16 =	Hundreds	Tens	Ones

86 25 + 18 =	Hundreds	Tens	Ones

68 38 + 13 =	Hundreds	Tens	Ones

Use place value to solve each problem. Wherever possible, make 10 ones or 10 tens to simplify the problem.

25 + **15** = _40_

20 + 5 + 10 + 5

30 + 10 = 40

28 + **12** + **36** = _____

20 + 8 + 10 + 2 + 30 + 6

59 + **51** + **33** = _____

19 + **41** + **23** = _____

LET'S START! GATHER THESE TOOLS AND MATERIALS.

4 dice

Paper

Markers

Scissors
(with an adult's help)

10 or more beans

10 or more pieces of dried pasta

10 or more cotton balls

10 or more cotton swabs

Tape or glue

LET'S TINKER!

Separate the four dice into groups of two. **Roll** each set of dice and record the numbers on a piece of paper. For example, if you roll a **1** and a **6** with one pair of dice, record the number as **16** or **61**—it's your choice. Then roll the other pair of dice for your second number. **Add** the two numbers together. What is the sum? Can you add the numbers in your head?

LET'S MAKE: SPINNER GAME!

1. Draw 2 large circles on 2 pieces of paper and cut them out.

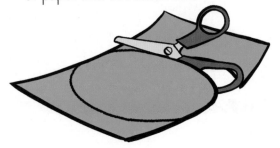

2. Draw lines to divide each circle into 6 equal wedges and write a 2-digit number between 20 and 50 in each wedge.

3. Place a marker in the middle of one circle as the spinner.

4. Play: Spin the marker and, on a separate piece of paper, record the number the cap of the marker lands on. **Repeat** with the other circle. **Add** the numbers together to get a sum. Now it's the other player's turn to do the same. Whoever is closest to 100 wins the round. Keep playing until one player wins three rounds.

LET'S ENGINEER!

The MotMots are competing in a crafting contest! They have to use 10 or more dried beans, 10 or more pieces of pasta, 10 or more cotton balls, and 10 or more cotton swabs to create a sculpture that looks like their favorite animal.

How can the MotMots design an animal sculpture using all those materials?

Construct your sculpture using 10 or more of each item listed. Make sure you **record** how many of each item you are using. **Add** up the number of items you used to make your sculpture. What is the sum? Can you make a sculpture using more materials? How many more items did you add?

PROJECT 6: DONE!
Get your sticker!

Subtraction Using Place Value

Draw the rest of each rope by connecting the expanded form of each number.

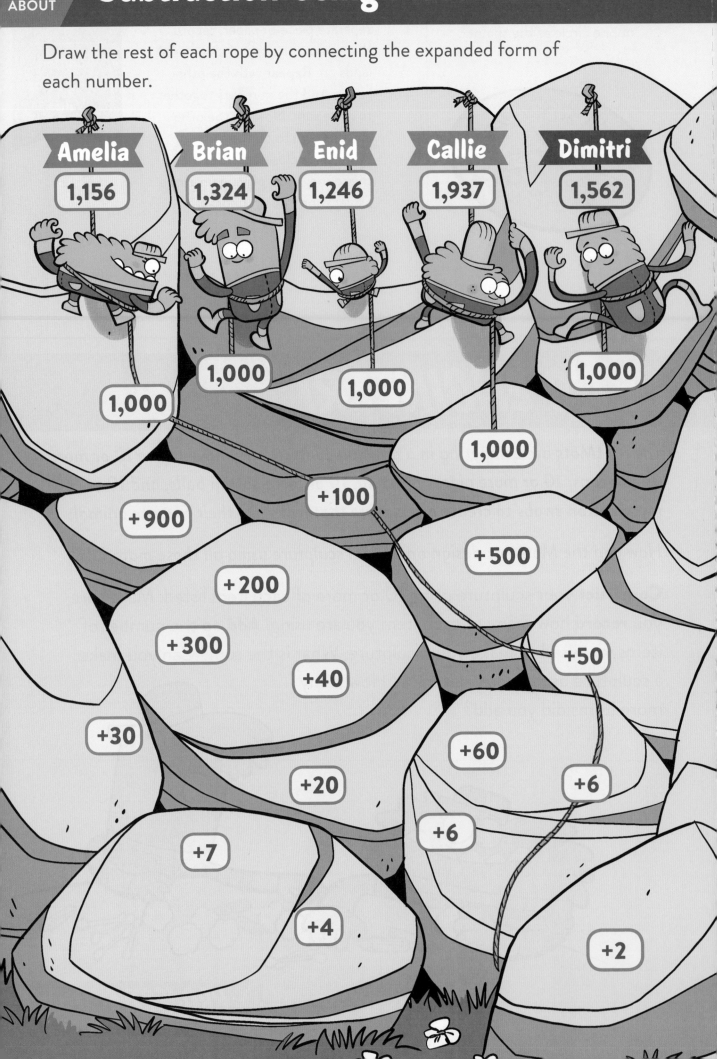

Subtract by using place value.

70 − 40 = ☐

7 tens − 4 tens =

_____

53 − 20 = ☐

5 tens, 3 ones − 2 tens =

_____

77 − 60 = ☐

7 tens, 7 ones − 6 tens =

_____

59 − 28 = ☐

5 tens, 9 ones − 2 tens, 8 ones =

_____

45 − 33 = ☐

4 tens, 5 ones − 3 tens, 3 ones =

_____

Subtract by using the expanded number form and jumping hundreds, tens, and ones.

34 – 11 = 23

−10   −1
34 → 24 → 23

48 – 35 =

−30   −5
48 → 18 → ___

68 – 17 =

86 – 48 =

643 − 126 =

427 − 213 =

866 − 542 =

981 − 580 =

Use the place value chart to solve each problem.

$39 - 12 =$ 27

Tens	Ones
●●✗	●●●●● ●●●✗✗
2	7

$58 - 26 =$

Tens	Ones

$76 - 43 =$

Tens	Ones

$98 - 25 =$

Tens	Ones

The MotMots are packing their backpacks for a nature hike! Draw a place value chart to solve each word problem.

Enid decided to pack **183** of her favorite cotton balls. But then she decided she didn't need **72** of them, so she unpacked them. How many does she have packed?

Frank packed **175** egg sandwiches, but he ate **30** of them. How many does he have left?

Dimitri packed **432** rubber bands. Callie packed **100** fewer. How many did Callie pack?

LET'S START!

GATHER THESE TOOLS AND MATERIALS.

Bowl of popcorn

Brushes

Paint, including:
black; red, pink, or orange; yellow or green;
blue or purple

30 flat stones
(10 large, 10 medium, 10 small)

LET'S TINKER!

Get a bowl of popcorn. **Count** each kernel in the bowl. **Eat** five! How many kernels do you have left? **Keep** eating, taking handfuls of 5, 10, 50, and 100 (you can use two hands!) at a time, and subtracting from the total.

LET'S MAKE: STACKING STONES!

1. Find 10 large stones, 10 medium stones, and 10 small stones. They should be large and flat enough for stacking. **Wash** and dry each stone.

2. Paint the large stones red, pink, or orange. **Let** them dry and write "100" on them with black paint.

3. Paint the medium stones yellow or green. **Let** them dry and write "10" on them with black paint.

4. Paint the small stones blue or purple. **Let** them dry and write "1" on them with black paint.

What numbers can you make by stacking stones together? For example, if you stack a red 100 stone, a yellow 10 stone, and a purple 1 stone, what number do you make? (111!) What happens to that number when you remove one of the stones?

LET'S ENGINEER!

The MotMots are creating their own numbers with their stacking stones. Enid's stack has a value of 434. Brian's stack has a value of 376. Callie wants to build a stack that is exactly the value of Enid's stack minus the value of Brian's stack.

How can Callie find out the value of her stack without writing it down?

Figure out the value of Callie's stack using only the stones, and then build it.

PROJECT 7: DONE!
Get your sticker!

Addition & Subtraction: Word Problems

Solve the word problems below.

At the Cotton Ball Festival, Amelia ate 9 pies. Then she ate 4 more. Enid ate 2 pies. How many pies did they eat altogether?

Brian won 19 tickets, and Amelia won 24 more tickets than Brian. How many tickets did Amelia win?

Brian got to level 5 in the strength contest. He tried again and reached 3 levels higher. On his third try, he reached 4 levels higher than on his second try. How high did he get?

Frank's cotton ball won the Fluff and Stuff competition by beating 27 other contestants. In the Bounce and Flounce competition, he beat 10 other contestants. And in the Wiggle and Waggle competition, he beat 2 others. How many contestants did he beat in total?

Enid won 27 prizes, and Amelia won 5 fewer prizes than Enid. How many prizes did Amelia win?

Callie stayed on the Spin Cycle ride for 12 seconds. The next time, she rode for a shorter amount of time. In total, she rode for 20 seconds. How long was her second ride?

Read the story. As you read, tally the costume photos on page 61 by drawing circles (O) to add or crossing circles out (Ø) to subtract.

Dimitri ran around the Cotton Ball Festival to take photos of all the different costumes. He saw **10** cowboy cotton balls in the cafeteria and **2** more by the water fountain.

He spotted **14** astronaut cotton balls on the trampolines. Then **4** more arrived. But then **10** of them took off their helmets and they were actually pirates!

Another **12** pirates were standing by the donut truck, along with **4** more cowboys.

Finally, in the dance hall at the Cotton Ball, he saw **7** cowboys, **2** pirates, **7** ninjas, and **1** astronaut.

That was when Dimitri saw that his camera's battery was almost dead. As he replaced the battery, he accidentally erased pictures of **10** cowboys and **3** astronauts.

Can you write your own word problem using cotton balls?

By the end of the
night, how many
pictures of each
costume did he have?

cowboys: _____

ninjas: _____

astronauts: _____

pirates: _____

Fill in the number sentences to solve. Then draw a line from each MotMot to the prize they can get using all their tickets.

Dimitri won **73** tickets from the carnival games. He gave **20** away. Then he won another **17**.

Step 1: 73 − 20 = __53__

Step 2: __53__ + 17 = __70__

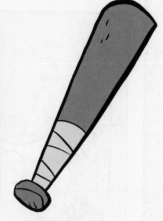

Frank won **84** tickets for his prize cotton ball. He won another **11** for the dance competition. Then he lost **20** through a hole in his pocket.

Step 1: 84 + 11 = _____

Step 2: _____ − 20 = _____

Callie won **81** tickets. She accidentally lost **30** of them when she went on the Spin Cycle ride. Then she won another **23**.

Step 1: 81 − 30 = _____

Step 2: _____

Enid won only **9** tickets because she could not see over the counter. Amelia gave her **65** tickets to make her feel better. But **40** of those tickets were covered in cherry pie and couldn't be used.

Step 1: _____

Step 2: _____

76

75

74

88

95

80

34

70

Frank

Callie

Dimitri

Enid

LET'S START!

20 or more
cotton balls

Construction paper

Scissors
(with an adult's help)

Glue

20 or more
craft sticks

10 or more rubber bands

3 or more bottle caps

Bucket or basket

LET'S TINKER!

Decorate the cotton balls as cowboys, astronauts, pirates, and ninjas. **Cut** out 3 cowboy hats from your construction paper for 3 cowboys. **Cut** out 5 helmets for 5 astronauts. **Cut** out 4 eye patches for 4 pirates. **Cut** out 5 throwing stars for 5 ninjas.

Glue the items above to your cotton balls. How many cottons balls are dressed up in total?

LET'S MAKE: COTTON-BALL CATAPULT!

1. Stack 3 craft sticks together and wrap each end with a rubber band.

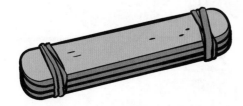

2. Do the same with another 2 craft sticks, but wrap only one end with a rubber band.

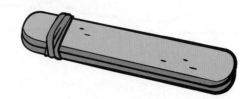

3. Place the stack of 3 craft sticks in between the stack of 2 craft sticks and attach them with a rubber band where they overlap.

4. Glue a bottle cap to the end of the top craft stick.

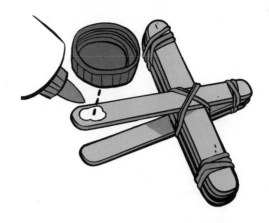

Your catapult is finished! **Shoot** a cotton ball with your catapult.

Modify your catapult by adding or subtracting craft sticks, rubber bands, and bottle caps. Does this change the accuracy of your catapult or how far your cotton ball can go?

LET'S ENGINEER!

The MotMots are playing a game of Toss That Cotton Ball! The MotMots get points for each cotton ball that goes into a bucket across the room. The pirates are worth 9 points. The astronauts are worth 7. The cowboys are worth 16. The ninjas are worth 24. Callie needs to get more than 47 points to beat Frank's record.

How can Callie beat Frank's record?

Use the catapult you made to launch the cotton balls into your bucket. **Try** to beat Frank's record for Callie. **Alter** the design of the catapult to make it shoot farther and be more accurate.

PROJECT 8: DONE!
Get your sticker!

Measurement

Every Thursday, the MotMots have a stacking competition. Measure each stack of MotMots in inches or in centimeters.

inches

centimeters

inches

inches

centimeters

centimeters

MotMots love to measure, so they have lots of measuring devices.
Circle the best tool to measure each object.

Ruler

Yardstick

Measuring tape

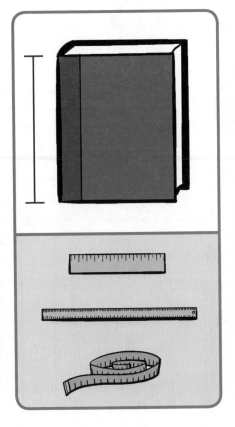

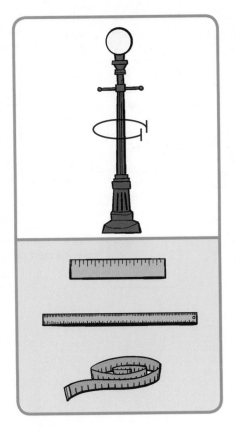

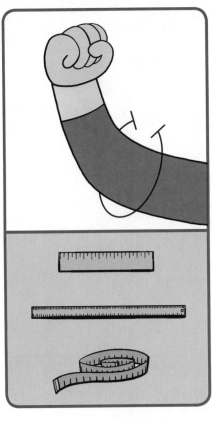

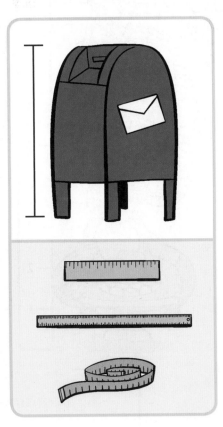

Circle the best unit of measurement for each object. Then estimate how tall each object is.

inches   feet   **yards**

Estimation: _____

inches   feet   **yards**

Estimation: _____

inches   feet   **yards**

Estimation: _____

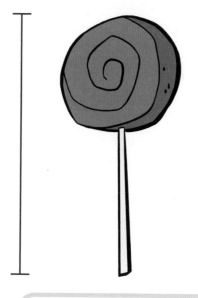

inches   feet   **yards**

Estimation: _____

Estimate the length of your own arm and then measure it. How close was the actual measurement to your guess?

69

Put your hand on the page and trace around it. Then use a ruler to measure each finger in inches and in centimeters. Write your measurements next to each finger. Then measure the length of your whole hand in inches and in centimeters and write your measurements below.

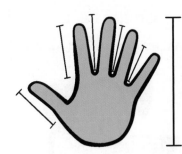

My hand is _____ inches or _____ centimeters long.

Put your foot on the page and trace around it. Then measure the length of your foot in inches and in centimeters. Write your measurements below.

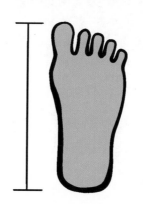

My foot is _____ inches or _____ centimeters long.

LET'S START!

GATHER THESE TOOLS AND MATERIALS.

5 bottle caps

Tape measure

Scissors
(with an adult's help)

Rubber band

2 beads or pieces
of dried tube pasta

Tape

Ruler

Markers

LET'S TINKER!

Find a large, smooth surface, like a countertop or an uncarpeted floor.

Slide the bottle caps across the surface. **Try** flicking, hitting, or sliding the caps. Is it easier to slide some bottle caps than others? Do some caps go farther than others?

Estimate how far each bottle cap slid. Then **use** your tape measure to measure the distances.

LET'S MAKE: MOTMOT LAUNCHER!

1. Cut the rubber band.

2. Thread each end of the rubber band through a bead or a piece of pasta.

3. Knot the ends to create handles.

4. Get stickers from page 385 and decorate your bottle caps.

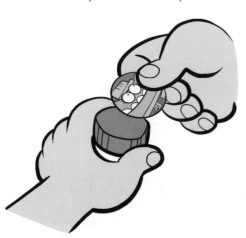

5. Launch the bottle caps by snapping your rubber band, and measure how far they fly.

LET'S ENGINEER!

Frank has been working on his Frank Launcher. It's finally able to launch Frank, but he can't control how far he goes. So if he tries it, he won't know where he'll land!

How can Frank modify his launcher so he goes exactly as far as he wants?

Stretch a tape measure on a table. **Stand** a marker up at a distance you think you can hit. Now **try** to knock it down by launching a bottle cap from your MotMot launcher. Did you knock over the marker? If not, **modify** the cap or launcher to try to hit it. If you did knock over the marker, **measure** another distance and try hitting that as well. How can you modify your cap or launcher to hit the marker at a different distance?

PROJECT 9: DONE!
Get your sticker!

Length

Estimate the length and height of each train. Then use a ruler to measure each train.

Amelia's Train

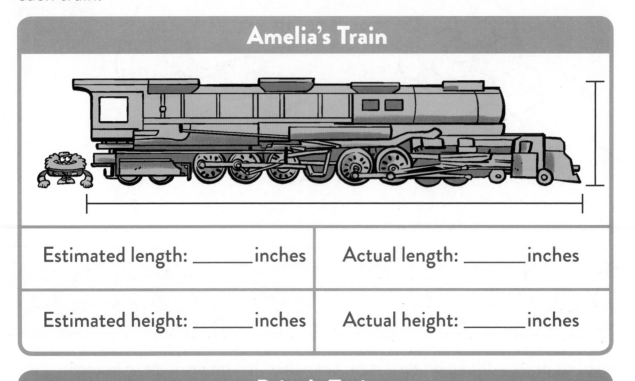

Estimated length: _____ inches | Actual length: _____ inches

Estimated height: _____ inches | Actual height: _____ inches

Brian's Train

Estimated length: _____ inches | Actual length: _____ inches

Estimated height: _____ inches | Actual height: _____ inches

Which train is longer? _____

How much longer is the longer train? _____

Which train is taller? _____

How much taller is the taller train? _____

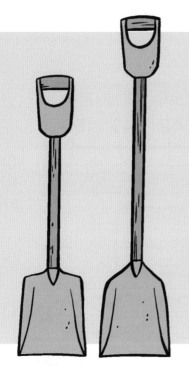

Amelia's shovel is 6 inches longer than Brian's. Brian's shovel is 52 inches long. How long is Amelia's?

_____inches

The crossing sign on Amelia's track is 10 centimeters shorter than Brian's. Brian's sign is 81 centimeters tall. How tall is Amelia's?

_____centimeters

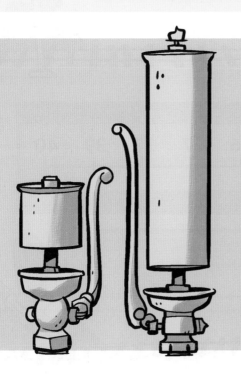

Amelia's steam whistle is 54 inches long. Brian's whistle is 14 inches shorter than Amelia's. How long is Brian's whistle?

_____inches

Use the number lines to solve the following problems.

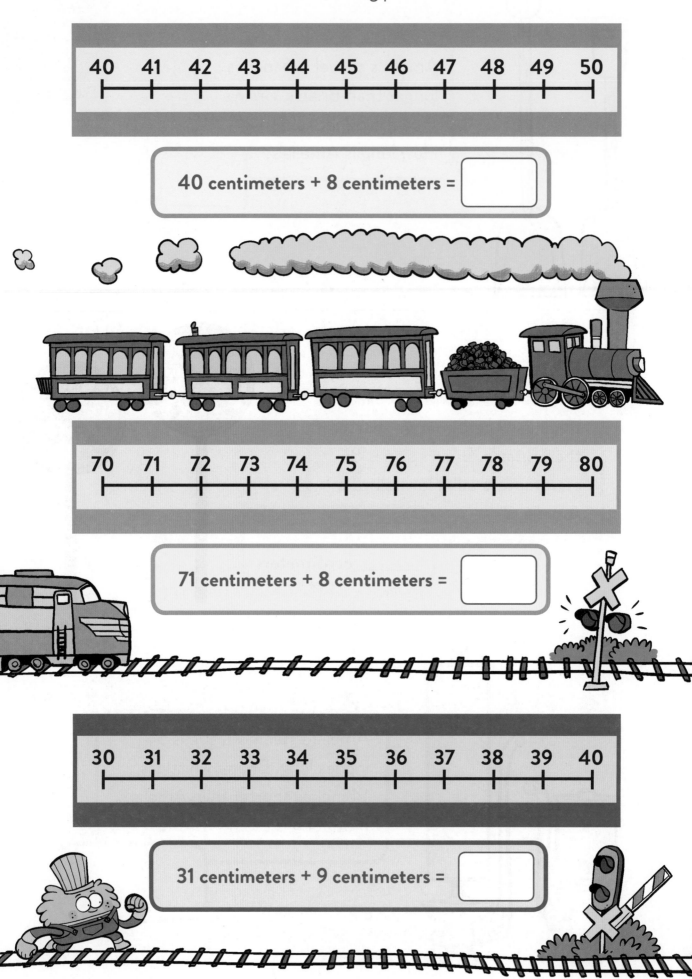

| 40 | 41 | 42 | 43 | 44 | 45 | 46 | 47 | 48 | 49 | 50 |

40 centimeters + 8 centimeters =

| 70 | 71 | 72 | 73 | 74 | 75 | 76 | 77 | 78 | 79 | 80 |

71 centimeters + 8 centimeters =

| 30 | 31 | 32 | 33 | 34 | 35 | 36 | 37 | 38 | 39 | 40 |

31 centimeters + 9 centimeters =

Draw number lines to solve the following problems.

31 centimeters + 16 centimeters = ☐

56 centimeters + 9 centimeters = ☐

65 centimeters + 12 centimeters = ☐

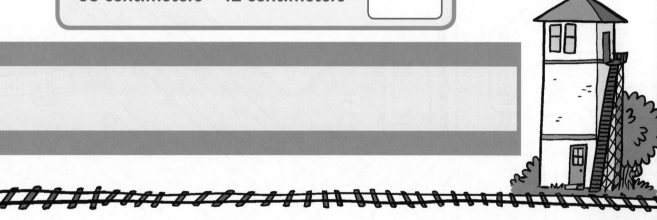

Get a few pencils and measure them. How long is the longest pencil? How long is the shortest pencil? How much longer is the longest pencil than the shortest?

Measure each track in inches.

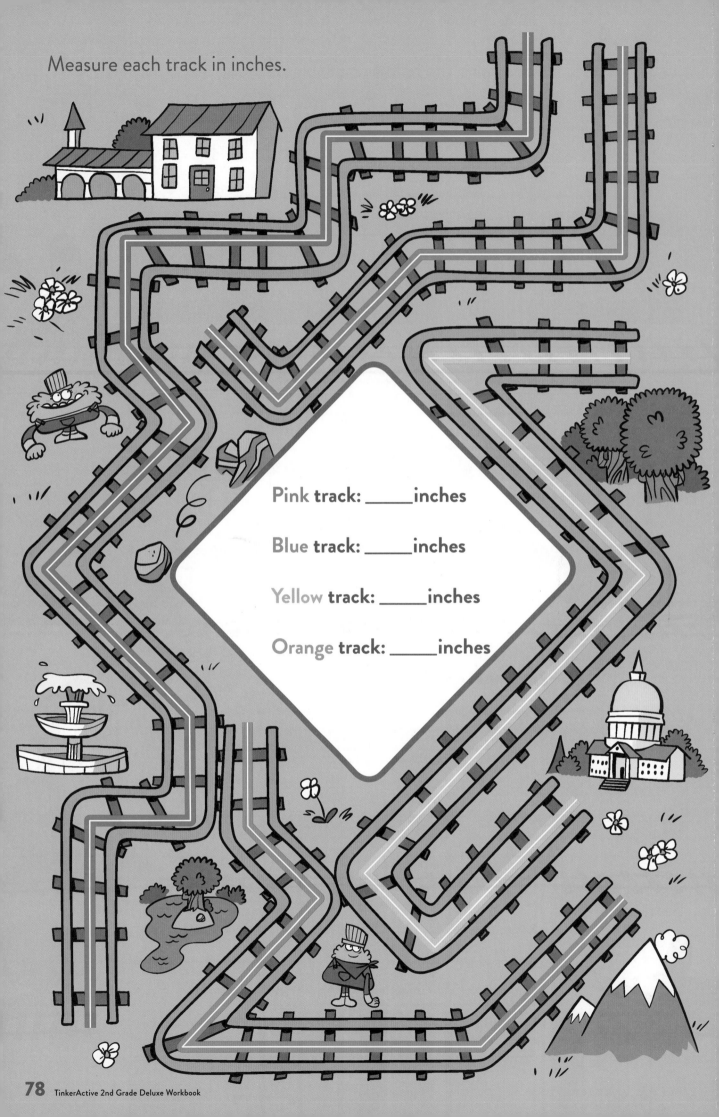

Pink track: _____inches

Blue track: _____inches

Yellow track: _____inches

Orange track: _____inches

Which path is shorter, **pink** or **blue**?

Which path is longer, **yellow** or **pink**?

How much shorter or longer is the **yellow** track than the **pink**?

If Amelia took the **pink** path, and Brian waited for her to get exactly halfway before starting on the **blue** path, who would have the shorter distance left to walk?

How much shorter or longer is the **orange** track than the **blue** ?

How much shorter or longer is the **yellow** track than the **orange**?

LET'S START!

GATHER THESE TOOLS AND MATERIALS.

Cardboard

10–15 marbles

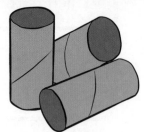
2 or more toilet paper or paper towel rolls

50 craft sticks

Tape

Scissors
(with an adult's help)

Glue sticks
or glue gun

LET'S TINKER!

Roll a marble on different surfaces, like tables, carpets, and tile.

Measure how far it rolls on each surface.

How much farther does the marble go on one surface versus another?

LET'S MAKE: MARBLE RUN!

1. Glue craft sticks together to make trays.

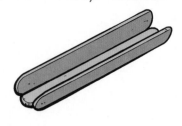

2. Cut toilet paper rolls to create more trays.

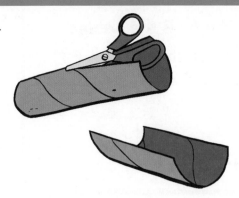

3. Glue or tape the trays to cardboard to create the run.

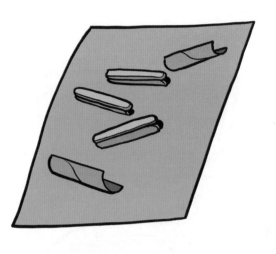

4. Tape the cardboard to a wall and test your marble run!

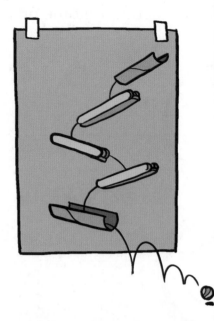

How long is your marble run? Measure each tray and add the lengths.

LET'S ENGINEER!

Enid is perfectly round, and that makes her perfectly suited for the MotMot Marble Madness Marathon. She wants to go at least 100 centimeters.

How can Enid roll more than 100 centimeters?

Extend your run so a marble can travel more than 100 centimeters. Remember, if a marble drops from one tray to another, you can count the distance between the trays.

PROJECT 10: DONE!
Get your sticker!

Time

Draw a line to match the time on the clocks.

Draw the hands on the clocks to show when each MotMot finished the course.

CALLIE 12:00

DIMITRI 2:15

BRIAN 3:30

AMELIA 2:45

ENID 1:35

FRANK 2:20

Count by fives to tell the time. Then fill in the missing numbers in each sentence.

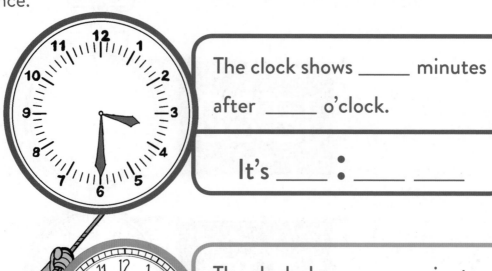

The clock shows _____ minutes after _____ o'clock.

It's _____ : _____ _____

The clock shows _____ minutes after _____ o'clock.

It's _____ : _____ _____

The clock shows _____ minutes after _____ o'clock.

It's _____ : _____ _____

The clock shows

_____ minutes after

_____ o'clock.

It's _____ : _____ _____

The clock shows

_____ minutes after

_____ o'clock.

It's _____ : _____ _____

When do you do each activity? Draw hands on the clock. Then fill in the missing time in the sentence, as well as a.m. or p.m.

I wake up at ___ : _____

I eat breakfast at ___ : _____

I go to school at ___ : _____

I eat lunch at ___ : _____

I have recess at ___ : _____

I go home at ___ : _____

I eat dinner at ___ : _____

I go to bed at ___ : _____

Cut out the clock's hands at the bottom of page 86. Then arrange the hands on the clock to show each MotMot's finishing time. Fill in the times on the digital clocks below each MotMot.

Amelia finished the obstacle course at 2:15 p.m.

Brian finished 15 minutes later.

Callie finished 1 hour and 30 minutes after Brian.

Dimitri finished at 15 minutes before 6.

Enid finished at half past 6.

Frank finished 2 hours and 20 minutes after Enid.

Amelia   Brian   Callie   Dimitri   Enid   Frank

LET'S START! GATHER THESE TOOLS AND MATERIALS.

Timer

1-5 sheets of colored construction paper

Scissors (with an adult's help)

Glue

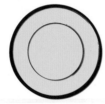

2 paper plates or shoebox lids

10-20 pieces of tube pasta

Crayons

1 marble

LET'S TINKER!

Plan an obstacle course that starts at your front door and ends in your bedroom. **Include** lots of different movements like crawling, hopping, and balancing, and challenges like tossing a toy into a laundry basket. Once you've designed your course, **try** it! **Time** yourself and then see if you can beat your own time.

LET'S MAKE: MINI OBSTACLE COURSE!

1. Cut the paper into strips.

2. Glue each end of the strips to the plate or shoebox lid to create tunnels.

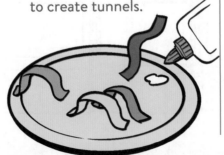

3. Glue the pasta down to create tracks.

4. Write START and FINISH, and draw arrows with a crayon to show the route.

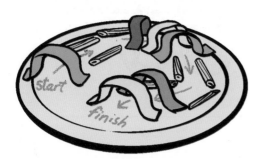

5. Drop a marble in and use a timer to measure how long it takes to complete your mini obstacle course.

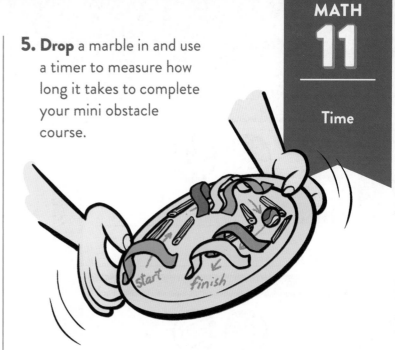

LET'S ENGINEER!

Dimitri has mastered his obstacle course and can finish it lickety-split. Now he wants a challenge!

How can Dimitri modify his obstacle course so it's harder, but also more fun?

Make your home obstacle course or marble obstacle course more difficult and more fun. **Try** changing the route or adding new materials and obstacles. Then **test** it out.

How long does it take you to complete the new course? Longer or shorter than before? Is it harder? Is it more fun? **Challenge** a friend or family member to beat your time.

PROJECT 11: DONE!
Get your sticker!

Money

Write the name and value for each type of coin.

Name: _____

Value: _____

Name: _____

Value: _____

Name: _____

Value: _____

Name: _____

Value: _____

Add the coins using place value and jumping. Include the symbols for dollars ($) or for cents (¢) in your answer.

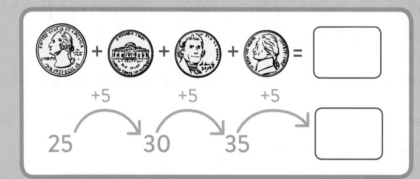

+5   +5   +5

25   30   35

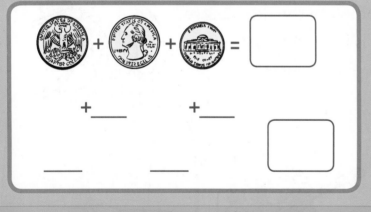

+___   +___

___   ___

+___   +___   +___   +___   +___

___   ___   ___   ___

Draw a line from each item on the menu to the matching amount of money.

What would you buy from Enid's Treat Truck if you had $1.00? Circle your choice!

How would you pay for each item? Write the amount of each coin or bill that you would use to buy each item.

$1.73

$2.15

$1.83

$3.91

Solve each word problem.

Frank has 98¢ and buys a teddy bear in a wagon.

How much money will he have left?

75¢

37¢

Enid has 50¢ and wants the basket of baskets.

How much money will she have left?

Brian wants a stuffed giraffe. He has one dollar.

How much money will he have left?

80¢

$1.00

Amelia has two dollars. She wants the volleyball.

How much money will she have left?

Do you have some coins? Write your own word problem based on what change you have and what you would like to buy. How much money will you have left?

Circle the money so 3 MotMots each get $1.00. Use each coin only once.

Draw a dollar bill for Frank.

Get the following coins: 4 quarters, 5 dimes, 10 nickels, and 10 pennies. Use the coins to answer each question below.

What is the fewest number of coins necessary to make 62¢?

Draw those coins.

What is the fewest number of coins necessary to make 48¢?

Draw those coins.

What are other ways to make 48¢ using your pennies, nickels, dimes, and quarters?

Draw two other ways.

LET'S START!

At least 15 pennies, 15 nickels, 15 dimes, and 15 quarters

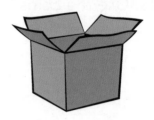

Cardboard or a cardboard box
(larger than 18 inches by 9 inches)

Tape

Glue

Scissors
(with an adult's help)

Pencil

Newspaper

LET'S TINKER!

Look at and touch your coins, then brainstorm different ways to sort them.

How can you sort coins in different ways?

What is unique about each coin?

LET'S MAKE: COIN-SORTING TRAY!

1. Ask an adult to cut the cardboard into 3 rectangles that are 18 by 3 inches.

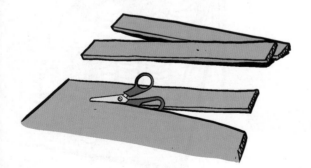

2. Place a dime, a penny, a nickel, and a quarter on the cardboard with space between each one, as shown below.

3. Draw a rectangle around each coin and ask an adult to cut out the rectangles.

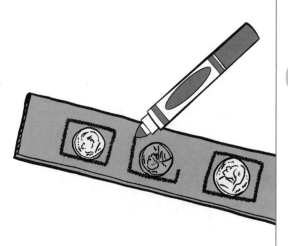

4. Glue the other 2 pieces of cardboard to the sides as the walls of your coin-sorting tray.

5. Slide your coins over the tray. Does it sort them?

LET'S ENGINEER!

Enid's Treat Truck is so popular that the MotMots are all giving her their piggy banks. Now she has too many coins to sort and count!

If Enid wants to find out how much money she has in quarters, how can she sort out just the quarters?

Modify your coin-sorting tray so you can pour lots of coins into it at once and sort out only the quarters. How much money do you have in quarters?

PROJECT 12: DONE!
Get your sticker!

Data & Graphs

Use the picture graph to answer each question below.

Number of Burgers Eaten — Amelia, Brian, Callie, Dimitri, Enid, Frank

How many burgers has Amelia eaten? _____

How many burgers has Dimitri eaten? _____

Which MotMots ate the same number of burgers? _____

How many burgers did Amelia and Enid eat altogether? _____

How many fewer burgers did Callie eat than Brian? _____

Which MotMots ate a combined total of 8 burgers? _____

Use the picture graph to answer each question below.

The MotMots' Favorite Sports

Soccer	🔺 🔺 🔺 🔺 🔺
Tennis	🔺 🔺 🔺 🔺 🔺 🔺
Hockey	🔺 🔺 🔺
Volleyball	🔺
Bowling	🔺 🔺 🔺 🔺 🔺 🔺 🔺 🔺 🔺 🔺

🔺 = 1 MotMot

What is the most popular sport? _____

What is the least popular sport? _____

How many MotMots like soccer best? _____

How many combined MotMots love volleyball and hockey? _____

How many fewer MotMots like hockey than tennis? _____

How many fewer MotMots like volleyball than bowling? _____

Tally the medals
that Brian won.

Number of Medals

Gold	Silver	Bronze

Use the tally chart to draw Brian's medals in each picture graph.

Number of Medals			
6			
5			
4			
3			
2			
1			
	Gold	Silver	Bronze

= 1 Medal

Gold	
Silver	
Bronze	

= 1 Medal

Ask 10 friends or family members the following question: Are the baseballs below the same size or is one bigger than the other? Then, in the graph below, color in one space to record each person's response.

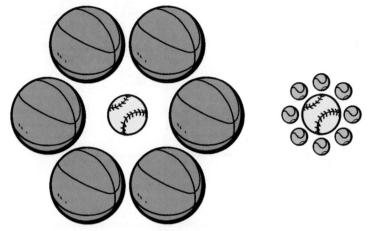

Number of People	Left is bigger	Right is bigger	Same size
10			
9			
8			
7			
6			
5			
4			
3			
2			
1			

Fun fact: The two baseballs are actually the **same size**! Try measuring them to see for yourself.

How many MotMots are participating in each MotMot Olympics event? Look at page 103 and collect the data you need. Then fill in the bar graph.

Number of MotMots	Cycling	Fencing	Race Walking	Volleyball
5				
4				
3				
2				
1				

Look carefully at all the MotMots on page 103. How many gold, silver, and bronze medals did they win? Use the space below to create a tally chart.

Gold	
Silver	
Bronze	

LET'S START! GATHER THESE TOOLS AND MATERIALS.

7 pieces of $8\frac{1}{2}$ x 11 paper

Construction paper

15 straws

12 inches of string

Glue or tape

Marker

LET'S TINKER!

Fold 3 different pieces of paper into 3 different shapes and flick them across the room. **Measure** and record the distance for each shape, flicking each 3 times. Did one shape do better than the others?

LET'S MAKE: FLYING FRANK!

1. Fold a piece of paper in half lengthwise.

2. Take a corner and fold it into a triangle. Keep folding until you reach the end.

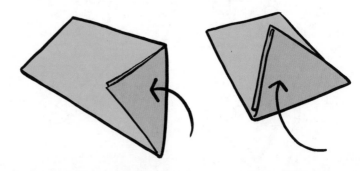

3. Tuck the extra paper into the triangle to secure it.

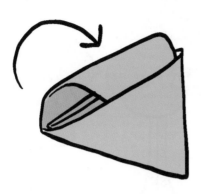

4. Apply the stickers from page 385 to each side.

5. Flick this shape 3 times across the room and add the results to the data for the three shapes you tried before.

LET'S ENGINEER!

Frankball is the MotMots' favorite pastime. The only problem is that no one ever remembers the score!

How can the MotMots keep score?

Use the straws and string to create different-size targets for Frank to fly through or land on. **Ask** friends or family members to play—you get one point for every successful flick. Then **create** a scoreboard to keep score as you play. What is the best way to label the scoreboard or count your points?

PROJECT 13: DONE!
Get your sticker!

Shape Attributes

Fill in the missing information in the chart below.

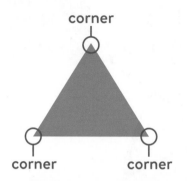
corner
corner   corner

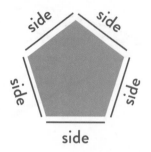
side side
side   side
side

Shape	Name	Number of Corners	Number of Sides
●		0	0
			3
■			
	rectangle		
▱	trapezoid		
	pentagon		
⬡			

Quadrilaterals have four sides. Circle the quadrilaterals.

Fill in the missing information for each shape.

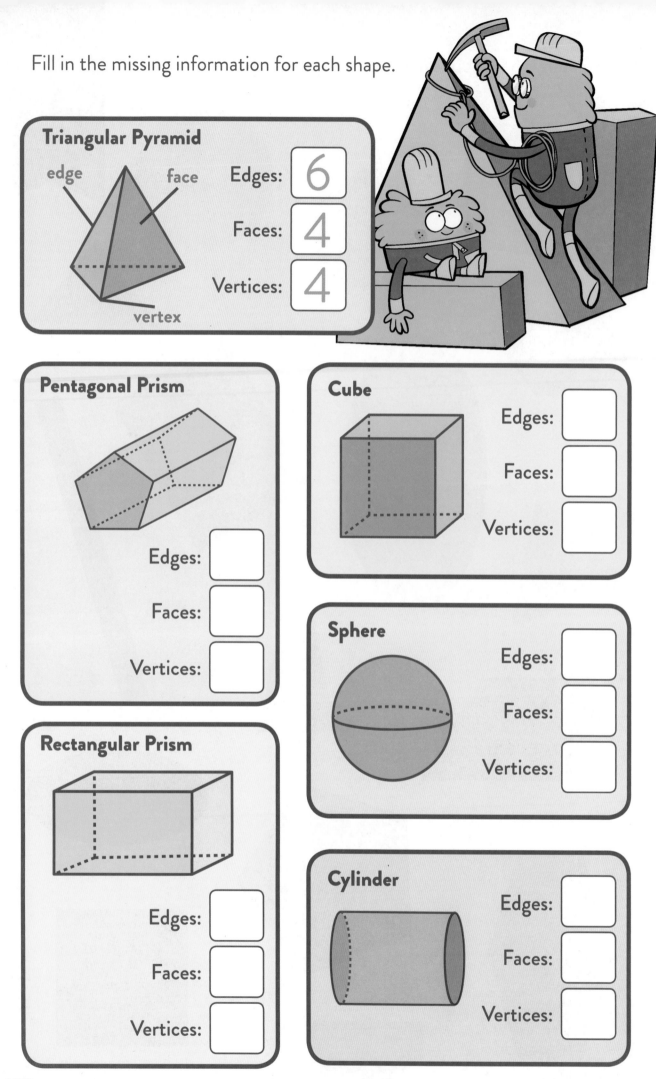

Triangular Pyramid

edge   face

vertex

Edges: 6

Faces: 4

Vertices: 4

Pentagonal Prism

Edges:

Faces:

Vertices:

Cube

Edges:

Faces:

Vertices:

Sphere

Edges:

Faces:

Vertices:

Rectangular Prism

Edges:

Faces:

Vertices:

Cylinder

Edges:

Faces:

Vertices:

Read the clues and draw each shape.

Amelia's favorite
2-dimensional shape has
4 corners and 4 equal sides.

Dimitri's favorite 3-dimensional
shape has 2 edges and 2 faces.

Enid's favorite
2-dimensional shape
has no sides.

Frank's favorite 2-dimensional shape
has 3 corners.

Color the image using the key below.

Draw a line to guide Brian through the maze to the exit.

Brian can only step on shapes that have 1 more or 1 less side than the previous shape he stepped on.

Brian cannot move diagonally.

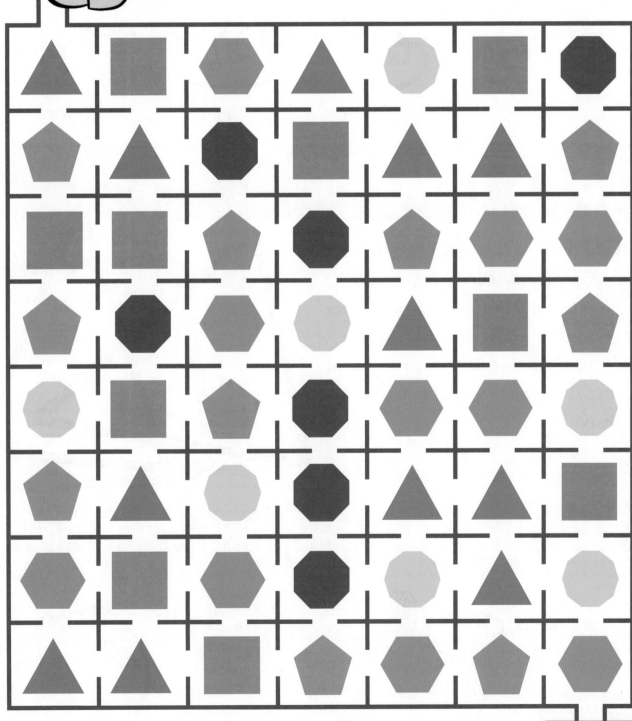

EXIT!

LET'S START!

GATHER THESE TOOLS AND MATERIALS.

10 pipe cleaners

5 plastic shopping bags

Scissors
(with an adult's help)

Paper clips

4 feet of string

Tape

6 coins

LET'S TINKER!

Fold the pipe cleaners into different 2-dimensional shapes. Then **make** 3-dimensional shapes. Can you make shapes by combining other shapes? Or how about making 3-dimensional shapes by combining 2-dimensional shapes?

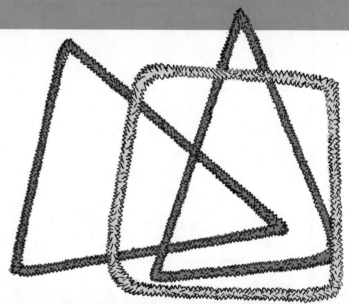

LET'S MAKE: PARACHUTE!

1. Cut a cone shape out of the corner of a plastic shopping bag.

2. Use a straightened paper clip to punch holes into four points along the edge. **Punch** the holes so there is equal distance between them.

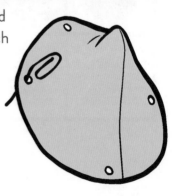

3. Thread a piece of string through each hole and tie it. If the bag tears, **use** tape to reinforce the holes.

4. Tie the strings to a pipe cleaner.

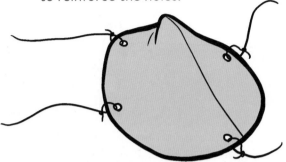

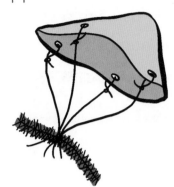

5. Wrap the pipe cleaner around a coin.

6. Test your parachute!

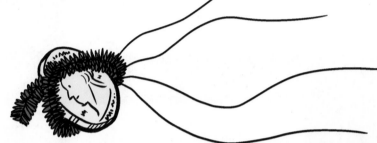

LET'S ENGINEER!

Now that the MotMots have parachutes, they are ready to go skydiving. But they want to float in the air as long as possible.

How can each MotMot float for a longer amount of time?

Apply the MotMot stickers from page 385 to some coins. **Drop** each MotMot with a parachute, and time how long it takes them to get to the ground. How could you modify each parachute so it stays in the air longer? **Try** some different designs and shapes, then time the skydives! Which design floats the longest?

PROJECT 14: DONE!
Get your sticker!

Geometry

Draw lines to divide each rectangle into parts that are the same size. Then count the number of parts.

Draw 1 line.

How many parts do you have now?

2

Draw 2 lines.

How many parts do you have now?

Draw 3 lines.

How many parts do you have now?

Draw 4 lines.

How many parts do you have now?

Draw 5 lines.

How many parts do you have now?

Color in the parts of each beam.

1 part out of 2

2 parts out of 3

2 parts out of 5

3 parts out of 8

4 parts out of 6

How many parts of each shape are missing?
Fill in each sentence. Then read it aloud.

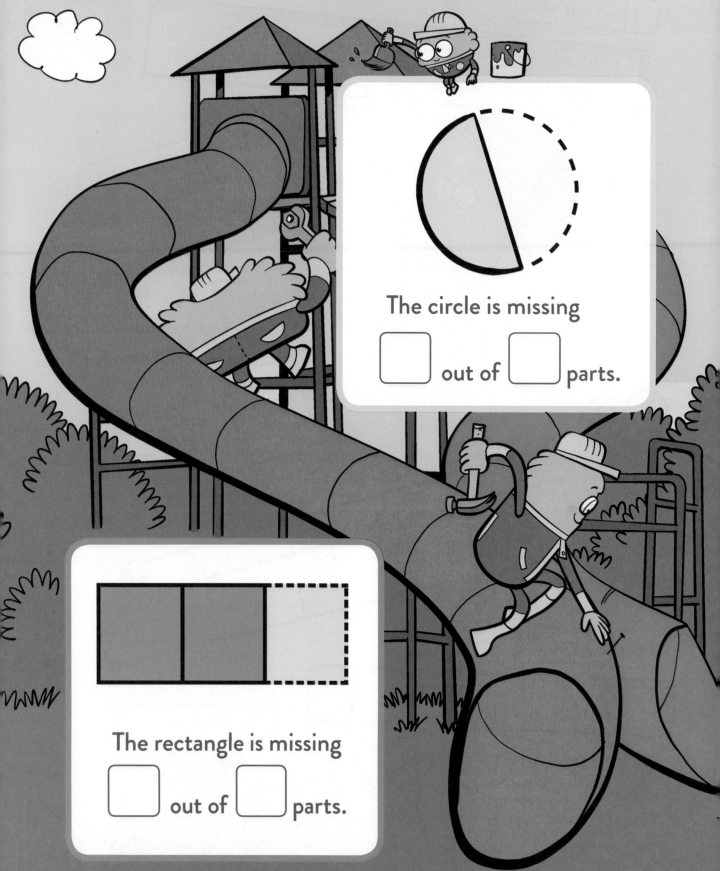

The circle is missing

⬜ out of ⬜ parts.

The rectangle is missing

⬜ out of ⬜ parts.

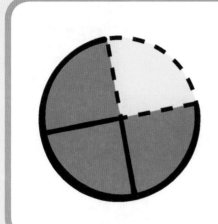

The circle is missing ☐ out of ☐ parts.

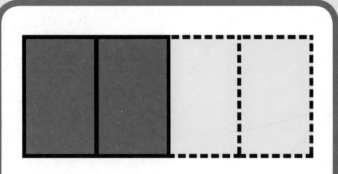

The rectangle is missing ☐ out of ☐ parts.

The rectangle is missing ☐ out of ☐ parts.

Match the shape to each description.

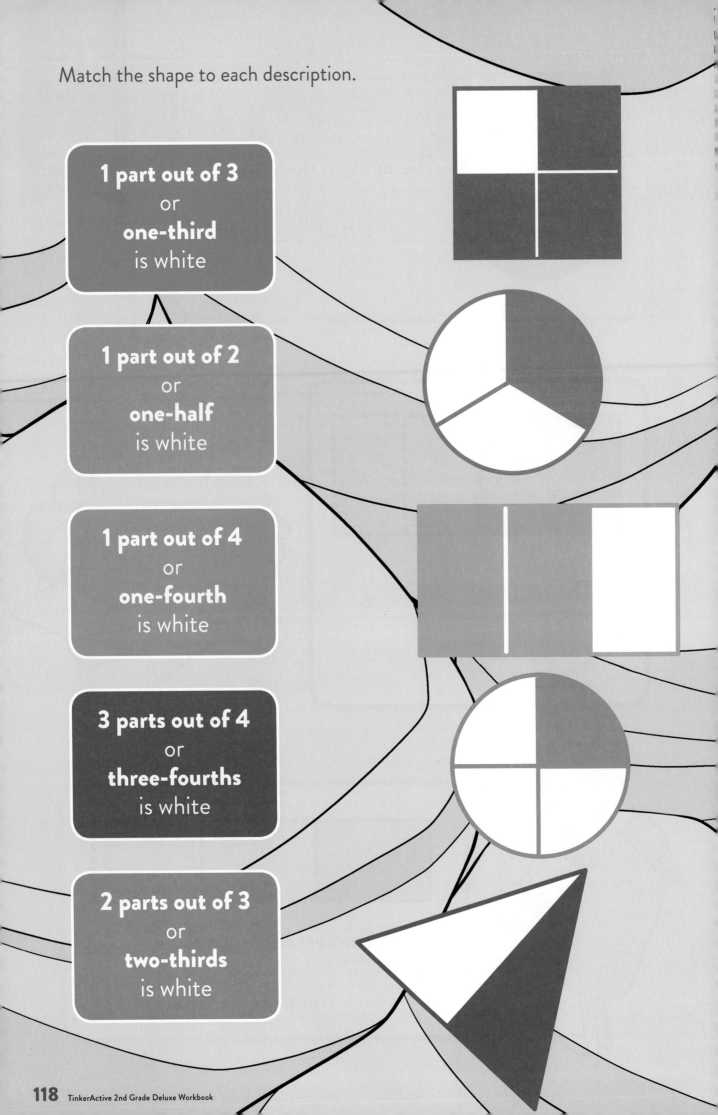

1 part out of 3
or
one-third
is white

1 part out of 2
or
one-half
is white

1 part out of 4
or
one-fourth
is white

3 parts out of 4
or
three-fourths
is white

2 parts out of 3
or
two-thirds
is white

Color the parts of each shape as labeled.

One-fourth

One-half

Two-thirds

Two-fifths

One-third

Two-thirds

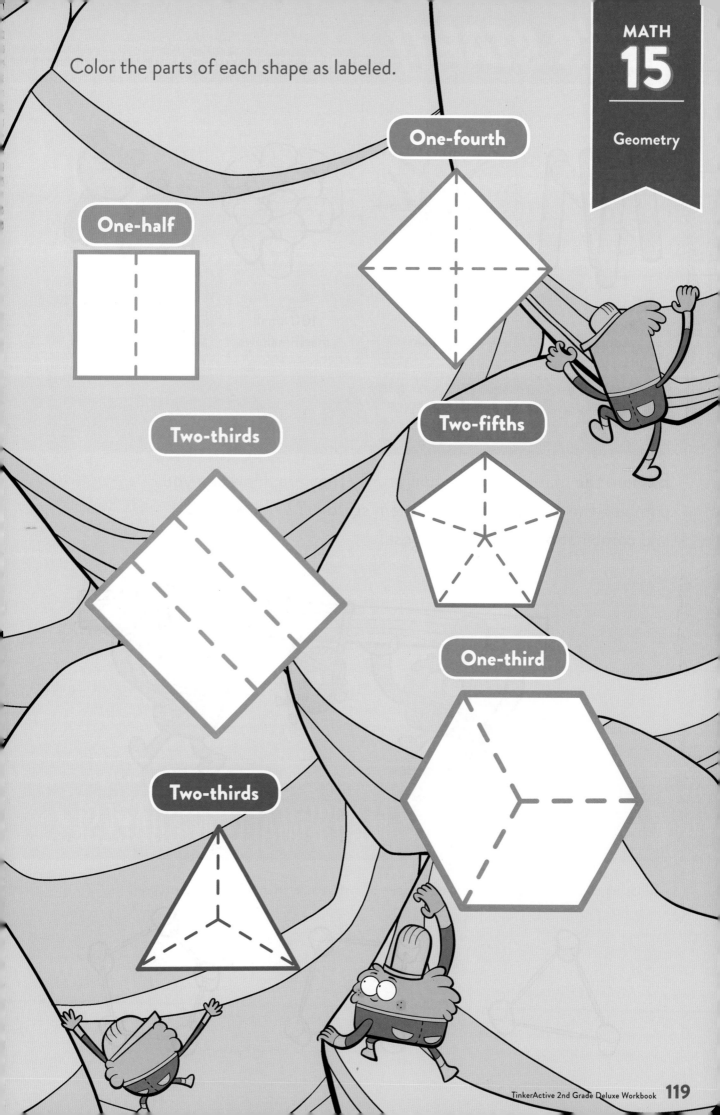

LET'S START! GATHER THESE TOOLS AND MATERIALS.

Craft sticks

Toothpicks

100 small marshmallows

Small figurines or or stuffed animals

LET'S TINKER!

Explore the materials to see how sturdy they are. How can you combine the materials to make them sturdier? What shapes and combinations are the strongest?

LET'S MAKE: MARSHMALLOW SHAPES!

1. Using toothpicks, **create** the base shapes of a square, a triangle, and a pentagon.

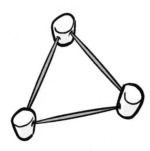

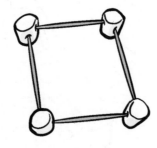

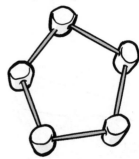

2. Make more of the base shapes from step 1 and combine them to make pyramids or cubes.

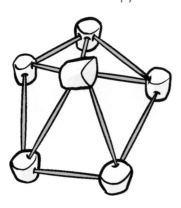
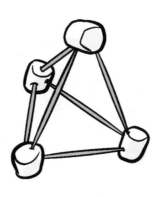
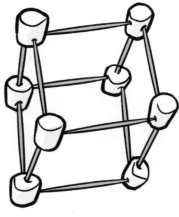

What other 2- and 3-dimensional shapes can you make?

LET'S ENGINEER!

The MotMots want to make a jungle gym to climb on at the playground, but they don't know what the strongest shape is.

How can the MotMots test the strength of different shapes?

Make a structure with your materials that reaches up to 12 inches using only one kind of shape. Then **make** another structure using another kind of shape. **Place** your stuffed animals or figurines on each structure to test its strength. Which shape is strongest?

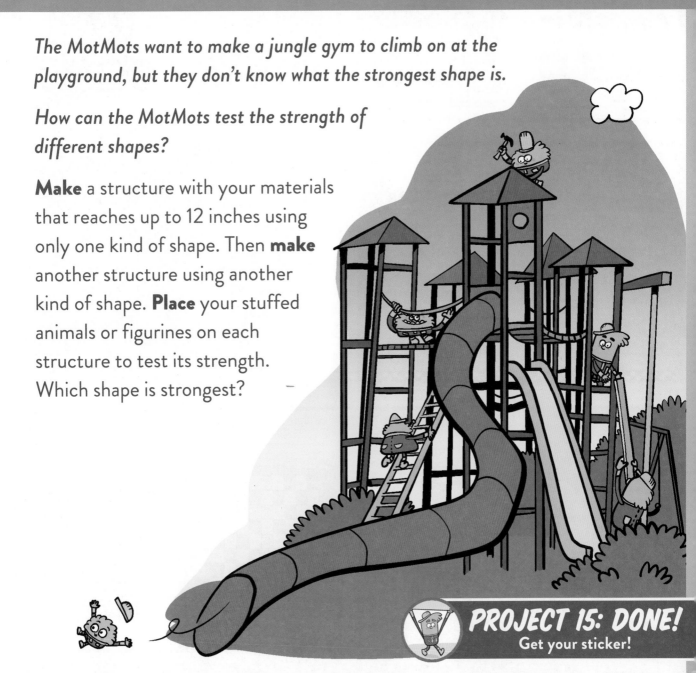

PROJECT 15: DONE!
Get your sticker!

ANSWER KEY

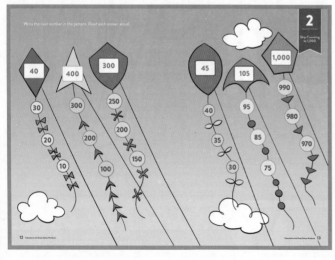

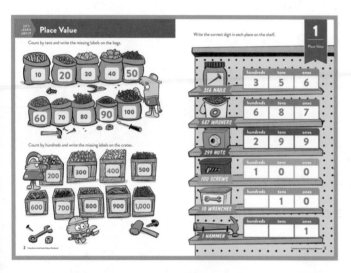

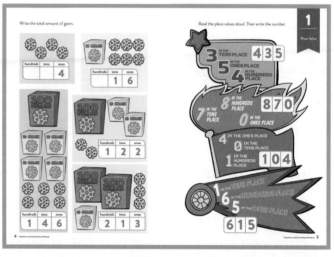

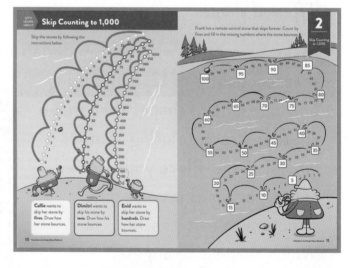

Comparing Numbers

Dimitri and Enid made a game called Less Than, Greater Than, Mot, Mot, Mot! Play it by yourself, or with a friend. Follow the directions, and when you reach each item, shout "MOT! MOT! MOT!"

Look around you. Can you touch something **SOFT** by taking less than three steps? Race to it and shout, "MOT, MOT, MOT!"

Now touch something **SHINY** in less than 2 hops.

Can you touch something **STRIPED** in greater than 9 skips?

Touch something **BIGGER** than you in less than 5 backward steps.

Can you touch something **BLUE** in greater than 12 side steps?

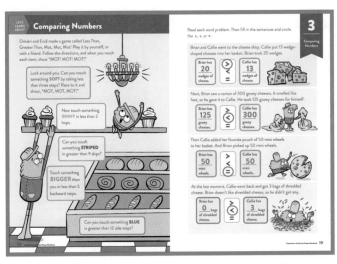

Read each word problem. Then fill in the sentences and circle the >, <, or =.

Brian and Callie went to the cheese shop. Callie put 13 wedge-shaped cheeses into her basket. Brian took 20 wedges.

Brian has **20** wedges of cheese. ⊙**>** ○< ○= Callie has **13** wedges of cheese.

Next, Callie saw a carton of 300 gooey cheeses. It smelled like feet, so he gave it to Callie. He took 125 gooey cheeses for himself.

Brian has **125** gooey cheeses. ○> ⊙**<** ○= Callie has **300** gooey cheeses.

Then Callie added her favorite pouch of 50 mini wheels to her basket. And Brian picked up 50 mini wheels.

Brian has **50** mini wheels. ○> ○< ⊙**=** Callie has **50** mini wheels.

At the last moment, Callie went back and got 3 bags of shredded cheese. Brian doesn't like shredded cheese, so he didn't get any.

Brian has **0** bags of shredded cheese. ○> ⊙**<** ○= Callie has **3** bags of shredded cheese.

Frank's pet alligator is hungry! Which containers have more food?

Compare the number on each container. Then write >, <, or = in each space.

747 > **724**

537 < **812**

981 = **981**

743 > **643**

619 < **632**

501 > **491**

15 = **15**

113 = **113**

Solve each problem.

Brian has **342** raisins. Amelia has **212**. Who has more? Write the comparison as a number sentence.
342 > **212**

Callie has **102** sunflower seeds, and Frank has **931** sunflower seeds. Who has more? Write the comparison as a number sentence.
102 < **931**

Enid has **113** raisins. Dimitri has **212** raisins. Who has more? Write the comparison as a number sentence.
113 < **212**

Compare Amelia and Dimitri. Who has more raisins? Write the comparison as a number sentence.
212 = **212**

Compare the number of chairs in your house to the number of doors. The next time you go outside, count the number of people wearing hats and people wearing glasses. Which is more?

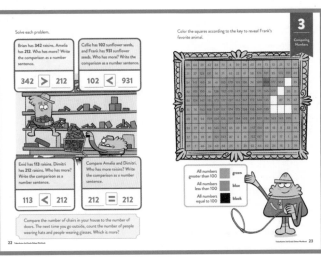

Color the squares according to the key to reveal Frank's favorite animal.

All numbers greater than 100 — green
All numbers less than 100 — blue
All numbers equal to 100 — black

Even & Odd

Callie and Brian are making chocolate bars. Color the squares in the chocolate mold to represent each number. Then circle whether the number is even or odd.

6 — Odd / **Even**
5 — **Odd** / Even
11 — **Odd** / Even
10 — Odd / **Even**
12 — Odd / **Even**
9 — **Odd** / Even

Follow the directions to reveal Brian's favorite filling for chocolates.

Color the squares with even numbers between 10 and 30 **red**.
Color the squares with odd numbers between 30 and 50 **green**.
Color the squares with even numbers between 51 and 60 **black**.

A number whose last digit is 0, 2, 4, 6, or 8 is even. All other numbers are odd.

Look at the chocolates and write the matching number sentence. Then solve the problem and circle whether the answer is even or odd.

4 + 4 = 8 (Even) Odd

3 + 3 + 3 = 9 Even (Odd)

2 + 2 + 2 + 2 = 8 (Even) Odd

3 + 3 + 3 + 3 + 3 + 3 = 18 (Even) Odd

Draw a line from each number sentence to its array. Then find the total and circle whether the answer is odd or even.

4 + 4 + 4 = 12 (Even) Odd

3 + 3 + 3 = 9 Even (Odd)

4 + 4 + 4 + 4 = 16 (Even) Odd

2 + 2 + 2 = 6 (Even) Odd

4 + 4 = 8 (Even) Odd

Answers will vary.

	Even	Odd
How many months till your birthday?		
How many chairs do you see right now?		
What is your age plus 7?		
How many steps are between your kitchen and the bathroom?		
What is the number of kids in your class plus 4?		
How many red objects can you count around you now?		

Answers will vary.

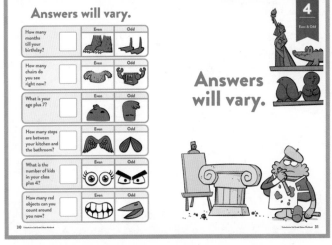

Addition & Subtraction

You can solve a subtraction problem by thinking of the related addition problem.

Solve each set of problems.

7 − 3 = **4** ; 3 + **4** = 7

11 − 6 = **5** ; 6 + 5 = 11

14 − 6 = **8** ; 6 + **8** = 14

13 − 8 = **5** ; 8 + 5 = 13

15 − 9 = **6** ; 9 + **6** = 15

16 − 9 = **7** ; 9 + **7** = 16

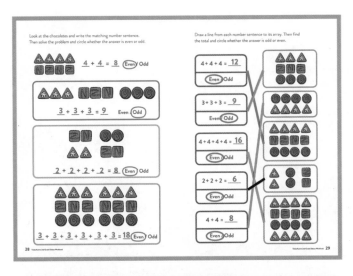

Use the treehouse chart below to solve the problems on the next page. Put your finger on the first number and then add or subtract by moving your finger by tens and then by ones. Fill in the sentences and write your answer.

1	2	3	4	5	6	7	8	9	10
11	12	13	14	15	16	17	18	19	20
21	22	23	24	25	26	27	28	29	30
31	32	33	34	35	36	37	38	39	40
41	42	43	44	45	46	47	48	49	50
51	52	53	54	55	56	57	58	59	60
61	62	63	64	65	66	67	68	69	70
71	72	73	74	75	76	77	78	79	80
81	82	83	84	85	86	87	88	89	90
91	92	93	94	95	96	97	98	99	100

43 + 17 = **60**
• Start at 43.
• Jump **10** spaces forward.
• Then move **7** more spaces forward.

74 − 19 = **55**
• Start at 74.
• Jump **10** spaces backward.
• Then move **9** more spaces backward.

25 + 28 = **53**
• Start at 25.
• Jump **20** spaces forward.
• Then move **8** more spaces forward.

93 − 19 = **74**
• Start at 93.
• Jump **10** spaces backward.
• Then move **9** more spaces backward.

18 + 53 = **71**
• Start at 18.
• Jump **50** spaces forward.
• Then move **3** more spaces forward.

55 − 26 = **29**
• Start at 55.
• Jump **20** spaces backward.
• Then move **6** more spaces backward.

46 + 16 = **62**
• Start at 46.
• Jump **10** spaces forward.
• Then move **6** more spaces forward.

84 − 77 = **7**
• Start at 84.
• Jump **70** spaces backward.
• Then move **7** more spaces backward.

Cut out the rooms in the tree house. Arrange each in the grid so every row and column adds up to 15.

Arrange the rooms so each row or column adds up to the number outside the grid.

Addition Using Place Value

Look at each addition sentence. Then look at each number as an array. Circle any groups of 10 blocks in the ones place, and circle any groups of 10 blocks in the tens place. Then solve.

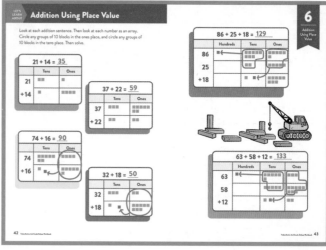

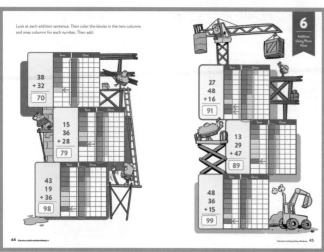

Look at each addition sentence. Then color the blocks in the tens columns and ones columns for each number. Then add.

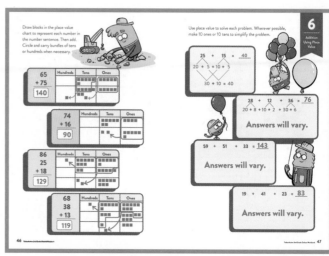

Draw blocks in the place value chart to represent each number in the number sentence. Then add. Circle and carry bundles of tens or hundreds when necessary.

Use place value to solve each problem. Wherever possible, make 10 ones or 10 tens to simplify the problem.

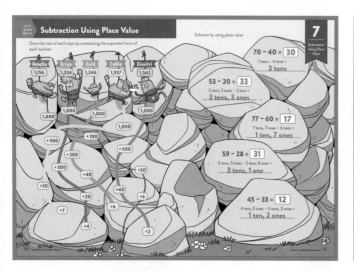

Subtraction Using Place Value

Draw the rest of each rope by connecting the expanded form of each number.

Subtract by using place value.

Subtract by using the expanded number form and jumping hundreds, tens, and ones.

Use the place value chart to solve each problem.

The MotMots are packing their backpacks for a nature hike! Draw a place value chart to solve each word problem.

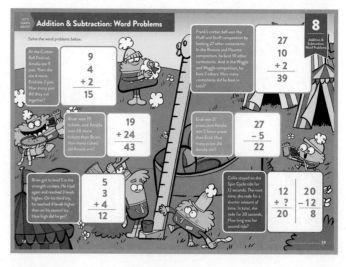

Addition & Subtraction: Word Problems

Solve the word problems below.

Read the story. As you read, tally the costume photos on page 45 by drawing circles (O) to add or crossing circles out (∅) to subtract.

Dimitri ran around the Cotton Ball Festival to take photos of all the different costumes. He saw **10** cowboy cotton balls in the cafeteria and **2** more by the water fountain.

He spotted **14** astronaut cotton balls on the trampolines. Then **4** more arrived. But then **10** of them took off their helmets and they were actually pirates!

Another **12** pirates were standing by the donut truck, along with **4** more cowboys.

Finally, in the dance hall at the Cotton Ball, he saw **7** cowboys, **2** pirates, **7** ninjas, and **1** astronaut.

That was when Dimitri saw that his camera's battery was almost dead. As he replaced the battery, he accidentally erased pictures of **10** cowboys and **3** astronauts.

Can you write your own word problem using cotton balls?

By the end of the night, how many pictures of each costume did he have?

cowboys: **13**   ninjas: **7**
astronauts: **6**   pirates: **24**

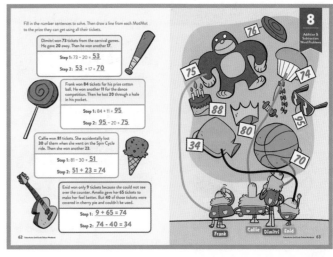

Fill in the number sentences to solve. Then draw a line from each MotMot to the prize they can get using all their tickets.

Dimitri won **73** tickets from the carnival games. He gave **20** away. Then he won another **17**.
Step 1: 73 − 20 = **53**
Step 2: **53** + 17 = **70**

Frank won **84** tickets for his prize cotton ball. He won another **11** for the dance competition. Then he lost **20** through a hole in his pocket.
Step 1: 84 + 11 = **95**
Step 2: **95** − 20 = **75**

Callie won **81** tickets. She accidentally lost **30** of them when she went on the Spin Cycle ride. Then she won another **23**.
Step 1: 81 − 30 = **51**
Step 2: **51** + 23 = **74**

Enid won only **9** tickets because she could not see over the counter. Amelia gave her **65** tickets to make her feel better. But **40** of those tickets were covered in cherry pie and couldn't be used.
Step 1: **9 + 65** = **74**
Step 2: **74 − 40 = 34**

Frank   Callie   Dimitri   Enid

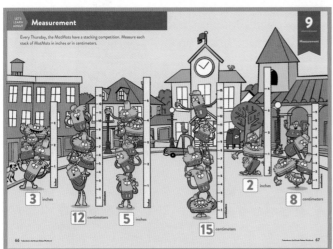

LET'S LEARN ABOUT

Measurement

Every Thursday, the MotMots have a stacking competition. Measure each stack of MotMots in inches or in centimeters.

3 inches
12 centimeters   **5** inches
15 centimeters
2 inches
8 centimeters

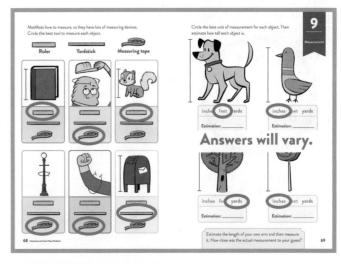

MotMots love to measure, so they have lots of measuring devices. Circle the best tool to measure each object.

Ruler   Yardstick   Measuring tape

Circle the best unit of measurement for each object. Then estimate how tall each object is.

inches **feet** yards
Estimation: _____

inches feet yards
Estimation: _____

inches feet **yards**
Estimation: _____

inches feet yards
Estimation: _____

Answers will vary.

Estimate the length of your own arm and then measure it. How close was the actual measurement to your guess?

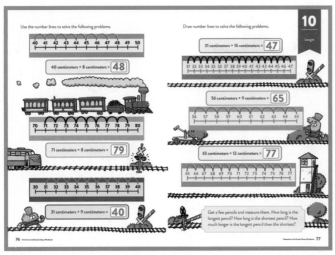

Put your hand on the page and trace around it. Then use a ruler to measure each finger in inches and in centimeters. Write your measurements next to each finger. Then measure the length of your whole hand in inches and in centimeters and write your measurements below.

Put your foot on the page and trace around it. Then measure the length of your foot in inches and in centimeters. Write your measurements below.

Answers will vary.

Answers will vary.

My hand is _____ inches or _____ centimeters long.

My foot is _____ inches or _____ centimeters long.

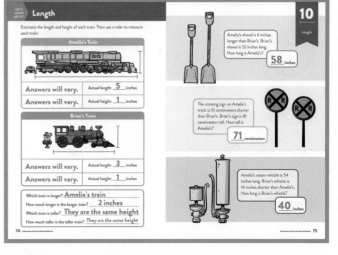

LET'S LEARN ABOUT

Length

Estimate the length and height of each train. Then use a ruler to measure each train.

Amelia's Train
Answers will vary.   Actual length: **5** inches
Answers will vary.   Actual height: **1** inches

Brian's Train
Answers will vary.   Actual length: **3** inches
Answers will vary.   Actual height: **1** inches

Which train is longer? **Amelia's train**
How much longer is the longer train? **2 inches**
Which train is taller? **They are the same height**
How much taller is the taller train? **They are the same height**

Amelia's shovel is 6 inches longer than Brian's. Brian's shovel is 52 inches long. How long is Amelia's? **58** inches

The crossing sign on Amelia's track is 10 centimeters shorter than Brian's. Brian's sign is 81 centimeters tall. How tall is Amelia's? **71** centimeters

Amelia's steam whistle is 54 inches long. Brian's whistle is 14 inches shorter than Amelia's. How long is Brian's whistle? **40** inches

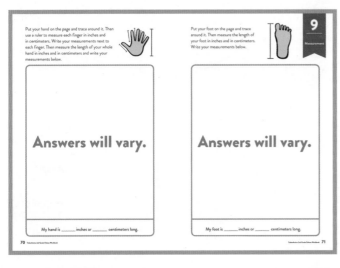

Use the number lines to solve the following problems.

40 centimeters + 8 centimeters = **48**

71 centimeters + 8 centimeters = **79**

31 centimeters + 9 centimeters = **40**

Draw number lines to solve the following problems.

31 centimeters + 16 centimeters = **47**

56 centimeters + 9 centimeters = **65**

65 centimeters + 12 centimeters = **77**

Get a few pencils and measure them. How long is the longest pencil? How long is the shortest pencil? How much longer is the longest pencil then the shortest?

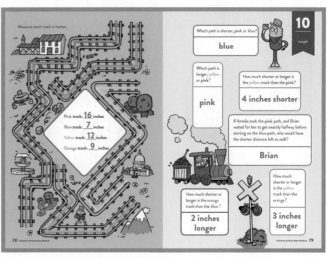

Measure each track in inches.

Pink track: **16** inches
Blue track: **7** inches
Yellow track: **12** inches
Orange track: **9** inches

Which path is shorter, pink or blue?
blue

Which path is longer, yellow or pink?
pink

How much shorter or longer is the yellow track than the pink?
4 inches shorter

If Amelia took the pink path, and Brian waited for her to get exactly halfway before starting on the blue path, who would have the shorter distance left to walk?
Brian

How much shorter or longer is the orange track then the blue?
2 inches longer

How much shorter or longer is the yellow track then the orange?
3 inches longer

Time

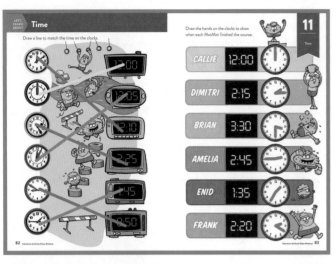

Draw a line to match the time on the clocks.

Draw the hands on the clocks to show when each MotMot finished the course.

CALLIE	12:00
DIMITRI	2:15
BRIAN	3:30
AMELIA	2:45
ENID	1:35
FRANK	2:20

Count by fives to tell the time. Then fill in the missing numbers in each sentence.

The clock shows **30** minutes after **3** o'clock.
It's **3** : **3** **0**

The clock shows **15** minutes after **4** o'clock.
It's **4** : **1** **5**

The clock shows **45** minutes after **2** o'clock.
It's **2** : **4** **5**

The clock shows **15** minutes after **9** o'clock.
It's **9** : **1** **5**

The clock shows **30** minutes after **7** o'clock.
It's **7** : **3** **0**

When do you do each activity? Draw hands on the clock. Then fill in the missing time in the sentence, as well as a.m. or p.m.

Answers will vary.

I wake up at ___ : ___.
I eat breakfast at ___ : ___.
I have recess at ___ : ___.
I go home at ___ : ___.
I eat dinner at ___ : ___.
I go to bed at ___ : ___.

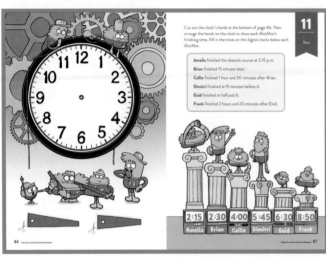

Cut out the clock's hands at the bottom of page 86. Then arrange the hands on the clock to show each MotMot's finishing time. Fill in the times on the digital clocks below each MotMot.

Amelia finished the obstacle course at 2:15 p.m.
Brian finished 15 minutes later.
Callie finished 1 hour and 30 minutes after Brian.
Dimitri finished at 15 minutes before 6.
Enid finished at half past 6.
Frank finished 2 hours and 20 minutes after Enid.

2:15	2:30	4:00	5:45	6:30	8:50
Amelia	Brian	Callie	Dimitri	Enid	Frank

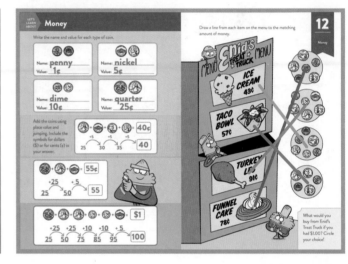

Money

Write the name and value for each type of coin.

Name: **penny** Value: **1¢**
Name: **nickel** Value: **5¢**
Name: **dime** Value: **10¢**
Name: **quarter** Value: **25¢**

Add the coins using place value and jumping. Include the symbols for dollars ($) or for cents (¢) in your answer.

40¢ / **40**
25 → 30 → 35 → 40

55¢ / **55**
25 → 50 → 55

$1 / **100**
25 → 50 → 75 → 85 → 95 → 100

Draw a line from each item on the menu to the matching amount of money.

ICE CREAM 43¢
TACO BOWL 57¢
TURKEY LEG 91¢
FUNNEL CAKE 78¢

What would you buy from Enid's Treat Truck if you had $1.00? Circle your choice!

How would you pay for each item? Write the amount of each coin or bill that you would use to buy each item.

Answers will vary. $1.73
Answers will vary. $2.15
Answers will vary. $1.83
Answers will vary. $3.91

Solve each word problem.

Frank has 98¢ and buys a teddy bear in a wagon. How much money will he have left?
23¢

Enid has 50¢ and wants the basket of baskets. How much money will she have left?
13¢

Brian wants a stuffed giraffe. He has one dollar. How much money will he have left?
20¢

Amelia has two dollars. She wants the volleyball. How much money will she have left?
$1.00

Do you have some coins? Write your own word problem based on what change you have and what you would like to buy. How much money will you have left?

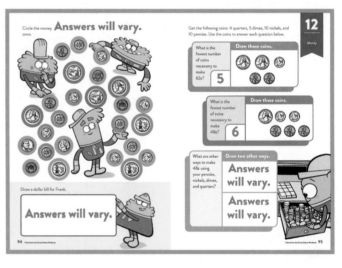

Circle the money **Answers will vary.** once.

Draw a dollar bill for Frank.
Answers will vary.

Get the following coins: 4 quarters, 5 dimes, 10 nickels, and 10 pennies. Use the coins to answer each question below.

What is the fewest number of coins necessary to make 62¢? **5** Draw those coins.

What is the fewest number of coins necessary to make 48¢? **6** Draw those coins.

What are other ways to make 48¢ using your pennies, nickels, dimes, and quarters? Draw two other ways.
Answers will vary.
Answers will vary.

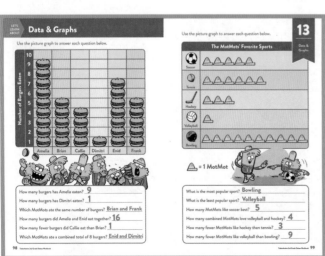

Data & Graphs

Use the picture graph to answer each question below.

How many burgers has Amelia eaten? **9**
How many burgers has Dimitri eaten? **1**
Which MotMots ate the same number of burgers? **Brian and Frank**
How many burgers did Amelia and Enid eat together? **16**
How many fewer burgers did Callie eat than Brian? **5**
Which MotMots ate a combined total of 8 burgers? **Enid and Dimitri**

Use the picture graph to answer each question below.

The MotMots' Favorite Sports

△ = 1 MotMot

What is the most popular sport? **Bowling**
What is the least popular sport? **Volleyball**
How many MotMots like soccer best? **5**
How many combined MotMots love volleyball and hockey? **4**
How many fewer MotMots like hockey than tennis? **3**
How many fewer MotMots like volleyball than bowling? **9**

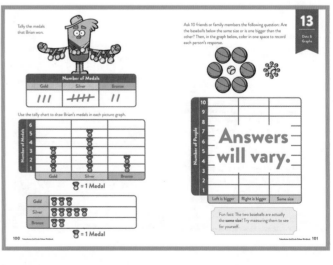

Tally the medals that Brian won.

Number of Medals

Gold	Silver	Bronze
III	HHT	II

Use the tally chart to draw Brian's medals in each picture graph.

= 1 Medal

Gold	Silver	Bronze

= 1 Medal

Ask 10 friends or family members the following question: Are the baseballs below the same size or is one bigger than the other? Then, in the graph below, color in one space to record each person's response.

Answers will vary.

Left is bigger | Right is bigger | Same size

Fun fact: The two baseballs are actually the **same size**! Try measuring them to see for yourself.

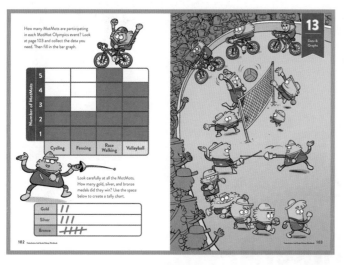

How many MotMots are participating in each MotMot Olympics event? Look at page 103 and collect the data you need. Then fill in the bar graph.

Number of MotMots				
5				
4				
3				
2				
1				
	Cycling	Fencing	Race Walking	Volleyball

Look carefully at all the MotMots. How many gold, silver, and bronze medals did they win? Use the space below to create a tally chart.

Gold	//
Silver	///
Bronze	‖‖‖‖

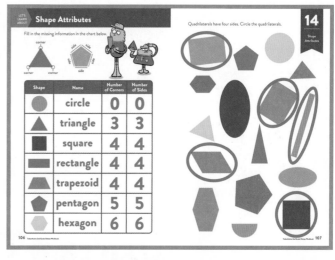

Fill in the missing information in the chart below.

Quadrilaterals have four sides. Circle the quadrilaterals.

Shape	Name	Number of Corners	Number of Sides
●	circle	0	0
▲	triangle	3	3
■	square	4	4
▬	rectangle	4	4
⬟	trapezoid	4	4
⬠	pentagon	5	5
⬡	hexagon	6	6

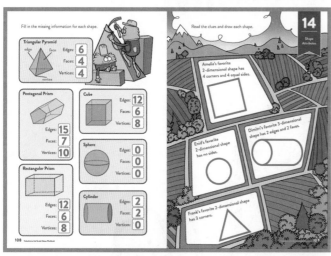

Fill in the missing information for each shape.

Read the clues and draw each shape.

Triangular Pyramid
Edges: 6
Faces: 4
Vertices: 4

Pentagonal Prism
Edges: 15
Faces: 7
Vertices: 10

Cube
Edges: 12
Faces: 6
Vertices: 8

Sphere
Edges: 0
Faces: 0
Vertices: 0

Rectangular Prism
Edges: 12
Faces: 6
Vertices: 8

Cylinder
Edges: 2
Faces: 2
Vertices: 0

Amelia's favorite 2-dimensional shape has 4 corners and 4 equal sides.

Enid's favorite 2-dimensional shape has no sides.

Dimitri's favorite 3-dimensional shape has 2 edges and 2 faces.

Frank's favorite 2-dimensional shape has 3 corners.

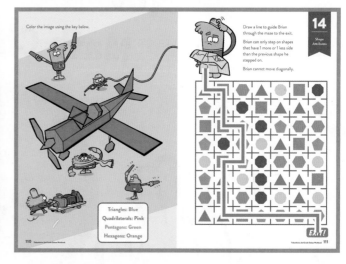

Color the image using the key below.

Draw a line to guide Brian through the maze to the exit.

Brian can only step on shapes that have 1 more or 1 less side than the previous shape he stepped on.

Brian cannot move diagonally.

Triangles: Blue
Quadrilaterals: Pink
Pentagons: Green
Hexagons: Orange

EXIT!

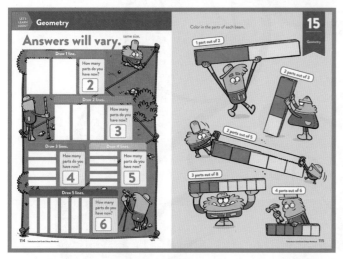

Answers will vary.

same size.

Color in the parts of each beam.

Draw 1 line.
How many parts do you have now? 2

Draw 2 lines.
How many parts do you have now? 3

Draw 3 lines.
How many parts do you have now? 4

Draw 4 lines.
How many parts do you have now? 5

Draw 5 lines.
How many parts do you have now? 6

1 part out of 2
2 parts out of 3
2 parts out of 5
3 parts out of 8
4 parts out of 6

How many parts of each shape are missing? Fill in each sentence. Then read it aloud.

The circle is missing 1 out of 4 parts.

The circle is missing 1 out of 2 parts.

The rectangle is missing 2 out of 4 parts.

The rectangle is missing 1 out of 3 parts.

The rectangle is missing 2 out of 3 parts.

Match the shape to each description.

Answers will vary.

1 part out of 3 or **one-third** is white

1 part out of 2 or **one-half** is white

1 part out of 4 or **one-fourth** is white

3 parts out of 4 or **three-fourths** is white

2 parts out of 3 or **two-thirds** is white

One-fourth
One-half
Two-thirds
Two-fifths
One-third
Two-thirds

TinkerActive WORKBOOKS

SECOND GRADE · SCIENCE · AGES 7–8

by Megan Hewes Butler

illustrated by Tae Won Yu

educational consulting by Lindsay Frevert

Odd Dot · New York

Properties of Matter

All things are made up of matter. All the objects around you, like a chair, a tree, or a pet, are matter. Matter can be described by how it looks, feels, and more!

Circle one word to describe each piece of matter.

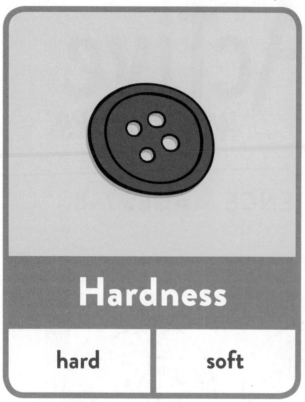

Hardness

| hard | soft |

Texture

| smooth | rough |

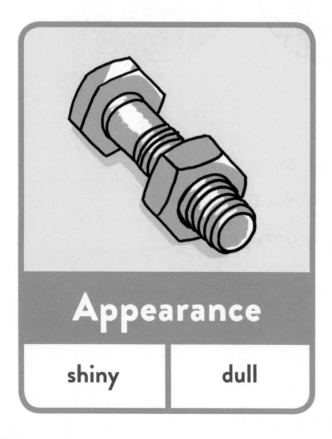

Appearance

| shiny | dull |

Flexibility

| flexible | stiff |

Observe your pencil. Then answer each question.

What color is it?

_____

_____

_____

What shape is it?

_____

_____

_____

What does it feel like?

_____

_____

_____

What does it sound like when you tap it?

_____

_____

_____

Matter has different properties—for example, paper is thin, while a tree trunk is thick. Because of these differences, different types of matter are useful for different needs.

Read the text aloud. Then circle the object that each MotMot needs and explain why you chose that object.

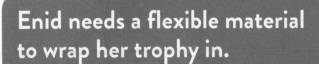
Enid needs a flexible material to wrap her trophy in.

or

Why? _____

_____

Frank needs a strong material to make a leash for his pet alligator.

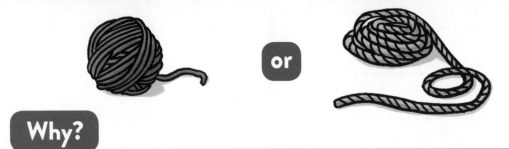

or

Why? _____

_____

Brian needs a soft material to clean this mirror with.

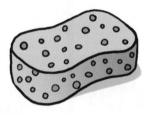 or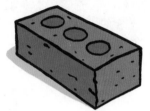

Why? _____

_____

Dimitri needs a heavy material to hold open this door.

 or

Why? _____

_____

Hunt for matter around you. Find an object that fits each description below. Then write its name or draw it.

A material that is
WARM

A material that is
STICKY

A material that is
RED

A material that is
WET

A material that is
BUMPY

A material that is
SOFT

A material that is
BENDABLE

Choose something of your own to observe, and draw it. Then circle all the descriptions that apply, or fill in your own.

My object is a _____ .

COLOR

Other: _____

SHAPE

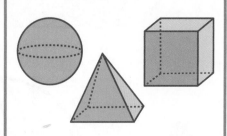

Other: _____

TEXTURE

- **Smooth**
- **Bumpy**
- **Hairy**

Other: _____

SIZE

- **Small**
- **Medium**
- **Large**

FLEXIBILITY

- **Flexible**
- **Rigid**
- **Mixed**

HARDNESS

- **Soft**
- **Hard**
- **Mixed**

I notice that my object is also _____

_____

_____ .

Markers

Paper

2 or more cans

10 or more craft sticks

10 or more plastic cups

Aluminum foil

LET'S TINKER!

Observe each of your materials.

- What color is it?
- Is it round?
- Pointed?
- Slippery?

Describe them all.

- How are they the same?
- How are they different?

Group materials that have something in common.

LET'S MAKE: TOWERING TOWER

Make a tall tower with your materials.

Ask yourself: What qualities should the materials have in order to make a tall tower?

Choose rigid and strong materials that can be stacked without bending. **Choose** wide materials that can't fall over. How can you stack the materials to make the tower taller and stronger?

LET'S ENGINEER!

Enid and Callie are playing hide-and-seek with the other MotMots. Enid wants to send a message to Callie, who is hiding behind the pantry door.

How can Enid send Callie a message?

Think about what shape of material can be passed under a door.

- What other properties should the material have?
- How can the materials be combined to solve the problem?

Write your own secret message. You can **add** stickers from page 387.

Test your ideas by trying to send a note under a door.

PROJECT 1: DONE!
Get your sticker!

Assemble and Disassemble Parts

Many objects around you are made up of multiple parts. Look at the swing and study its parts. Next,

- Cross out the chains.
- Underline the seat.
- Circle the hangers.

Which parts are left over? _____

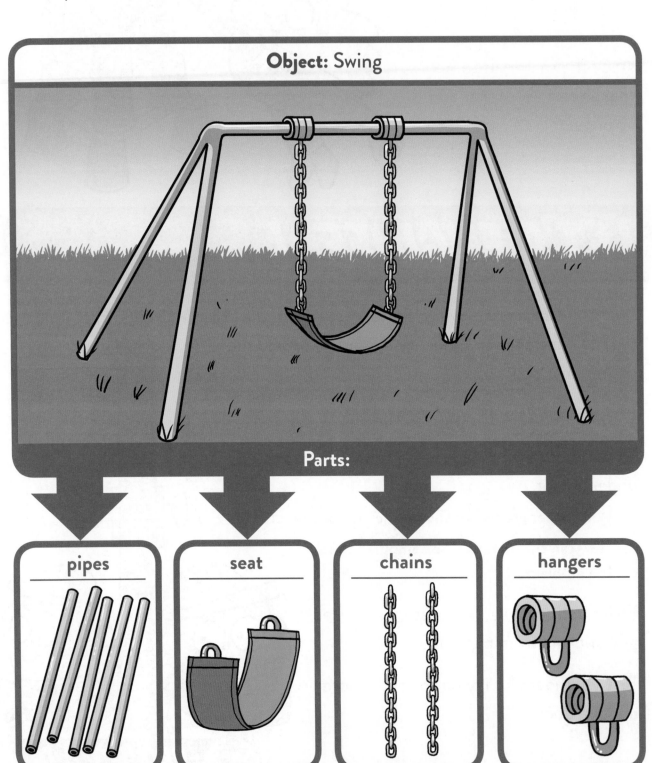

Object: Swing

Parts:

| pipes | seat | chains | hangers |

Write the names of and draw the parts that make up this object.

Object: Tire Swing

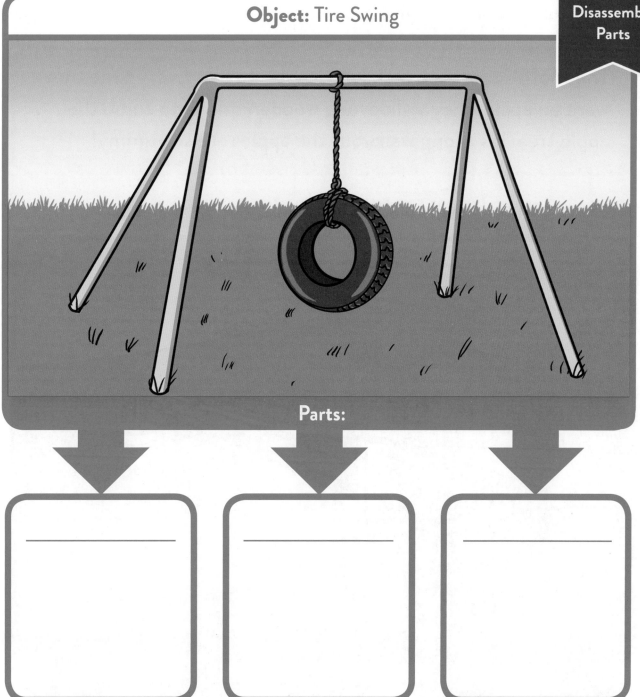

Parts:

Find one object around you that is made up of multiple parts. Then write about the object and its parts.

_____

_____

_____

Many objects can be broken into parts. Then the parts can be used to build something new.

Read the story aloud. Then follow the instructions.

The MotMots love to pick juicy apples to eat. Every time they want an apple, they walk over a wooden bridge to climb the apple tree. It's a long walk, but the apples are so yummy!

Write the names of and draw the parts that make up the bridge.

Parts of the bridge:

buckets

Enid loves apples the most. If she rides her bike, she can get to the apple tree more quickly and pick apples more often. She rides to the park, but she can't get her bike over the bridge.

What could Enid build with the same parts so she could ride her bike over the stream? Draw it.

Callie and her friends are camping. They want to picnic, but it looks like it will rain soon. How can Callie keep her friends and the food dry?

Look at the materials and parts that Callie has at the campsite.

butterfly net

sleeping bag

picnic basket

leaves

picnic blanket

jump rope

rocks

sticks

Describe how Callie can solve the problem.

_____

_____

_____

Draw what she can build to solve the problem.

LET'S START!

Tape

Paper

Markers

Aluminum foil

4–6 toothpicks

4–6 cotton balls

4–6 rubber bands

1 or more toilet paper rolls

Beans, nuts, or dried pasta

LET'S TINKER!

Put your materials together so they make a new object or do something new.
Stack them, fit one inside another, or attach them.

What new object did you make?

What can it do?

LET'S MAKE: ROBOT PARTS

Make a robot. **Choose** parts for the body, legs, and other features—like a head, arms, antennae, and buttons. You can **add** stickers from page 387. How can you make the parts stay together?

LET'S ENGINEER!

Amelia wants to play music with her friends. But there are no instruments left!

How can Amelia make music with her friends?

Combine your materials to make an instrument.

- How can the materials be combined to make sound?
- Is your instrument quiet or loud?
- What kind of sound does it make?

PROJECT 2 DONE!
Get your sticker!

States of Matter

Matter can exist in different forms, including a solid, a liquid, or a gas.

| A **solid** has shape and volume. | A **liquid** has volume, but no shape. It flows. | A **gas** has no volume or shape. It fills the volume of its container. |

Read about the matter. Then draw what you predict will happen when these cups are emptied.

A grape is a solid, so each one has a shape.

Grape juice is a liquid, so it has no shape.

Brian is searching for solids, liquids, and gases. Fill in the state of matter of each object.

Solids, liquids, and gases have different properties, and each can be used for different purposes.

Read what each MotMot needs aloud. Then circle the material that will solve each problem, and fill in whether it is a solid, a liquid, or a gas.

Dimitri needs something to drink.

He needs a _____.

Callie needs something firm to stay between two cookies.

MILK

Milk

She needs a _____.

Frank needs something that can expand to fill this balloon.

Enid needs something she can pour into this vase.

He needs a _____.

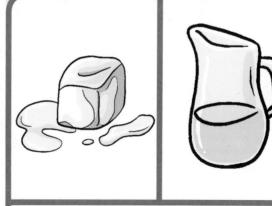

She needs a _____.

The molecules that make up a solid, a liquid, and a gas act differently.

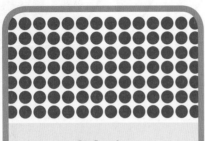

In a **solid**, the molecules are tightly packed. They jiggle only a little.

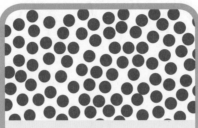

In a **liquid**, the molecules are close together but have some room to move and slide around.

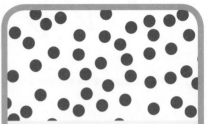

In a **gas**, the molecules have lots of space to move around quickly and freely!

Join the MotMots and move your body like a molecule! Then draw yourself dancing in each state: solid, liquid, and gas.

Jiggle your body a little like a **solid**.

Move and slide your body around like a **liquid**.

Stretch your body to move freely and quickly like a **gas**.

Matter is in different states all around you. Hunt for examples in your home and follow the directions below.

Describe and draw a **solid**.

_____

_____

_____

Describe and draw a **liquid**.

_____

_____

_____

Can you see a **gas** in your home? If so, describe and draw it. If not, why do you think you can't see any gases?

_____

_____

_____

_____

Aluminum foil	Plastic wrap	1 or more plastic cups	4–6 rubber bands	4–6 drinking straws

Water	Toys	Measuring cup	5–8 spoonfuls of cornstarch	Small backpack or bag

LET'S TINKER!

Solids have their own shape—they do not need a container to hold them. **Change** the shapes of the foil, plastic wrap, cup, rubber bands, or straws. **Fold**, tear, bend, and twist the materials.

Liquids cannot hold their own shape—they need a container. **Make** something that can hold a liquid and fill it with water.

Air is a gas that is all around us, but we cannot see it. **Make** bubbles of air that you can see! **Fill** a cup halfway with water. **Lower** your straw to the bottom of the cup and blow softly. What do you see?

LET'S MAKE: PLAY GOOP!

1. Measure $\frac{1}{4}$ cup of water into your bowl.

2. Stir in 5 to 8 heaping spoonfuls of cornstarch, one at a time. The goop is ready when you can still stir it, even though it is hard to do so.

3. Play!

- Does it feel like a liquid or a solid?

- Does it move like a liquid or a solid?

- Can you make a ball—a solid—with it?

- In what ways does the goop act like a liquid?

- In what ways does it act like a solid?

Caution: When you are done experimenting, do not wash the goop down a sink drain. Instead, throw it in the trash.

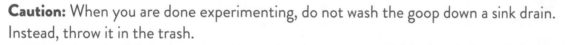

LET'S ENGINEER!

Frank is packing for a trip. He needs to fit all his things into his sack, but it is filling up fast. Each item is a solid and takes up space.

How can Frank fit all his things into his sack?

Try to fit all your materials in your bag, as if you are going on a trip. How can you make the materials take up less space? Can any of them change shape?

PROJECT 3: DONE!
Get your sticker!

Temperature

Temperature is a measure of how much heat is in an object. Heating up an object or cooling it down can cause changes that we can see.

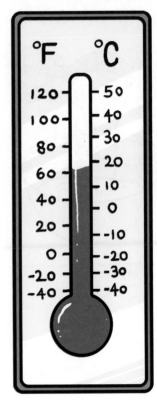

When ice cream heats up enough, it changes from a solid to a liquid.

Write about and draw what happens when an ice-cream cone is in the hot sun.

_____

_____

_____

When water cools down enough, it changes from a liquid to a solid.

Write about and draw what happens when a pond full of water is in freezing cold weather.

Some changes that happen from heating and cooling are reversible. This means that the matter can change back to the way it was.

Some changes that happen from heating and cooling are *not* reversible. This means that the matter *cannot* go back to the way it was.

Observe each change below. Then write a ✔ next to the sentence that accurately describes the temperature changes.

☐ The water freezes and becomes ice. Then the ice thaws and becomes water.

☐ The water freezes and becomes ice. The ice cannot become water again.

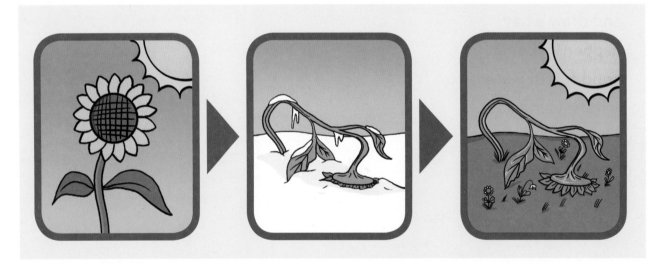

☐ The flower freezes and dies. The flower is alive again when it gets warm.

☐ The flower freezes and dies. The flower cannot come back to life when it gets warm again.

Look at each object as it heats up and cools down. Then write a ✔ next to "reversible" or "not reversible."

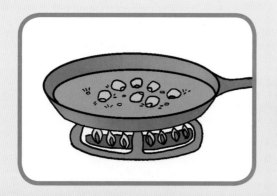

This change is:

☐ reversible   ☐ not reversible

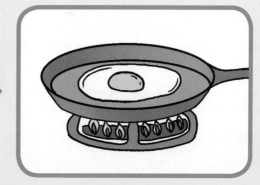

This change is:

☐ reversible   ☐ not reversible

This change is:

☐ reversible   ☐ not reversible

Hunt for objects around you that are affected by temperature. Draw what you find. Then answer each question.

Something that is cold

What happens if it becomes hot?

_____

_____

_____

Something that is warm

What happens if it becomes cold?

_____

_____

_____

Something that is a solid

What happens if it becomes hot?

_____

_____

_____

Something that is a liquid

What happens if it becomes cold?

_____

_____

_____

Find food in your kitchen that changes when you cook it. Then draw or write to answer each question.

What does it look like before it is cooked?	What does it look like after it is cooked?

The change is:

☐ reversible   ☐ not reversible

Find something in your freezer that you can thaw. Then draw or write to answer each question.

What does it look like before it is thawed?	As it warms up, what changes do you observe?

The change is:

☐ reversible   ☐ not reversible

LET'S START! GATHER THESE TOOLS AND MATERIALS.

Ice cubes

Leaf

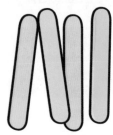
Craft sticks

Crayons

Cup of water

Piece of string
2–3 feet long

Aluminum foil

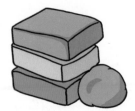
Modeling Clay

LET'S TINKER!

Change the temperature of your materials by blowing on them.

- **Which materials change?**

- **Are the changes reversible or not reversible?**

LET'S MAKE: FREEZER EXPERIMENT

1. **Observe** your materials.

- What do they feel like? Look like? Smell like?

- Do they bend or break when you touch them?

2. Put the materials in the freezer. **Predict** what will happen to them.

3. Take the materials out of the freezer in a few hours and make new observations.

- How did they change?

- Do any of them look different? Feel different? Smell different?

- Were your predictions correct?

LET'S ENGINEER!

Callie wants an ice-cold drink, so she breaks off some icicles for her juice. But when she holds the cold icicles in her warm hands, they start to melt!

How can she carry the icicles to her kitchen without melting them?

Design a container that can keep ice colder than your hands do. How can you keep the ice cubes away from the warmth of your hands? **Use** ice cubes to test which materials can keep ice frozen.

PROJECT 4: DONE!
Get your sticker!

Water Cycle

Over 70% of Earth's surface is covered in water. Water is the only thing that can naturally be found on Earth as a solid, a liquid, and a gas.

Write a ✔ next to the correct form of water.

☐ Solid
☐ Liquid

☐ Solid
☐ Liquid

☐ Solid
☐ Liquid

☐ Solid
☐ Liquid

☐ Solid
☐ Liquid

☐ Solid
☐ Liquid

Animals live on and in the water—both solid and liquid—all over Earth. Draw a line to connect each animal to its water habitat.

sailfish

dolphin

emperor penguin

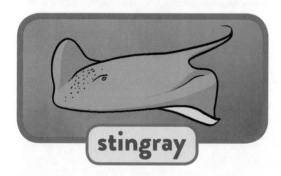

stingray

polar bear

POLAR HABITAT

OPEN OCEAN HABITAT

The water cycle describes the way water moves to and from the land, sky, and ocean. Water that starts on the land becomes a gas in the sky, and then becomes a solid or liquid that falls back to Earth. The water cycle repeats over and over again.

Look at the water cycle, and read the descriptions aloud. Then answer each question.

Evaporation

Water from rivers, lakes, streams, and oceans changes to water vapor when the Sun heats Earth.

Condensation

Water vapor in the air changes into small drops of liquid water when it gets colder. The small water drops come together to make clouds.

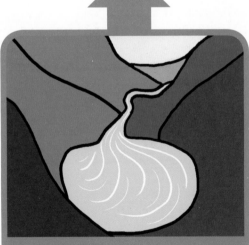

Collection

Liquid water collects in rivers, lakes, streams, and oceans.

Precipitation

Water falls to Earth from clouds as rain, hail, or snow.

You breathe on a cold day and you can see your breath.

Is this water vapor a **liquid** or a **gas**?

_____

Clouds become heavy with water and raindrops fall to Earth.

Are these drops **precipitation** or **evaporation**?

_____

You leave a bucket of water outside for a few days, and later you find less water in the bucket.

Is the water **evaporating** or **precipitating**?

_____

You add ice to a glass of water, and water drops form on the outside as it cools.

Are these drops **condensation** or **evaporation**?

_____

Which parts of the water cycle have you seen for yourself?

_____

All forms of water can be seen in the weather. Observe and record your weather for a week.

	Draw the weather outside your home.	Is there any precipitation?	Is it a solid, liquid, or gas?
Sunday		☐ yes ☐ no	_____
Monday		☐ yes ☐ no	_____
Tuesday		☐ yes ☐ no	_____
Wednesday		☐ yes ☐ no	_____
Thursday		☐ yes ☐ no	_____
Friday		☐ yes ☐ no	_____
Saturday		☐ yes ☐ no	_____

Severe weather events often have precipitation. Read each definition. Then draw a line to the matching picture.

In a **hailstorm**, balls and lumps of ice, called hail, fall like rain.

In a **thunderstorm**, heavy rain falls. There is thunder, lightning, and sometimes wind or hail.

A **hurricane** is a storm that forms over the ocean. Fast-spinning winds pick up water, move at over 74 miles per hour, and make heavy rain.

A **blizzard** is a cold-weather storm with strong winds. Snow is blown so quickly that seeing is difficult.

LET'S START!

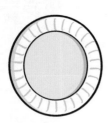
Paper plate

Permanent markers

2 or more plastic sandwich bags

Water

Tape

Water bottle

Ice cubes

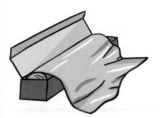
Aluminum foil

LET'S TINKER!

Place some of your materials in the bowl of water. **Watch** what happens when they get wet.

- How do they change?
- Do any of them stay the same?
- How do they move in the water?
- What else do you notice?

LET'S MAKE: YOUR OWN WATER CYCLE

1. Using the permanent markers, **draw** an ocean at the bottom of a plastic bag and clouds at the top.

2. Fill your bag with about 1 inch of water and seal the top tightly.

3. Tape the bag to a window with lots of sunlight.

4. Watch the water inside your bag "cycle" over several days! Can you tell when the water evaporates, condenses, and precipitates?

LET'S ENGINEER!

Dimitri wants to put ice cubes in his water bottle, but the ice cubes he has won't fit through the neck of the bottle.

How can he freeze more water so the cubes fit into the bottle?

Design a new ice cube shape that can fit into the bottle. What shapes can solve the problem?

Make a mold with your foil, pour in water, and put it in your freezer. After a few hours, **remove** your new ice cube. Does it fit into a water bottle?

PROJECT 5: DONE!
Get your sticker!

Earth's Surface

Earth's surface is made of rocks and dirt, and it is constantly changing. Many things cause these changes, including animals, plants, people, and the weather.

Look at each each picture. Then write a ✔ next to what caused the change to Earth's surface.

☐ Animals   ☐ People
☐ Plants   ☐ Weather

☐ Animals   ☐ People
☐ Plants   ☐ Weather

☐ Animals   ☐ People
☐ Plants   ☐ Weather

☐ Animals   ☐ People
☐ Plants   ☐ Weather

☐ Animals   ☐ People
☐ Plants   ☐ Weather

☐ Animals   ☐ People
☐ Plants   ☐ Weather

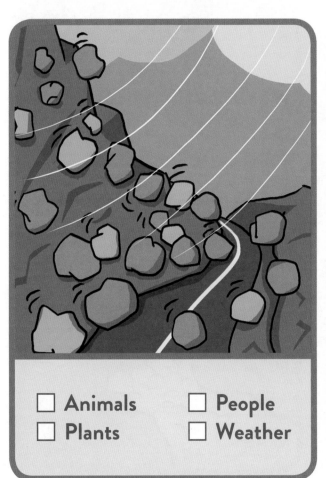

☐ Animals   ☐ People
☐ Plants   ☐ Weather

☐ Animals   ☐ People
☐ Plants   ☐ Weather

Some effects of wind and water on Earth's surface can be slowed down or even stopped.

Read each definition aloud. Then draw a line to the matching picture.

A **windbreak** is a row of trees or other plants used to protect the ground from erosion by the wind.

A **dam** is a barrier built in a river to hold back or slow down the water. Dams also release water when needed.

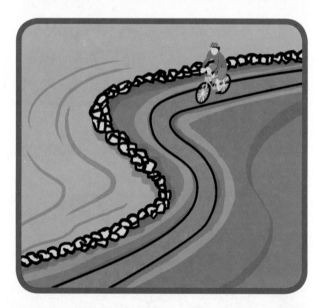

A **levee** is a large wall or mound of earth that provides protection from high water and storms. A levee does not move.

When it rains, the river in Tinker Town usually overflows. The water floods onto the playground where the MotMots play. They can't play there until the water is absorbed by the ground and the ground dries again.

What could stop the flooding? Draw your solution.

Describe your solution.

_____

_____

_____

_____

Circle the MotMot in each pair of pictures who is doing something to protect Earth's surface.

Write about and draw what you can do at school to help protect Earth's surface.

_____

_____

Write about and draw what you can do at home to help protect Earth's surface.

_____

_____

LET'S START!

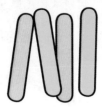
4 or more craft sticks

5 or more rocks

5 or more buttons

Large metal tray or pan

Dirt, mud, or modeling clay

Sticks

3 or more leaves

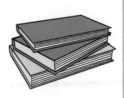
Stack of books

Large paper cup

Water

LET'S TINKER!

One way that animals change the surface of Earth is by making prints and impressions on the dirt.

Make your own fingerprints or handprints. **Find** materials you can use to make the prints in.

- Which materials do not work for making prints? Why?

- What other kinds of prints can you make?

LET'S MAKE: RECYCLED TIC-TAC-TOE

1. Lay 4 craft sticks in a grid.

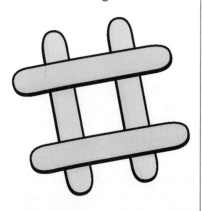

2. Get 5 rocks for yourself and 5 buttons for the other player.

3. Play tic-tac-toe!

LET'S ENGINEER!

Enid wants to put a bench in a sunny spot so she can sit and read outside. But the only sunny spot is exactly where a stream runs.

How can Enid change the path of the stream using natural materials?

Make a model to find out how to change the path of a stream. **Work** outdoors, or work indoors using a sink or a bathtub.

- Place a smooth layer of natural materials in the bottom of the tray. Try using mud, dirt, rocks, sticks, and leaves, or use modeling clay.

- Then tilt the tray and put a stack of books under one side to keep it slanted.

- Using a cup, pour a little bit of water at the top of your tray. Watch where the water goes.

- Use the natural materials in the tray to build a dam, walls, barriers, and hills to change the path of the water. Pour water in again and observe what happens.

PROJECT 6: DONE!
Get your sticker!

Changes on Earth

Some changes on Earth's surface happen slowly, and other changes happen quickly. For example, most volcanoes erupt quickly. But each volcano is unique. Some volcanoes take weeks or even years to finish erupting.

Read the stages of a volcanic eruption. Then write the numbers 1, 2, and 3 to put the eruption in order.

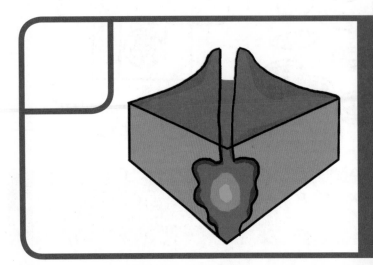

When a volcano becomes active, magma gathers beneath the volcano. Sometimes Earth shakes, like an earthquake, as the volcano begins to erupt.

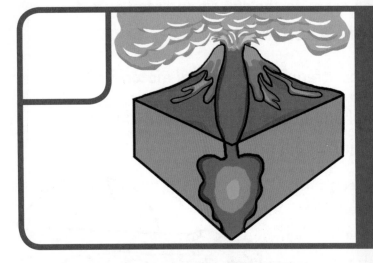

An explosion of gases pushes the magma out of the volcano. Once it is on Earth's surface, we call it lava. Lava oozes down the slopes, and ash fills the sky.

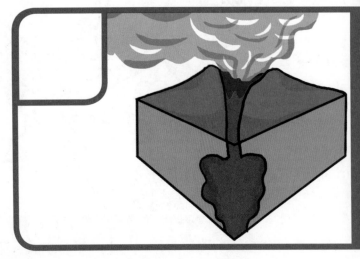

The lava finishes erupting. The empty volcano is weak and often collapses into the magma chamber, leaving a crater.

Read about each way Earth changes quickly. Then follow the directions.

An earthquake is when the ground shakes because Earth's crust moves deep inside it.

Draw how this place might look just after an **earthquake**.

A landslide is when rocks, mud, or other parts of Earth's surface slide down a mountain or hill.

Draw how this place might look just after a **landslide**.

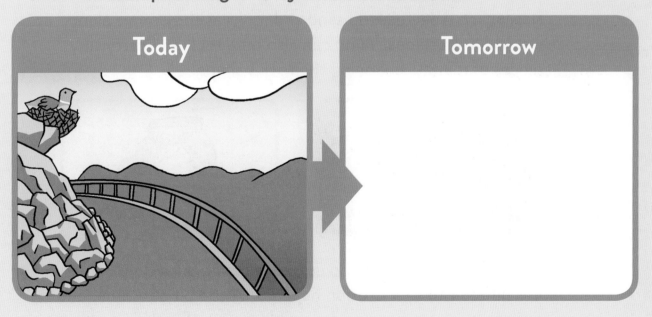

Some changes on Earth happen slowly—so slowly that no one can observe them.

Read the report aloud.

All About Erosion

Erosion is when Earth's surface is slowly worn away. Over time, the shape of the land changes.

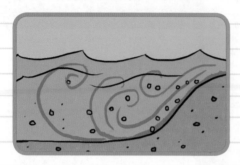 

Water causes most erosion. Bits of sand and small rocks are picked up by a river and moved. The Grand Canyon, in Arizona, is an example of water erosion over a very long time.

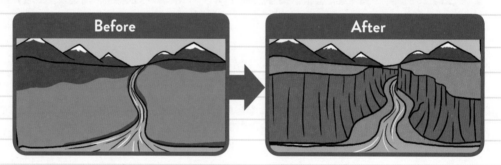

Ice and **wind** can cause erosion, too. Glaciers are made of flowing ice. They pick up sand and rocks as they move along, just like a river does. Wind can also hit a rock and carry tiny pieces of it away, changing the rock's shape!

Erosion happens all around us, but it happens so slowly that it is difficult to see. Erosion happens a little bit at a time, but over many years it can make big changes to Earth.

Draw how erosion might make this place look next year and in one hundred years.

Today

Tomorrow

Next Year

100 Years

Do these events change Earth slowly or quickly? Write a ✔ next to the correct speed.

A hurricane changes Earth:

☐ quickly   ☐ slowly

A glacier changes Earth:

☐ quickly   ☐ slowly

An earthquake changes Earth:

☐ quickly   ☐ slowly

Erosion changes Earth:

☐ quickly   ☐ slowly

Which event do you think can change Earth the fastest? Why?

_____

_____

_____

_____

Which event do you think can change Earth the slowest? Why?

_____

_____

_____

_____

Draw how Earth's surface around you changes.

Are the changes you see fast or slow? Write about what you observe.

_____

_____

_____

_____

LET'S START!

4–6 cotton balls

4–6 pieces of dried pasta

Aluminum foil

Aluminum foil

4–6 paper clips

Tall plastic or glass cup

Baking soda

Dish soap

Large metal pan

Vinegar

LET'S TINKER!

Which of the following materials can be changed: cotton balls, dried pasta, aluminum foil, and paper clips? **Make** them change if you can. **Bend** them, crush them, wet them, scratch them, expand them, or try something else.

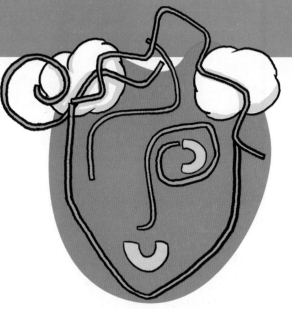

- Do the materials change slowly or quickly?
- Are there any materials that you can't change? Why?

LET'S MAKE: A VOLCANIC ERUPTION

1. Pour 2 spoonfuls of baking soda and a squirt of dish soap into a cup.

2. Place the cup on a tray or pan, and use the other materials to build a model volcano around the cup.

3. Dump about a cup of vinegar into the container.

4. Watch the "lava" flow!

LET'S ENGINEER!

Brian's little brother loves building sandcastles at the playground. But every time they return to the playground, the sandcastle is gone. And every time, Brian's little brother doesn't understand why and cries. Brian wants to teach his brother about the way weathering breaks rocks into smaller bits, and then erosion slowly moves the smaller rock pieces over time.

How can Brian show his little brother weathering and erosion?

Choose some materials that can be broken into smaller pieces. **Break** them apart. **Ask** yourself: How can I create wind to blow the pieces away? **Describe** the process of weathering and erosion aloud as you show it to a friend or family member.

PROJECT 7: DONE!
Get your sticker!

Maps

Maps show where things are located. Some maps show where land and water features are, while other maps show roads and where people live. Maps can be big or small, flat, round, or even digital—like on a computer or phone.

Draw a line from each map name to the matching map in Enid's home.

a globe

a trail map

a weather map

a train map

a star map

What kinds of maps do you and your family use?

_____

_____

Physical maps show the geography of an area. This includes the shape of the land, types of land, and bodies of water.

The MotMots are meeting friends for a picnic. Read the directions aloud. Then draw their path on the map. Use the landforms and bodies of water as your guides.

cape

bay

cliff

delta

- Move three spaces and turn right at the cliff.
- Move two steps and turn left.
- Move five spaces toward the river.
- Turn left and move two spaces.
- Turn right and move four steps toward the marsh.
- Turn right and move seven steps toward the lake.
- Turn right, move two steps, and stop to have a picnic!

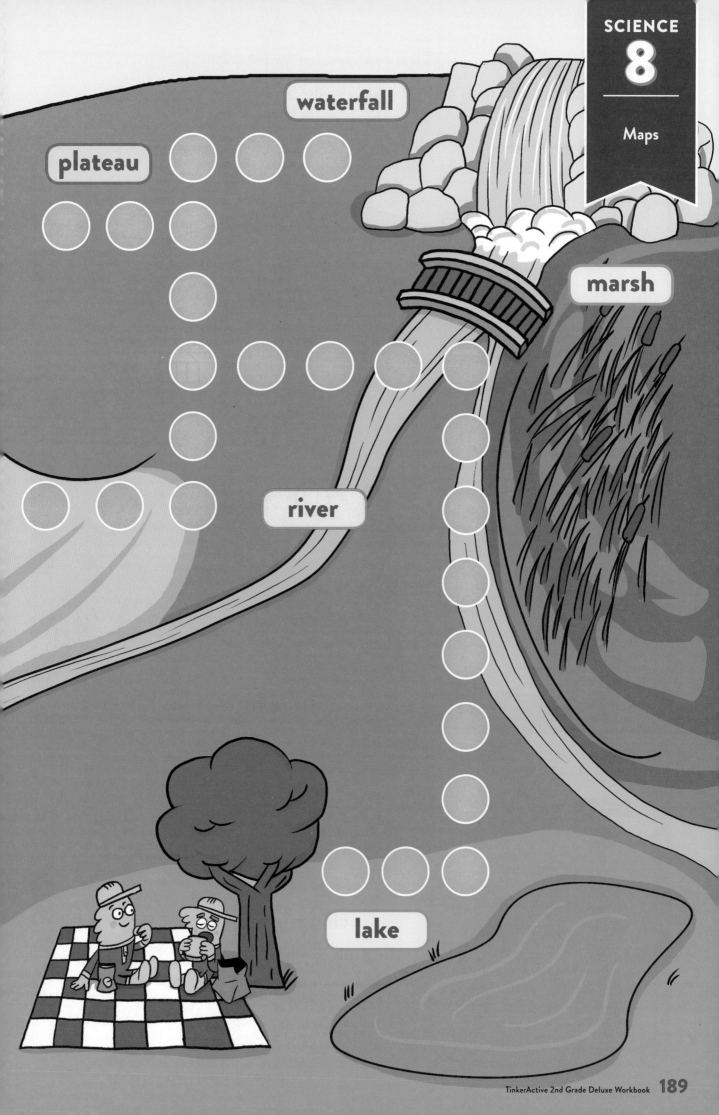

waterfall

plateau

marsh

river

lake

Maps often have features that help users read and decode the information. Look at this map and read the title, key, scale, and compass.

MAKER CITY

Key

- ▦ road
- 🌳 orchard
- 〰️ sea
- 🗼 lighthouse
- 🏛 city hall
- ⚾ sports field

Scale

0 5 10

1 inch = 10 miles

Compass

N
W   E
S

Draw a map of your home. Include a title, a key, and any other features you need on your map.

_____
Title

Key

LET'S START!

Cups

Cereal boxes or cardboard boxes

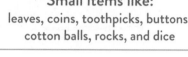
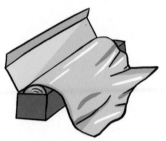

Small items like:
leaves, coins, toothpicks, buttons, cotton balls, rocks, and dice

Toilet paper or paper towel rolls

Aluminum foil

LET'S TINKER!

Use your materials to represent different features of your neighborhood. For example, a cup turned upside down can represent a hill.

- Which materials can represent natural features like land, water, and trees?
- Which materials can represent man-made features like bridges, roads, and buildings?
- How can you use your materials alone or assembled together?

LET'S MAKE: DREAM ISLAND MAP

Make and draw a map of your own imaginary island. **Choose** materials that can be used to show the edges of the island and different landforms. Which materials can represent the water—both the water around your island and any features like a river, lake, or waterfall? What else is on your island? A city? A volcano?

LET'S ENGINEER!

Amelia is designing her dream playground for a new park in her neighborhood. Her playground will be very large—so large, MotMots might get lost!

How can Amelia show others where everything is?

Draw a map of your dream playground. **Use** the materials to show the natural and man-made features you will include.

How can you be sure that other people can read your map correctly? **Show** your map to someone else and ask questions about what they see.

PROJECT 8: DONE!
Get your sticker!

Underwater Habitats

There are many different types of underwater habitats on Earth. The oceans, Earth's biggest habitat, are filled with salt water. Most lakes, rivers, ponds, and wetlands are freshwater habitats. Each type of underwater habitat has great diversity, which means different kinds of plants and animals live there.

Read about each animal. Then draw a line to its freshwater habitat.

Lake sturgeon are big fish. They can weigh up to 200 pounds and live in big, open bodies of water.

The **electric eel** lives in rivers. It makes an electric current to shock its prey.

The **bowfin** is also called a mudfish because it can live in shallow, muddy water.

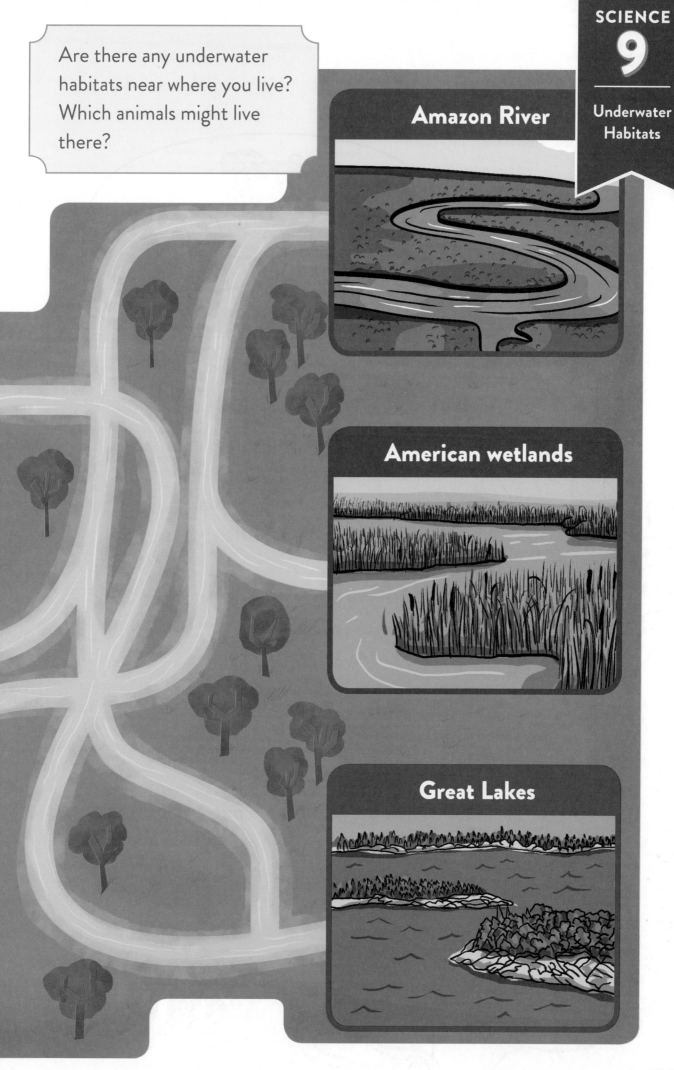

Are there any underwater habitats near where you live? Which animals might live there?

Amazon River

American wetlands

Great Lakes

The Great Barrier Reef is a saltwater ocean habitat off Australia. It is an enormous, colorful coral reef that thousands of plants and animals call home. Over a hundred different species of sharks live in the Great Barrier Reef habitat!

Read the poem aloud.

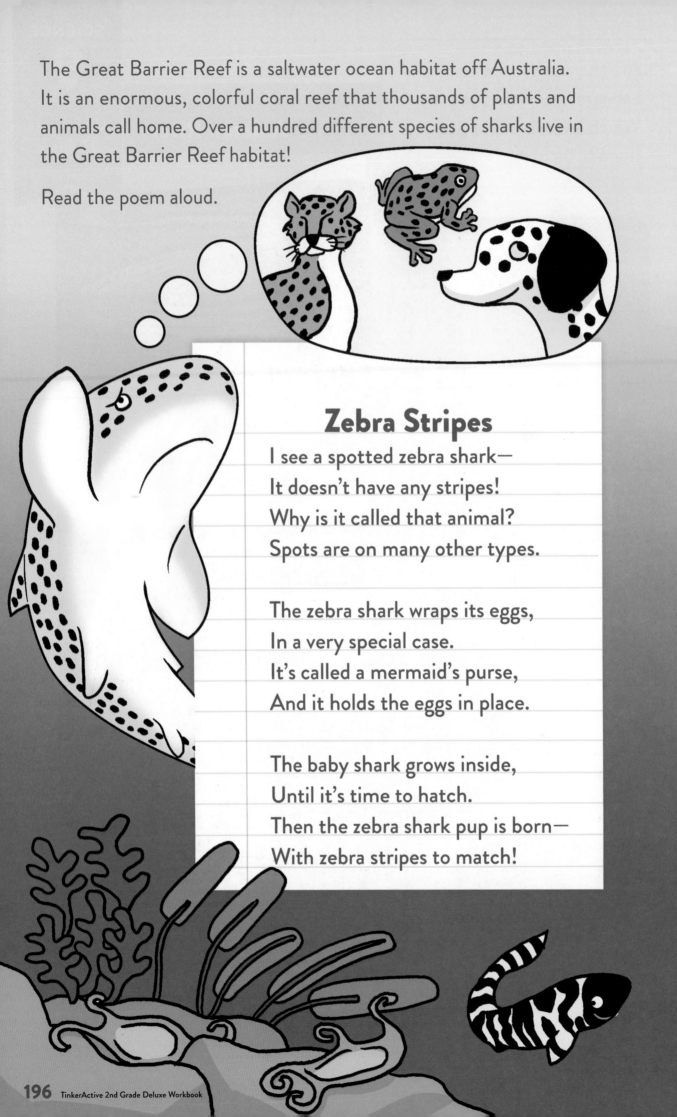

Zebra Stripes

I see a spotted zebra shark—
It doesn't have any stripes!
Why is it called that animal?
Spots are on many other types.

The zebra shark wraps its eggs,
In a very special case.
It's called a mermaid's purse,
And it holds the eggs in place.

The baby shark grows inside,
Until it's time to hatch.
Then the zebra shark pup is born—
With zebra stripes to match!

Look at the different sharks in this picture. Then draw a line connecting your two favorite sharks.

How are they the same?

_____

_____

_____

How are they different?

_____

_____

_____

A shark can lose hundreds, or even thousands, of teeth in its lifetime. Can you find eleven lost shark's teeth?

There are many different habitats at all levels of the ocean. There are tide pools along the shore, kelp forests underwater, seafloor trenches so deep people have never explored them, and many others.

Look at the levels of the ocean. Draw a line to lead the submarine to the the ocean trench.

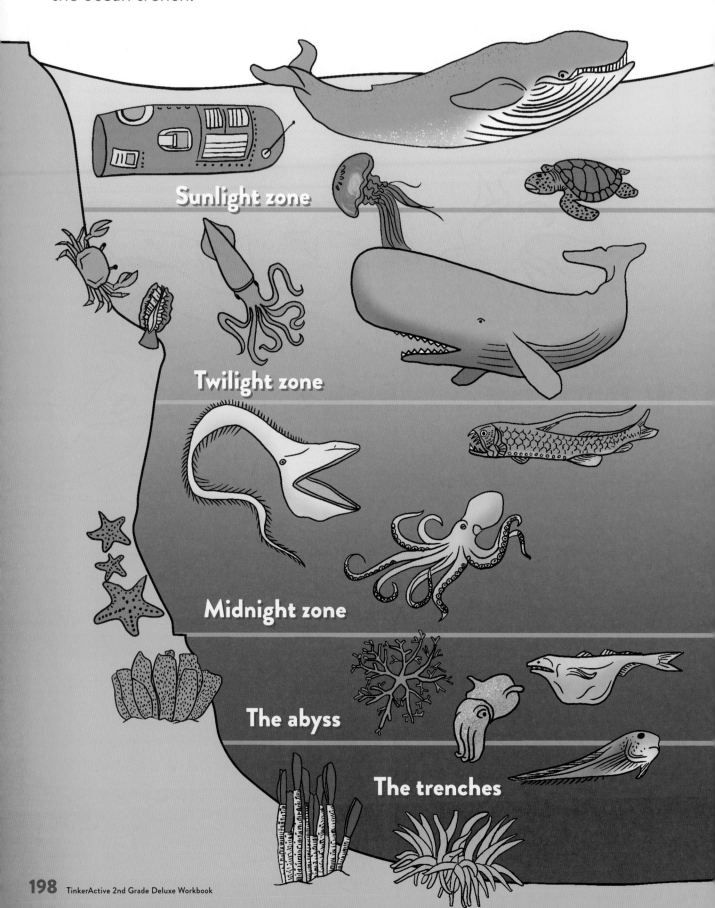

Sunlight zone

Twilight zone

Midnight zone

The abyss

The trenches

Two of these ocean creatures are real, but one is made up. Cross out the animal you predict is not real, and write about how you came to this conclusion.

The **dumbo octopus** has two fins that look like ears. The octopus flaps these fins to move. It swims along the seafloor looking for snails, worms, and other food.

The **fangtooth fish** has giant teeth, but its entire body isn't much larger than your hand. Its teeth help it capture prey of any size that wanders its way.

The **tube shark** has rows of tubes on its back to help it blend in with tube worms on the ocean floor. It lives and hunts in the sunlight zone.

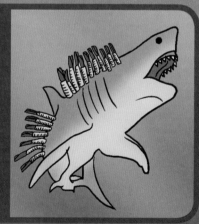

_____

_____

_____

LET'S START!

Flashlight

Sheets or pillowcases

Markers

Paper

6 or more drinking straws

Scissors

Glue

Shoebox

4–6 rocks

4–6 rubber bands

LET'S TINKER!

There is plenty of bright light at the top of the ocean, but in some places, the water goes so deep that no light reaches there—it is completely dark.

Go to a dark place, like a closet. Then **use** your materials to show light and dark. If you can, **show** some shades of light in between as well.

LET'S MAKE: COLORFUL CORAL

Corals are colorful animals that live together in the ocean. They make hard outer shells that form coral reefs. Make a model of corals with your materials.

1. Color each drinking straw a different color.

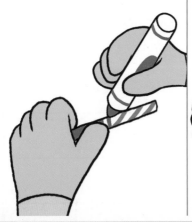

2. Cut them into small pieces.

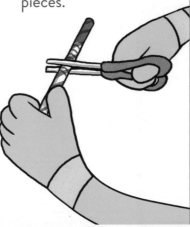

3. Glue the pieces to the paper upright like coral.

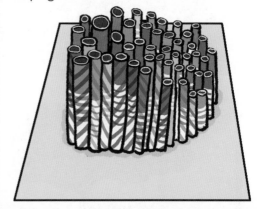

LET'S ENGINEER!

Dimitri is thinking about getting a pet goldfish. But he doesn't know what his goldfish will need, and he's worried that it won't like living with him.

How can Dimitri prepare for his goldfish?

Build a model of a fish tank using the shoebox. Think about a goldfish's natural habitat.

- What plants should live in the tank?
- Should there be other animals in it?
- Which materials can represent these plants and animals?

PROJECT 9: DONE!
Get your sticker!

Land Habitats

There are many types of land habitats, and each one is filled with unique plants and animals. The desert is a habitat that gets little rain. The plants and animals there have features and skills that help them survive with little water.

Read about each desert plant or animal. Then follow the instructions and answer each question.

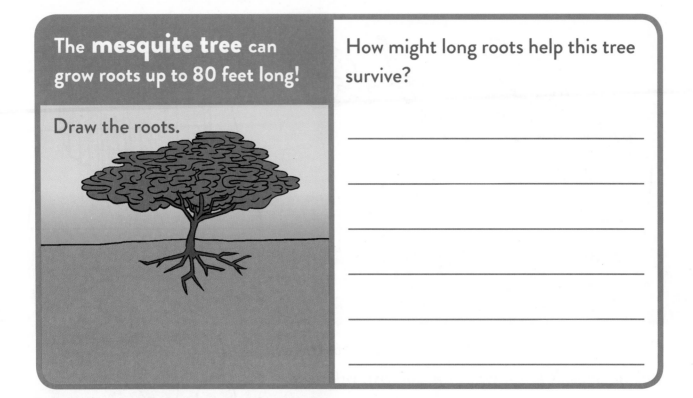

The **mesquite tree** can grow roots up to 80 feet long!

Draw the roots.

How might long roots help this tree survive?

_____

_____

_____

_____

_____

_____

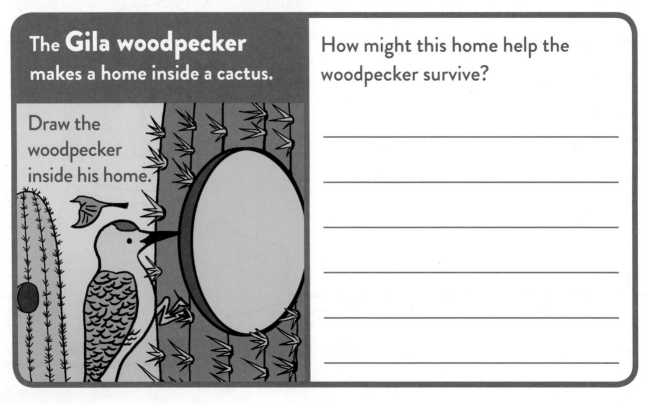

The **Gila woodpecker** makes a home inside a cactus.

Draw the woodpecker inside his home.

How might this home help the woodpecker survive?

_____

_____

_____

_____

_____

_____

In the desert, where food is scarce, the **dung beetle** finds something to eat—dung. It rolls the poop of other animals into balls!

Draw balls of food.

How might rolling the dung into balls help the beetles survive?

_____

_____

_____

_____

_____

_____

The **barrel cactus** has spines up to 4 inches long.

Draw the spines.

How might the spines help this cactus survive?

_____

_____

_____

_____

_____

_____

_____

The rain forest is the land habitat with the greatest diversity on Earth. This means that rain forests have the largest variety of different plants and animals.

Read the travel journal aloud. Then answer each question.

Yesterday we explored the Amazon rain forest! We walked on the **forest floor** past large red and orange mushrooms. It was dark and wet—the tall trees blocked most of the light. It smelled like soggy dirt after it rains. I didn't want to run into any jaguars or anteaters! But Callie did see a bright blue poison dart frog.

Next, we climbed a wooden staircase and stepped onto a hanging walkway through the **understory**. It was hot, and I had to push a lot of giant, waxy leaves out of my way. We saw leafcutter ants marching up the smooth tree bark!

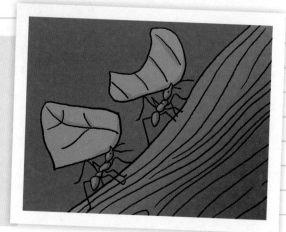

Last, we climbed over 100 feet up the **canopy**. I was tired! Lots of vines and ferns hung from the trees. I liked the sweet-smelling purple orchid flowers. There were animals all around—I could even hear monkeys squeaking, grunting, and howling! Dimitri grabbed some sweet mangoes as he walked by.

From there, I could see the very top, the **emergent layer**, where a few trees stretched 200 feet into the sky! It was bright and very hot. We watched the trees sway in the wind, but we didn't see many animals that high up.

What might you HEAR in the rain forest?

_____

_____

_____

What might you SEE in the rain forest?

_____

_____

_____

What might you TOUCH in the rain forest?

_____

_____

_____

What might you TASTE in the rain forest?

_____

_____

_____

What might you SMELL in the rain forest?

_____

_____

_____

There are grassland habitats all over the world, and they are all covered in grasses.

The MotMots went on a safari in the grasslands of South Africa and printed photos of the animals they saw. But photos from other trips got mixed in with them. Cross out the photos of animals that do not live in the grasslands.

Go on a safari outside your home. What plants and animals live near you? Draw what you observe in your habitat and write any plant or animal's name.

MY SAFARI

LET'S START!

Jar with a lid

Sand and dirt

Rocks

Moss or small plants

Cereal boxes or cardboard boxes

Water

Aluminum foil

LET'S TINKER!

Earth has a great diversity of plants and animals—each type of living thing is unique.

Think about how your materials are alike and how they are different. Then **sort** them by a trait like color, texture, or size. What other ways can the materials be sorted?

LET'S MAKE: MINI RAIN FOREST

1. Using a clear jar with a lid, **place** a layer of sand and rocks in the jar.

2. **Add** dirt on top, piling it high on the sides.

3. Put moss and/or small plants on top.

4. Carefully **add** water to the lowest part of the jar to make a "lake" next to the "mountain" of dirt and rocks. **Close** the lid.

5. Check back in a day, several days, and then a week. How does it change?

LET'S ENGINEER!

Callie's friends the dung beetles are rolling their food into balls so they can move them around and store them easily. They want to move the balls to the other side of the yard, but a large stone wall is in the way. Callie wants to help, but she doesn't want to touch the dung balls.

How can Callie help her friends without touching the dung balls?

Crumple some aluminum foil into balls to represent the dung balls. **Think** about how you might try to push objects up and over something. **Use** your materials to make something that helps the dung beetles push their balls up and over the stone wall.

PROJECT 10: DONE!
Get your sticker!

Plant Growth

Plants need air, sunlight, water, and nutrients from the dirt to grow. They have specialized parts to help meet their needs.

Dimitri is taking pictures of his garden. Label the part of a plant that you see in each picture.

roots	**leaves**	**trunk**	**fruit**
stem	**flower**	**branches**	**seeds**

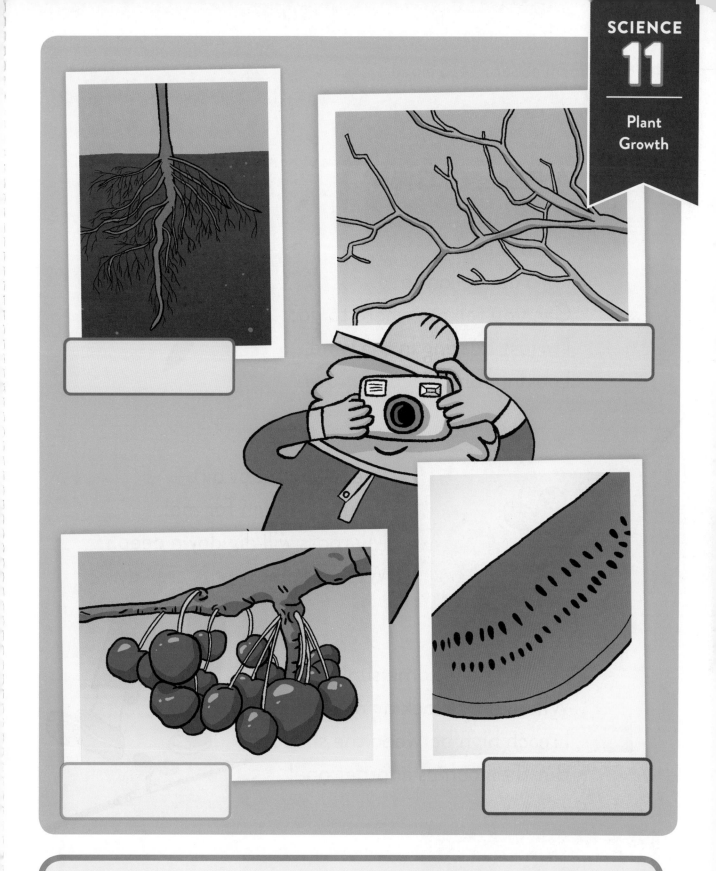

Circle the plant part that soaks up water and nutrients from the ground.

Draw a triangle around the plant part that collects sunlight and makes food for the plant.

Draw a rectangle around the plant part that protects seeds.

Read the poem about a seed aloud.

A Place to Grow

Hello there!
I'm a dandelion seed.
Can you tell me where to go?
I'm just floating in the wind,
Looking for a place to grow.

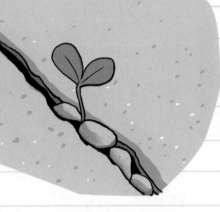

I needed a bit of dirt—
I found enough for me!
My roots will dig down deep.
Water and nutrients are key.

I know I need some sunlight—
What keeps blocking out the sun?
I reach high between the shadows,
But then comes another one!

Describe a habitat near your home where a dandelion seed could get all the air, sunlight, water, and nutrients it needs to grow.

_____

_____

_____

_____

Draw a line to match each plant to the habitat where it grows.

The **oak tree** has thick bark to protect the water inside while living in a dry habitat.

Cattails have fast-growing roots to anchor them in moving water.

Seagrass has many wide leaves to absorb the sunlight in shallow water.

Predict what will happen at the end of each experiment.

Callie plants two seeds in two pots.

Then she covers one plant so it won't get any light.

Plants collect sunlight with their leaves to make food. They do that by using chlorophyll, which keeps their leaves green. Plants need sunlight to make them grow.

Draw your prediction.

Brian plants two seeds in two pots.

Then he stops watering one plant.

Plants soak up water with their roots. Then the water travels to the leaves, where it helps to make food. Plants need water to make food and to keep from drying out.

Draw your prediction.

Look for plants inside or outside your home. Where do they get the sunlight and water that they need?

LET'S START! GATHER THESE TOOLS AND MATERIALS.

Paper

Scissors

20 or more drinking straws

Piece of string 2–3 feet long

Paper towel roll

Tape

Glue

Crayons

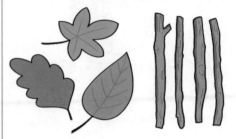
Sticks and leaves

LET'S TINKER!

Leaves come in all shapes, sizes, and colors. Leaves are important to plants because they gather light and make food.

Cut paper to make different leaf shapes and color them. What other materials can you add to your leaves to make them look more real?

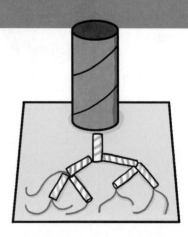

LET'S MAKE: PLANT PARTS

1. **Cut** and glue pieces of straws or string onto paper to represent plant roots.

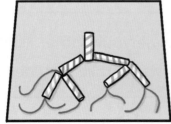

2. **Glue** on a paper towel roll to represent a stem or trunk.

3. Draw a line to represent the ground.

4. Does your plant have branches, leaves, a flower, or a fruit? What other parts can you make and add? **Put** them all together to complete your plant.

LET'S ENGINEER!

The tall tree in Enid's yard loves sunlight—and Enid loves her tree. She wants to show her classmates how it uses its roots, trunk, and branches to hold its leaves up high, where the sunlight can reach them.

How can Enid show her classmates how her tree works?

Make a model of a tree. **Use** only your drinking straws as a trunk and branches. **Use** tape to connect the straws. **Choose** the best material to represent roots.

- How can you connect the straws to build a strong base like a trunk?
- How can you keep your tree from falling over, like roots do for plants?
- Can you build your tree as tall as your knee? Or taller?

PROJECT 11: DONE!
Get your sticker!

Plant Pollination

Plants grow in one place and can't move. They need help with pollination—moving pollen between flowering plants of the same type to make seeds. Wind, water, and animals all help pollinate plants and spread their seeds.

Read about how each animal helps flowers pollinate. Then draw a line to lead each animal from one flower to the flower bush.

Bees collect nectar and pollen from flowers to make honey. As they fly from flower to flower, they spread pollen.

Hummingbirds can drink nectar from over 1,000 flowers a day! Pollen sticks to their beaks and is spread to new flowers.

How do you think wind or water helps spread pollen?

_____

_____

_____

When **butterflies** drink nectar from flowers, pollen sticks to their legs, tongues, and bodies. They can spread the pollen over long distances as they fly.

Read aloud some of the ways that animals can move seeds. Then draw a line to match each method to an animal.

Some animals eat fruits and vegetables full of seeds. Later, when they poop, the seeds are left on the ground to grow new plants.

Some animals move seeds around when they store their food. They might even bury seeds underground. If they forget about the seeds, new plants grow.

Some animals get burs full of seeds stuck in their fur. Then the burs fall off in other places to grow new plants.

Draw your own bur—a seed with a sticky or spiky covering. Then draw a line to an animal that could help move it.

SQUIRREL

LIZARD

BEAR

Wind and water also help move and spread seeds. Circle the seeds you predict can spread by flying, floating, or even spinning in the wind.

Draw what you predict happens when the wind blows by a dandelion.

People can also move seeds. Look in your kitchen for fruits and vegetables. Write about and draw the fruits and vegetables with seeds that your family has moved.

_____

_____

_____

Draw the inside and outside of your favorite fruit or favorite vegetable. Circle the seeds. Then write whether the seeds are on the inside or outside.

_____

LET'S START!

Tissue paper

4–6 twist ties

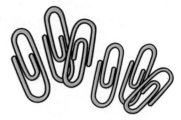

4–6 paper clips

4–6 toothpicks

Paper

Scissors

LET'S TINKER!

Which materials can move like a seed in the wind? **Make** your materials float, fly, or spin.

Change or combine your materials to alter how they move.

LET'S MAKE: SEED COVERINGS

Make a seed that sticks like a bur and is ready to go for a ride!

Choose or make materials that act like spines or small hooks that will attach to your shirt or hair.

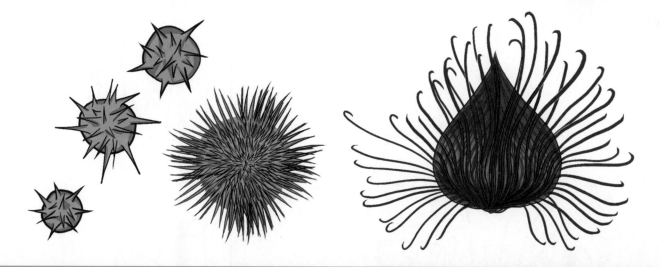

LET'S ENGINEER!

Enid is throwing a birthday party for Frank! She wants a big celebration with balloons and the best confetti. She wants the confetti to move through the air in different ways—parachuting, flying on wings, twisting, twirling, gliding, and fluttering.

How can Enid make confetti that moves through the air in different ways?

Cut your paper into small pieces to make confetti. **Think** about how seeds fly in different ways. What can you do to your paper to make it more like those different seeds? **Try** a few designs. Could any of your other materials be added to help?

PROJECT 12: DONE!
Get your sticker!

Engineering Design: Shoe

It's time to go to lunch, but Amelia is having trouble with one of her shoes. Why?

RESEARCH THE PROBLEM!

OBSERVE

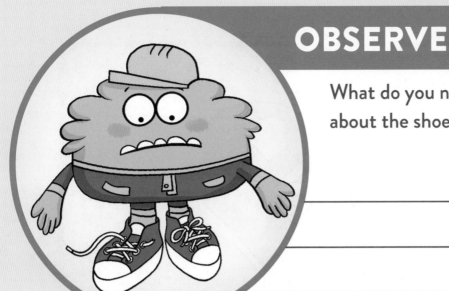

What do you notice about the shoe?

_____

_____

_____

GATHER INFORMATION

What can you learn by touching the shoe?

_____

_____

_____

ASK QUESTIONS

What would you ask Amelia about her shoe?

_____

_____

_____

Look at the picture. Why isn't Amelia's shoe tied?

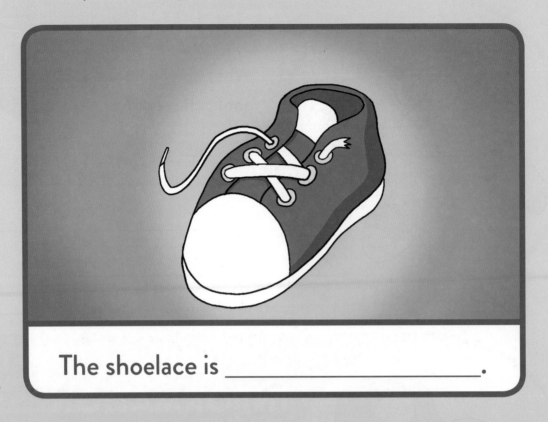

The shoelace is _____.

What caused the problem? Write about and draw possible causes.

Think about possible solutions for Amelia's problem. Then write about and draw an idea that can fix the problem.

What can the MotMots **do** that might help Amelia? Write about and draw a solution.

What materials can Amelia **use** to fix the shoe? Write about and draw a solution.

What can Amelia **do** to fix the shoe? Write about and draw a solution.

Each possible solution to a problem has strong points and weak points. You can compare solutions to choose the best design. Choose two solutions from the previous page to test. Write a name for each solution and follow the directions.

Solution 1: _____

Draw one solution and what you think will happen when Amelia tries to walk to lunch.

What works?

_____

_____

_____

What doesn't work?

_____

_____

_____

How can you fix what doesn't work or improve your design?

_____

_____

Solution 2: _____

Draw the other solution and what you think will happen when Amelia tries to walk to lunch.

What works?

_____

_____

_____

What doesn't work?

_____

_____

_____

How can you fix what doesn't work or improve your design?

_____

_____

Circle the solution you think Amelia should use.

LET'S START! GATHER THESE TOOLS AND MATERIALS.

Aluminum foil

Tape

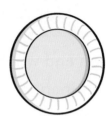
Paper plate

Pencil, marker, or crayon

Cardboard
(about the size of a piece of paper)

String

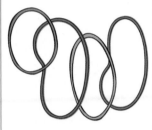
4–6 rubber bands

Stuffed animal

LET'S TINKER!

Look at your materials. How can they be worn? **Try** making a bracelet, hat, helmet, belt, crown, or even armor. How can the materials be combined to make something that you can wear?

LET'S MAKE: MOTMOT SHOES

A shoe is made of many parts working together.

1. Choose materials that are strong enough to walk on the ground like the soles of shoes do.

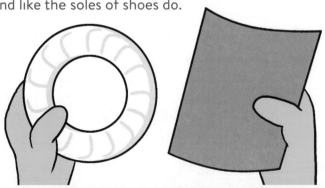

2. Trace your feet on the material and cut them out.

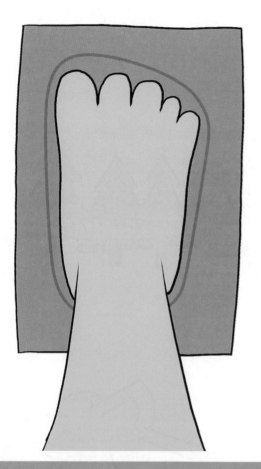

3. Make a cover for each foot as the top of the shoe. You can **add** stickers from page 387 to decorate your shoes.

4. Add materials like rubber bands or string to hold the parts together and to keep the shoes on your feet—like laces or straps!

LET'S ENGINEER!

Frank loves taking his best friend, MotBot, to the park. But his robot's feet keep getting dirty!

How can Frank protect MotBot's feet?

Use a stuffed animal or doll as a model for MotBot. Then **use** your materials to protect your toy's feet.

- How can you combine the materials to keep its feet clean?

- What happens to the "shoes" when you pick up your stuffed animal or doll?

- How will your invention stay on the toy as you play?

PROJECT 13: DONE!
Get your sticker!

Engineering Design: Fountain

The MotMots are thirsty from playing.
They would like a drink from the water fountain,
but no water is coming out. Why?

RESEARCH THE PROBLEM!

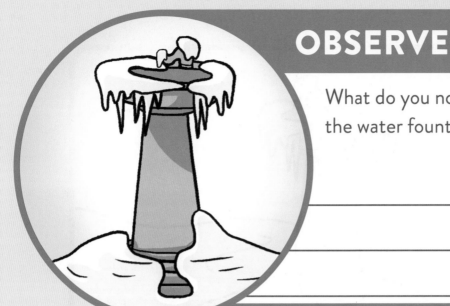

OBSERVE

What do you notice about
the water fountain?

_____

_____

_____

GATHER INFORMATION

What can you learn by touching
the water fountain?

_____

_____

_____

ASK QUESTIONS

What can you ask the MotMots
about the water fountain or the
environment?

_____

_____

_____

Look at the picture. Why isn't the fountain on?

The fountain is_____.

What caused the problem? Write about and draw possible causes.

Think about possible solutions for the MotMots' problem.
Then write about and draw an idea that can fix the problem.

What can the MotMots **do** that might help? Write about and draw a solution.

What materials can the MotMots **use** that might help? Write about and draw a solution.

What can the MotMots **bring** to the park that might help? Write about and draw a solution.

Each possible solution to a problem has strong points and weak points. You can compare solutions to choose the best design. Choose two solutions from the previous page to test. Write a name for each solution and follow the directions.

Solution 1: _____

Draw one solution and what you think will happen the next time the MotMots press the fountain's button for a drink.

What works?

_____

_____

_____

What doesn't work?

_____

_____

_____

How can you fix what doesn't work or improve your design?

_____

_____

Solution 2: _____

Draw the other solution and what you think will happen the next time the MotMots press the fountain's button for a drink.

What works?

_____

_____

_____

What doesn't work?

_____

_____

_____

How can you fix what doesn't work or improve your design?

_____

_____

Circle the solution you think the MotMots should use.

LET'S START! GATHER THESE TOOLS AND MATERIALS.

Sandwich bag

Aluminum foil

4–6 drinking straws

Assorted liquids
(with an adult's help):

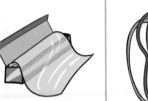
Plastic wrap

Rubber bands

Tall, clear drinking glass

- honey (or maple syrup)
- milk
- dish soap
- water
- vegetable oil
- rubbing alcohol

LET'S TINKER!

Dip or dunk the sandwich bag, aluminum foil, straws, plastic wrap, and rubber bands in water. What happens?

- How does the water react when you jiggle or tilt the materials?
- Do any of the materials absorb the water?

Shake the water off these materials to see if you can get them dry.

LET'S MAKE: LIQUID RAINBOW

Some liquids are denser and heavier than water. Make a rainbow with liquids of different densities!

1. **Pour** about 1 inch of honey into the glass without pouring any on the sides.

2. Slowly **add** about 1 inch of each of the rest of the liquids, in this order: milk, dish soap, and then water. Don't pour any of the liquids on the sides of the glass.

3. Slowly **pour** the last two liquids down the sides of the glass, in this order: vegetable oil and then rubbing alcohol. Because these are the lightest liquids, pour them slowly.

4. What do you think the density of an ice cube is? Is it heavier, lighter, or the same as water? Carefully **drop** an ice cube into the glass, and observe what happens. When it stops moving, which layer is it in?

TIP: If any of the layers were poured too quickly, let the glass sit for a bit and the liquids will settle into a rainbow (with no mixing of the layers).

LET'S ENGINEER!

Callie is going on a hike, but she can't find her water bottle!

How can Callie carry water with her?

Choose materials that can hold water and design a container for Callie to use. **Think** about the features of a water bottle.

- How can Callie get water in and out of her container?
- How will Callie drink from it?
- Do you need more than one material?

PROJECT 14: DONE!
Get your sticker!

Engineering Design: Slide

It's a busy day at the playground.
But no one is using the slide. Why?

RESEARCH THE PROBLEM!

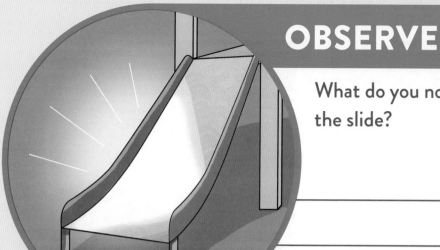

OBSERVE

What do you notice about the slide?

_____

_____

_____

GATHER INFORMATION

What might you learn by touching the slide?

_____

_____

_____

ASK QUESTIONS

What would you ask the MotMots about the slide?

_____

_____

_____

Look at the picture. Why aren't the MotMots playing on the slide?

The slide is_____.

What caused the problem? Write about and draw possible causes.

Think about possible solutions for the MotMots' problem.
Then write about and draw an idea that can fix the problem.

What can the MotMots **wear** so they can use the slide? Write about and draw a solution.

What materials **can** the MotMots **use** so they can go down the slide? Write about and draw a solution.

What can the MotMots **build** so they can use the slide? Write about and draw a solution.

Each possible solution to a problem has strong points and weak points. You can compare solutions to choose the best design. Choose two solutions from the previous page to test. Write a name for each solution and follow the directions.

Solution 1: _____

Draw one solution and what you think will happen the next time the MotMots play at the playground.

What works?

_____

_____

_____

What doesn't work?

_____

_____

_____

How can you fix what doesn't work or improve your design?

_____

_____

Solution 2: _____

Draw the other solution and what you think will happen the next time the MotMots play at the playground.

What works?

_____

_____

_____

What doesn't work?

_____

_____

_____

How can you fix what doesn't work or improve your design?

_____

_____

Circle the solution you think the MotMots should use.

LET'S START!

GATHER THESE TOOLS AND MATERIALS.

Aluminum foil

Toilet paper rolls and/or paper towel rolls

Tape

Marble
(or other small rolling object)

Cardboard

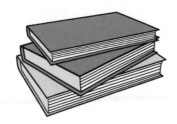
Books

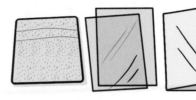
Flat materials like:
washcloth, waxed paper, and napkin

LET'S TINKER!

A slide is made of many materials that have unique properties. Which of these materials is slippery like a slide?

- How can you tell?
- Are any reflective?

Test each one by sliding a book or other small objects across them.

LET'S MAKE: MARBLE SLIDE

A slide is an inclined plane—its surface is tilted at an angle so things slide down it. Make a slide using inclined planes.

1. Tape a toilet paper roll or paper towel roll to a wall, tilted at an angle.

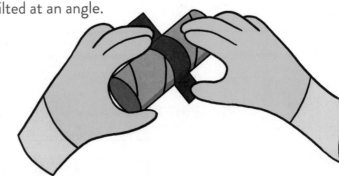

2. Drop a marble in through the top. What happens?

3. Add to your slide by connecting a roll at the top or bottom with tape. **Place** each roll tilted at an angle, like a slide.

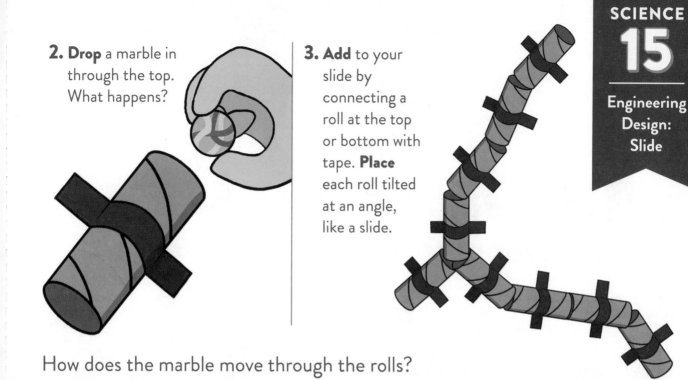

How does the marble move through the rolls?
Where does it move fastest? And slowest?

LET'S ENGINEER!

The school is getting a new slide for the school playground. Amelia is in charge of choosing the material the slide will be made of.

How can she choose the best material for the slide?

Compare and test different materials for a slide. First, **create** an inclined plane, like a slide. **Place** a piece of cardboard at an angle by holding one side up with books and taping the bottom. Next, **cover** the slide with a material such as foil. Last, **test** the slide. **Drop** a marble from the top. How does it move?

- Is it fast or slow?

- Bumpy or smooth?

Test more materials for covering the slide to see how they perform. What type of material makes the best surface for the new slide? Which materials do not make a good surface for sliding?

PROJECT 15: DONE!
Get your sticker!

ANSWER KEY

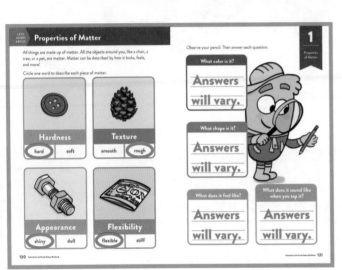

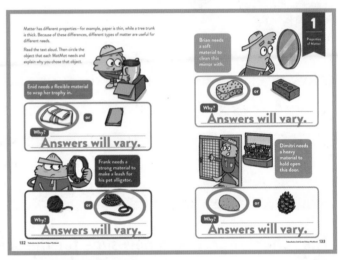

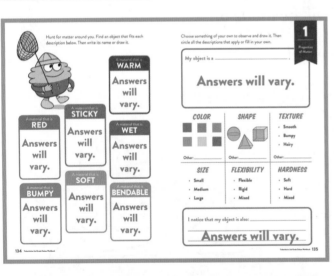

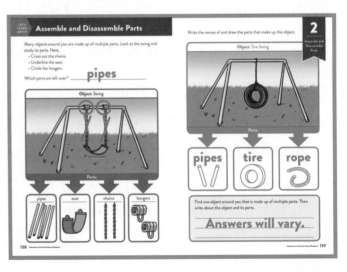

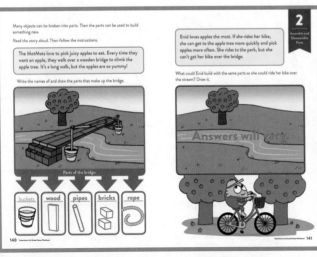

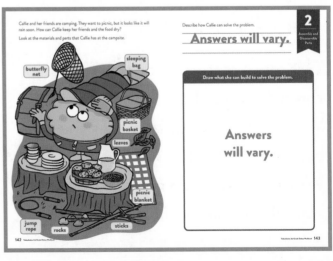

States of Matter

Matter can exist in different forms, including a solid, a liquid, or a gas.

A **solid** has shape and volume.

A **liquid** has volume, but no shape. It flows.

A **gas** has no volume or shape. It fills the volume of its container.

Read about the matter. Then draw what you predict will happen when these cups are emptied.

A grape is a solid, so each one has a shape.

Answers will vary.

Grape juice is a liquid, so it has no shape.

Answers will vary.

Brian is searching for solids, liquids, and gases. Fill in the state of matter of each object.

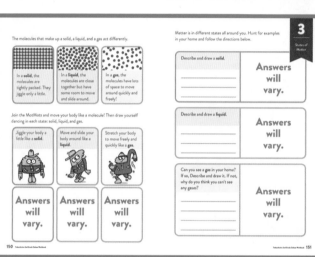

liquid
gas
solid
solid
liquid
liquid
solid
solid

Solids, liquids, and gases have different properties, and each can be used for different purposes.

Read what each MotMot needs aloud. Then circle the material that will solve each problem, and fill in whether it is a solid, a liquid, or a gas.

Dimitri needs something to drink.

Callie needs something firm to stay between two cookies.

Frank needs something that can expand to fill this balloon.

Enid needs something she can pour into this vase.

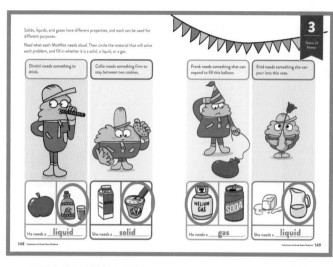

He needs a **liquid**

She needs a **solid**

He needs a **gas**

She needs a **liquid**

The molecules that make up a solid, a liquid, and a gas act differently.

In a **solid**, the molecules are tightly packed. They jiggle only a little.

In a **liquid**, the molecules are close together but have some room to move and slide around.

In a **gas**, the molecules have lots of space to move around quickly and freely!

Join the MotMots and move your body like a molecule! Then draw yourself dancing in each state: solid, liquid, and gas.

Jiggle your body a little like a **solid**.

Move and slide your body around like a **liquid**.

Stretch your body to move freely and quickly like a **gas**.

Answers will vary.

Answers will vary.

Answers will vary.

Matter is in different states all around you. Hunt for examples in your home and follow the directions below.

Describe and draw a **solid**.

Answers will vary.

Describe and draw a **liquid**.

Answers will vary.

Can you see a **gas** in your home? If so, Describe and draw it. If not, why do you think you can't see any gases?

Answers will vary.

Temperature

Temperature is a measure of how much heat is in an object. Heating up an object or cooling it down can cause changes that we can see.

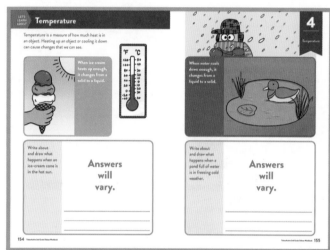

When ice cream heats up enough, it changes from a solid to a liquid.

When water cools down enough, it changes from a liquid to a solid.

Write about and draw what happens when an ice-cream cone is in the hot sun.

Answers will vary.

Write about and draw what happens when a pond full of water is in freezing cold weather.

Answers will vary.

Some changes that happen from heating and cooling are reversible. This means that the matter can change back to the way it was.

Some changes that happen from heating and cooling are not reversible. This means that the matter cannot go back to the way it was.

Observe each change below. Then write a ✔ next to the sentence that matches the temperature changes.

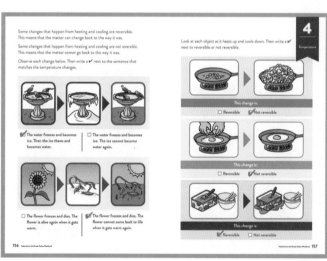

☑ The water freezes and becomes ice. Then the ice thaws and becomes water.

☐ The water freezes and becomes ice. The ice cannot become water again.

☐ The flower freezes and dies. The flower is alive again when it gets warm.

☑ The flower freezes and dies. The flower cannot come back to life when it gets warm again.

Look at each object as it heats up and cools down. Then write a ✔ next to reversible or not reversible.

This change is:
☐ Reversible   ☑ Not reversible

This change is:
☐ Reversible   ☑ Not reversible

This change is:
☑ Reversible   ☐ Not reversible

Hunt for objects around you that are affected by temperature. Draw what you find. Then answer each question.

Something that is cold
Answers will vary.
What happens if it becomes hot?

Something that is warm
Answers will vary.
What happens if it becomes cold?

Something that is a solid
Answers will vary.
What happens if it becomes hot?

Something that is a liquid
Answers will vary.
What happens if it becomes cold?

Find food in your kitchen that changes when you cook it. Then draw or write to answer each question.

What does it look like before it is cooked?
Answers will vary.

What does it look like after it is cooked?
Answers will vary.

The change is:
☐ Reversible   ☐ Not reversible

Find something in your freezer that you can thaw. Then draw or write to answer each question.

What does it look like now, before it is thawed?
Answers will vary.

As it warms up, what changes do you observe?
Answers will vary.

The change is:
☐ Reversible   ☐ Not reversible

Water Cycle

Over 70% of Earth's surface is covered in water. Water is the only thing that can naturally be found on Earth as a solid, a liquid, and a gas. Write a ✔ next to the correct form of water.

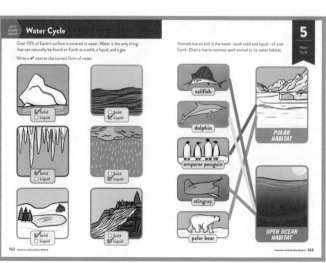

☑ Solid   ☐ Liquid
☐ Solid   ☑ Liquid
☑ Solid   ☐ Liquid
☐ Solid   ☑ Liquid
☑ Solid   ☐ Liquid
☐ Solid   ☑ Liquid

Animals live on and in the water—both solid and liquid—all over Earth. Draw a line to connect each animal to its water habitat.

sailfish
dolphin
emperor penguin
stingray
polar bear

POLAR HABITAT

OPEN OCEAN HABITAT

The water cycle describes the way water moves to and from the land, sky, and ocean. Water that starts on the land becomes a gas in the sky, and then becomes a solid or liquid that falls back to Earth. The water cycle repeats over and over again.

Look at the water cycle, and read the descriptions aloud. Then answer each question.

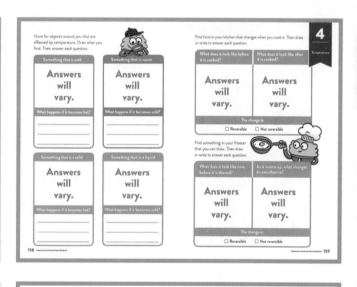

Evaporation
Water from rivers, lakes, streams, and oceans changes to water vapor when the sun heats Earth.

Condensation
Water vapor in the air changes into small drops of liquid water when it gets colder. The small water drops come together to make clouds.

Collection
Liquid water collects in rivers, lakes, streams, and oceans.

Precipitation
Water falls to Earth from clouds full of water. Precipitation can be rain, hail, or snow.

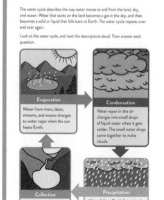

When you breathe on a cold day and you can see your breath.
Is this water vapor a **liquid** or a gas?
gas

When clouds become heavy with water and raindrops fall to Earth.
Are these drops **precipitation** or evaporation?
precipitation

When you leave a bucket of water outside for a few days and you find less water in the bucket.
Is the water **evaporating** or precipitating?
evaporating

When you add ice to a glass of water and water drops form on the outside as it cools.
Are these drops **condensation** or evaporation?
condensation

Which parts of the water cycle have you seen for yourself?
Answers will vary.

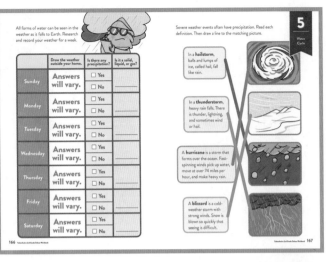

All forms of water can be seen in the weather as it falls to Earth. Research and record your weather for a week.

	Draw the weather outside your home.	Is there any precipitation?	Is it a solid, liquid, or gas?
Sunday	Answers will vary.	☐ Yes ☐ No	___
Monday	Answers will vary.	☐ Yes ☐ No	___
Tuesday	Answers will vary.	☐ Yes ☐ No	___
Wednesday	Answers will vary.	☐ Yes ☐ No	___
Thursday	Answers will vary.	☐ Yes ☐ No	___
Friday	Answers will vary.	☐ Yes ☐ No	___
Saturday	Answers will vary.	☐ Yes ☐ No	___

5 Water Cycle

Severe weather events often have precipitation. Read each definition. Then draw a line to the matching picture.

In a **hailstorm**, balls and lumps of ice, called hail, fall like rain.

In a **thunderstorm**, heavy rain falls. There is thunder, lightning, and sometimes wind or hail.

A **hurricane** is a storm that forms over the ocean. Fast-spinning winds pick up water, move at over 74 miles per hour, and make heavy rain.

A **blizzard** is a cold-weather storm with strong winds. Snow is blown so quickly that seeing is difficult.

LET'S LEARN ABOUT

Earth's Surface

6 Earth's Surface

Earth's surface is made of rocks and dirt, and it is constantly changing. Many things cause these changes, including animals, plants, people, and the weather.

Look at each picture. Then write a ✔ next to what caused the change to Earth's surface.

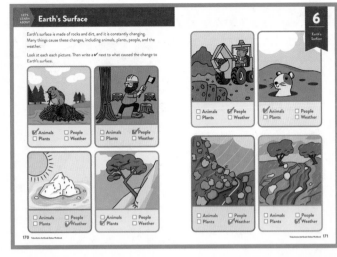

☑ Animals ☐ People
☐ Plants ☐ Weather

☐ Animals ☑ People
☐ Plants ☐ Weather

☑ Animals ☐ People
☐ Plants ☐ Weather

☐ Animals ☑ People
☐ Plants ☐ Weather

☐ Animals ☐ People
☐ Plants ☑ Weather

☐ Animals ☐ People
☑ Plants ☐ Weather

☐ Animals ☐ People
☐ Plants ☑ Weather

☐ Animals ☐ People
☐ Plants ☑ Weather

Some effects of wind and water on Earth's surface can be slowed down or even stopped.

Read each definition aloud. Then draw a line to the matching picture.

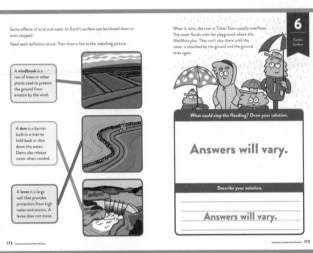

A **windbreak** is a row of trees or other plants used to protect the ground from erosion by the wind.

A **dam** is a barrier built in a river to hold back or slow down the water. Dams also release water when needed.

A **levee** is a large wall that provides protection from high water and storms. A levee does not move.

6 Earth's Surface

When it rains, the river in Tinker Town usually overflows. The water floods onto the playground where the MotMots play. They can't play there until the water is absorbed by the ground and the ground dries again.

What could stop the flooding? Draw your solution.

Answers will vary.

Describe your solution.

Answers will vary.

Circle the MotMot in each pair of pictures that is doing something to protect Earth's surface.

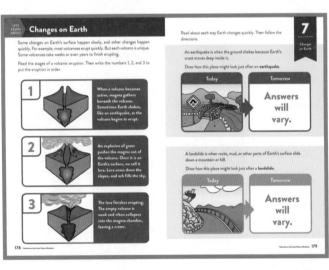

6 Earth's Surface

Write about and draw what you can do at **school** to help protect Earth's surface.

Answers will vary.

Write about and draw what you can do at **home** to help protect Earth's surface.

Answers will vary.

LET'S LEARN ABOUT

Changes on Earth

7 Changes on Earth

Some changes on Earth's surface happen slowly, and other changes happen quickly. For example, most volcanoes erupt quickly. But each volcano is unique. Some volcanoes take weeks or even years to finish erupting.

Read the stages of a volcanic eruption. Then write the numbers 1, 2, and 3 to put the eruption in order.

1 When a volcano becomes active, magma gathers beneath the volcano. Sometimes Earth shakes, like an earthquake, as the volcano begins to erupt.

2 An explosion of gases pushes the magma out of the volcano. Once it is on Earth's surface, we call it lava. Lava oozes down the slopes, and ash fills the sky.

3 The lava finishes erupting. The empty volcano is weak and often collapses into the magma chamber, leaving a crater.

Read about each way Earth changes quickly. Then follow the directions.

An **earthquake** is when the ground shakes because Earth's crust moves deep inside it.

Draw how this place might look just after an **earthquake**.

Today | Tomorrow
Answers will vary.

A **landslide** is when rocks, mud, or other parts of Earth's surface slide down a mountain or hill.

Draw how this place might look just after a **landslide**.

Today | Tomorrow
Answers will vary.

Some changes on Earth happen slowly—so slowly that no one can observe them.

Read the report aloud.

All About Erosion

Erosion is when Earth's surface is slowly worn away. Over time, the shape of the land changes.

Water causes most erosion. Bits of sand and small rocks are picked up by a river and moved. The Grand Canyon, in Arizona, is an example of water erosion over a very long time.

Before | After

Ice and **wind** can cause erosion, too. Glaciers are made of flowing ice. They pick up sand and rocks as they move along, just like a river does. Wind can also hit a rock and carry tiny pieces of it away, changing the rock's shape!

Erosion happens all around us, but it happens so slowly that it is difficult to see. Erosion happens a little bit at a time, but over many years it can make big changes to Earth.

7 Changes on Earth

Draw how erosion might make this place look next year and in one hundred years.

Today
Tomorrow
Next Year — Answers will vary.
100 Years — Answers will vary.

Do these events change Earth slowly or quickly? Write a ✔ next to the correct speed.

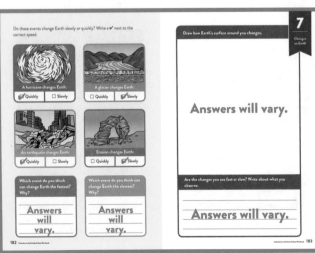

A hurricane changes Earth:
☑ Quickly ☐ Slowly

A glacier changes Earth:
☐ Quickly ☑ Slowly

An earthquake changes Earth:
☑ Quickly ☐ Slowly

Erosion changes Earth:
☐ Quickly ☑ Slowly

Which event do you think can change Earth the fastest? Why?
Answers will vary.

Which event do you think can change Earth the slowest? Why?
Answers will vary.

7 Changes on Earth

Draw how Earth's surface around you changes.

Answers will vary.

Are the changes you see fast or slow? Write about what you observe.
Answers will vary.

LET'S LEARN ABOUT

Maps

8 Maps

Maps show where things are located. Some maps show where land and water features are, while other maps show roads and where people live. Maps can be big or small, flat, round, or even digital—like on a computer or phone.

Draw a line from each map name to the matching map in Enid's home.

a globe

a trail map

a weather map

a train map

a star map

What kinds of maps do you and your family use?
Answers will vary.

Physical maps show the geography of an area. This includes the shape of the land, types of land, and bodies of water.

The MatMots are meeting friends for a picnic. Read the directions aloud. Then draw their path on the map. Use the landforms and bodies of water as your guides.

- Move three spaces and turn right at the cliff.
- Move two steps and turn left.
- Move five spaces toward the river.
- Turn left and move two spaces.
- Turn right and move four steps toward the marsh.
- Turn right and move seven steps toward the lake.
- Turn right, move two steps, and stop to have a picnic!

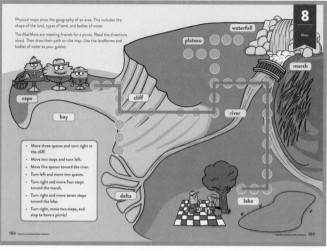

waterfall · plateau · cape · bay · cliff · river · marsh · delta · lake

---

Maps often have features that help users read and decode the information. Look at this map and read the title, key, scale, and compass.

Draw a map of your home. Include a title, a key, and any other features you need on your map.

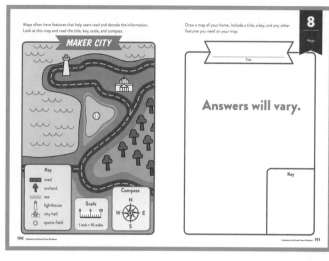

MAKER CITY

Key
- road
- orchard
- sea
- lighthouse
- city hall
- sports field

Compass N E S W

Scale
0 5 10
1 inch = 10 miles

Title

Answers will vary.

Key

Underwater Habitats

There are many different types of underwater habitats on Earth. The oceans, Earth's biggest habitat, are filled with salt water. Lakes, rivers, ponds, and wetlands are freshwater habitats. Each type of underwater habitat has great diversity, which means different kinds of plants and animals live there.

Read about each animal. Then draw a line to its freshwater habitat.

Are there any underwater habitats near where you live? Which animals might live there?

Amazon river

American wetlands

Great Lakes

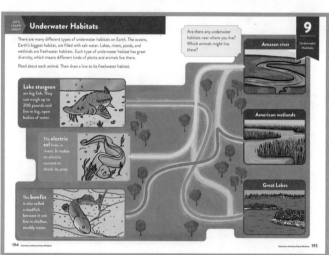

Lake sturgeon are big fish. They can weigh up to 200 pounds and live in big, open bodies of water.

The **electric eel** lives in rivers. It makes an electric current to shock its prey.

The **bowfin** is also called a mudfish because it can live in shallow, muddy water.

The Great Barrier Reef is a saltwater ocean habitat off Australia. It is an enormous, colorful coral reef that thousands of plants and animals call home. Over a hundred different species of sharks live in the Great Barrier Reef habitat!

Read the poem aloud.

Look at the different sharks in this picture. Then draw a line connecting your two favorite sharks.

How are they the same? Answers will vary.

How are they different? Answers will vary.

Zebra Stripes

I see a spotted zebra shark—
It doesn't have any stripes!
Why is it called that animal?
Spots are on many other types.

The zebra shark wraps its eggs,
In a very special case.
It's called a mermaid's purse,
And it holds the eggs in place.

The baby shark grows inside,
Until it's time to hatch.
Then the zebra shark pup is born—
With zebra stripes to match!

A shark can lose hundreds, or even thousands, of teeth in its lifetime. Can you find eleven lost shark's teeth?

There are many different habitats at all levels of the ocean. There are tide pools along the shore, kelp forests underwater, seafloor trenches so deep people have never explored them, and many others.

Look at the levels of the ocean. Draw a line to lead the submarine to the ocean trench. **Answers will vary.**

Sunlight zone
Twilight zone
Midnight zone
The abyss
The trenches

Two of these ocean creatures are real, but one is made up. Cross out the animal you predict is not real, and write about how you came to this conclusion.

The **dumbo octopus** has two fins that look like ears. The octopus flaps these fins to move. It swims along the seafloor looking for snails, worms, and other food.

The **fangtooth fish** has giant teeth, but its entire body isn't much larger than your hand. Its teeth help it capture prey of any size that wanders in the trenches.

The **tube shark** has rows of tubes on its back to help it blend in with tube worms on the ocean floor. It lives and hunts in the sunlight zone.

Answers will vary.

Land Habitats

There are many types of land habitats, and each one is filled with unique plants and animals. The desert is a habitat that gets little rain. The plants and animals there have features and skills that help them survive with little water.

Read about each desert plant or animal. Then follow the instructions and answer each question.

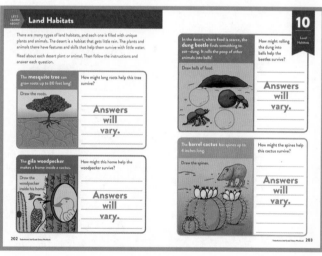

The **mesquite tree** can grow roots up to 80 feet long!

Draw the roots.

How might long roots help this tree survive? Answers will vary.

The **gila woodpecker** makes a home inside a cactus.

Draw the woodpecker inside his home.

How might this home help the woodpecker survive? Answers will vary.

In the desert, where food is scarce, the **dung beetle** finds something to eat—dung. It rolls the poop of other animals into balls!

Draw balls of food.

How might rolling the dung into balls help the beetles survive? Answers will vary.

The **barrel cactus** has spines up to 4 inches long.

Draw the spines.

How might the spines help this cactus survive? Answers will vary.

The rain forest is the land habitat with the greatest diversity on Earth. This means that rain forests have the largest variety of different plants and animals.

Read the travel journal aloud. Then answer each question.

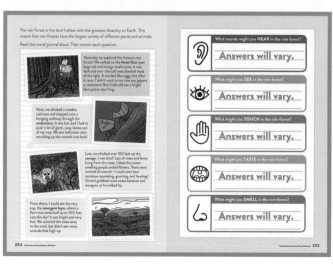

Yesterday we explored the Amazon rain forest! We walked on the forest floor past large red and orange mushrooms. It was dark and wet—the tall trees blocked most of the light. It smelled like soggy dirt after it rains. I didn't want to run into any jaguars or anteaters! But Callie did see a bright blue poison dart frog.

Next, we climbed a wooden staircase and stepped onto a hanging walkway through the understory. It was hot, and I had to push a lot of giant, waxy leaves out of my way. We saw leafcutter ants marching up the smooth tree bark!

Last, we climbed over 100 feet up the canopy. I was tired! Lots of vines and ferns hung from the trees. I liked the sweet-smelling purple orchid flowers. There were animals all around—I could even hear monkeys squeaking, grunting, and howling! Dimitri grabbed some sweet bananas and mangoes as he walked by.

From there, I could see the very top, the emergent layer, about a few trees stretched up to 200 feet into the sky! It was bright and very hot. We watched the trees sway in the wind, but didn't see many animals that high up.

What sounds might you **HEAR** in the rain forest? Answers will vary.

What might you **SEE** in the rain forest? Answers will vary.

What might you **TOUCH** in the rain forest? Answers will vary.

What might you **TASTE** in the rain forest? Answers will vary.

What might you **SMELL** in the rain forest? Answers will vary.

There are grassland habitats all over the world, and they are all covered in grasses.

The MatMots went on a safari in the grasslands of South Africa and printed photos of the plants and animals they saw. But photos from other trips got mixed in with them. Cross out the photos of plants and animals that do not live in the grasslands.

Go on a safari outside your home. What plants and animals live near you? Draw what you observe in your habitat and write any plant or animal's name.

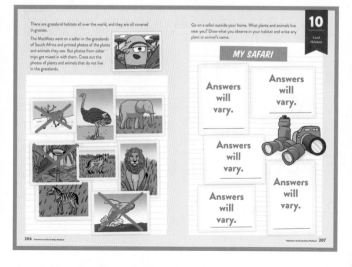

MY SAFARI

Answers will vary. · Answers will vary. · Answers will vary. · Answers will vary. · Answers will vary.

Plant Growth

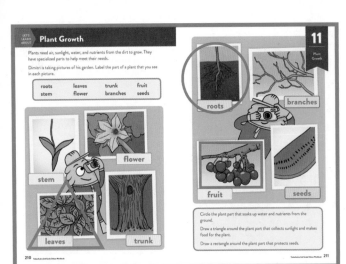

Plants need air, sunlight, water, and nutrients from the dirt to grow. They have specialized parts to help meet their needs.

Dimitri is taking pictures of his garden. Label the part of a plant that you see in each picture.

roots	leaves	trunk	fruit
stem	flower	branches	seeds

11 Plant Growth

roots · branches · flower · stem · fruit · seeds · leaves · trunk

Circle the plant part that soaks up water and nutrients from the ground.

Draw a triangle around the plant part that collects sunlight and makes food for the plant.

Draw a rectangle around the plant part that protects seeds.

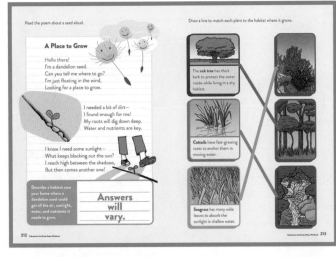

Read the poem about a seed aloud.

A Place to Grow

Hello there!
I'm a dandelion seed.
Can you tell me where to go?
I'm just floating in the wind,
Looking for a place to grow.

I needed a bit of dirt—
I found enough for me!
My roots will dig down deep.
Water and nutrients are key.

I know I need some sunlight—
What keeps blocking out the sun?
I reach high between the shadows,
But then comes another one!

Describe a habitat near your home where a dandelion seed could get all the air, sunlight, water, and nutrients it needs to grow.
Answers will vary.

Draw a line to match each plant to the habitat where it grows.

The **oak tree** has thick bark to protect the water inside while living in a dry habitat.

Cattails have fast-growing roots to anchor them in moving water.

Seagrass has many wide leaves to absorb the sunlight in shallow water.

Predict what will happen at the end of each experiment.

Callie plants two seeds in two pots.

Then she covers one plant so it won't get any light.

Plants collect sunlight with their leaves to make food. They do that by using chlorophyll, which keeps their leaves green. Plants need sunlight to make them grow.

Draw your prediction.

Brian plants two seeds in two pots.

Then he stops watering one plant.

Plants soak up water with their roots. Then the water travels to the leaves, where it helps to make food. Plants need water to make food and to keep from drying out.

Draw your prediction.

Look for plants inside or outside your home. Where do they get the sunlight and water that they need?

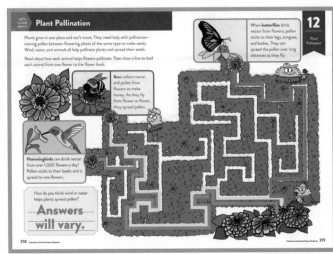

Plant Pollination

12 Plant Pollination

Plants grow in one place and can't move. They need help with pollination—moving pollen between flowering plants of the same type to make seeds. Wind, water, and animals all help pollinate plants and spread their seeds.

Read about how each animal helps flowers pollinate. Then draw a line to lead each animal from one flower to the flower bush.

Bees collect nectar and pollen from flowers to make honey. As they fly from flower to flower, they spread pollen.

Hummingbirds can drink nectar from over 1,000 flowers a day! Pollen sticks to their beaks and is spread to new flowers.

When **butterflies** drink nectar from flowers, pollen sticks to their legs, tongues, and bodies. They can spread the pollen over long distances as they fly.

How do you think wind or water helps plants spread pollen?
Answers will vary.

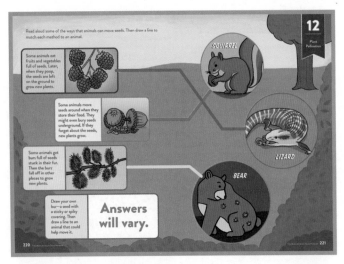

12 Plant Pollination

Read aloud some of the ways that animals can move seeds. Then draw a line to match each method to an animal.

SQUIRREL

Some animals eat fruits and vegetables full of seeds. Later, when they poop, the seeds are left on the ground to grow new plants.

Some animals move seeds around when they store their food. They might even bury seeds underground. If they forget about the seeds, new plants grow.

LIZARD

Some animals get burs full of seeds stuck in their fur. Then the burs fall off in other places to grow new plants.

BEAR

Draw your own bur—a seed with a sticky or spiky covering. Then draw a line to an animal that could help move it.
Answers will vary.

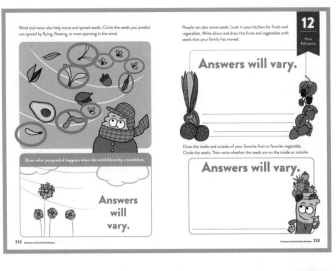

Wind and water also help move and spread seeds. Circle the seeds you predict can spread by flying, floating, or even spinning in the wind.

Draw what you predict happens when the wind blows by a dandelion.
Answers will vary.

People can also move seeds. Look in your kitchen for fruits and vegetables. Write about and draw the fruits and vegetables with seeds that your family has moved.
Answers will vary.

Draw the inside and outside of your favorite fruit or favorite vegetable. Circle the seeds. Then write whether the seeds are on the inside or outside.
Answers will vary.

12 Plant Pollination

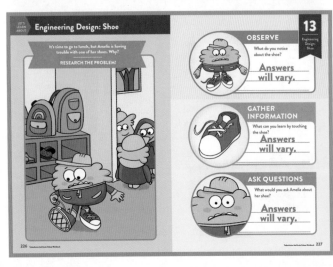

Engineering Design: Shoe

13 Engineering Design: Shoe

It's time to go to lunch, but Amelia is having trouble with one of her shoes. Why?
RESEARCH THE PROBLEM!

OBSERVE
What do you notice about her shoe?
Answers will vary.

GATHER INFORMATION
What can you learn by touching the shoe?
Answers will vary.

ASK QUESTIONS
What would you ask Amelia about her shoe?
Answers will vary.

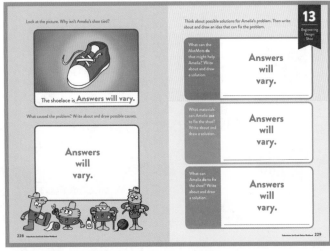

Look at the picture. Why isn't Amelia's shoe tied?

The shoelace is **Answers will vary.**

What caused the problem? Write about and draw possible causes.
Answers will vary.

Think about possible solutions for Amelia's problem. Then write about and draw an idea that can fix the problem.

What can the MintMoits do that might help Amelia? Write about and draw a solution.
Answers will vary.

What materials can Amelia use to fix the shoe? Write about and draw a solution.
Answers will vary.

What can Amelia do to fix the shoe? Write about and draw a solution.
Answers will vary.

13 Engineering Design: Shoe

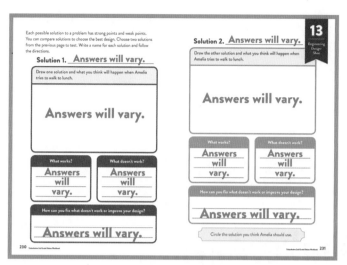

Each possible solution to a problem has strong points and weak points. You can compare solutions to choose the best design. Choose two solutions from the previous page to test. Write a name for each solution and follow the directions.

Solution 1. Answers will vary.

Draw one solution and what you think will happen when Amelia tries to walk to lunch.

Answers will vary.

What works? Answers will vary.

What doesn't work? Answers will vary.

How can you fix what doesn't work or improve your design? Answers will vary.

Solution 2. Answers will vary.

Draw the other solution and what you think will happen when Amelia tries to walk to lunch.

Answers will vary.

What works? Answers will vary.

What doesn't work? Answers will vary.

How can you fix what doesn't work or improve your design? Answers will vary.

Circle the solution you think Amelia should use.

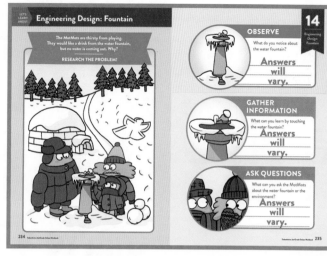

Engineering Design: Fountain

The MotMots are thirsty from playing. They would like a drink from the water fountain, but no water is coming out. Why?

RESEARCH THE PROBLEM!

OBSERVE
What do you notice about the water fountain?
Answers will vary.

GATHER INFORMATION
What can you learn by touching the water fountain?
Answers will vary.

ASK QUESTIONS
What can you ask the MotMots about the water fountain or the environment?
Answers will vary.

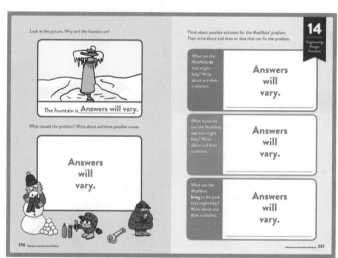

Look at the picture. Why isn't the fountain on?

The fountain is Answers will vary.

What caused the problem? Write about and draw possible causes.

Answers will vary.

Think about possible solutions for the MotMots' problem. Then write about and draw an idea that can fix the problem.

What can the MotMots **do** that might help? Write about and draw a solution.
Answers will vary.

What materials can the MotMots **use** that might help? Write about and draw a solution.
Answers will vary.

What can the MotMots **bring** to the park that might help? Write about and draw a solution.
Answers will vary.

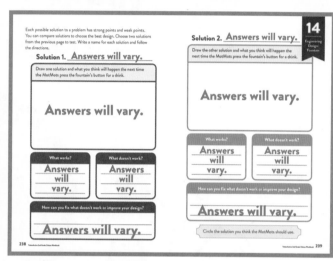

Each possible solution to a problem has strong points and weak points. You can compare solutions to choose the best design. Choose two solutions from the previous page to test. Write a name for each solution and follow the directions.

Solution 1. Answers will vary.

Draw one solution and what you think will happen the next time the MotMots press the fountain's button for a drink.

Answers will vary.

What works? Answers will vary.

What doesn't work? Answers will vary.

How can you fix what doesn't work or improve your design? Answers will vary.

Solution 2. Answers will vary.

Draw the other solution and what you think will happen the next time the MotMots press the fountain's button for a drink.

Answers will vary.

What works? Answers will vary.

What doesn't work? Answers will vary.

How can you fix what doesn't work or improve your design? Answers will vary.

Circle the solution you think the MotMots should use.

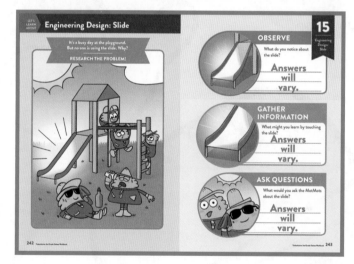

Engineering Design: Slide

It's a busy day at the playground. But no one is using the slide. Why?

RESEARCH THE PROBLEM!

OBSERVE
What do you notice about the slide?
Answers will vary.

GATHER INFORMATION
What might you learn by touching the slide?
Answers will vary.

ASK QUESTIONS
What would you ask the MotMots about the slide?
Answers will vary.

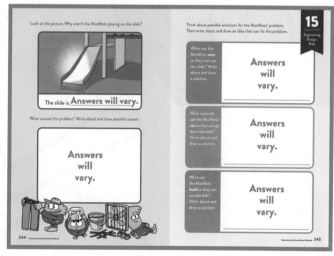

Look at the picture. Why aren't the MotMots playing on the slide?

The slide is Answers will vary.

What caused the problem? Write about and draw possible causes.

Answers will vary.

Think about possible solutions for the MotMots' problem. Then write about and draw an idea that can fix the problem.

What can the MotMots **wear** so they can use the slide? Write about and draw a solution.
Answers will vary.

What materials can the MotMots **use** so they can go down the slide? Write about and draw a solution.
Answers will vary.

What can the MotMots **build** so they can use the slide? Write about and draw a solution.
Answers will vary.

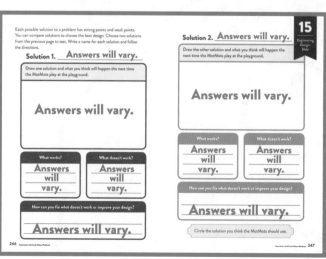

Each possible solution to a problem has strong points and weak points. You can compare solutions to choose the best design. Choose two solutions from the previous page to test. Write a name for each solution and follow the directions.

Solution 1. Answers will vary.

Draw one solution and what you think will happen the next time the MotMots play at the playground.

Answers will vary.

What works? Answers will vary.

What doesn't work? Answers will vary.

How can you fix what doesn't work or improve your design? Answers will vary.

Solution 2. Answers will vary.

Draw the other solution and what you think will happen the next time the MotMots play at the playground.

Answers will vary.

What works? Answers will vary.

What doesn't work? Answers will vary.

How can you fix what doesn't work or improve your design? Answers will vary.

Circle the solution you think the MotMots should use.

CONGRATS!

You're a TinkerActive Science Champion!

TinkerActive

WORKBOOKS

2ND GRADE · ENGLISH LANGUAGE ARTS · AGES 7–8

by Megan Hewes Butler

illustrated by Chad Thomas

educational consulting by Lindsay Frevert

Odd Dot · New York

Vowel Sounds

A **fictional text** is a text that describes imaginary events and people. Read this fiction story aloud.

Troubles with Bubbles

Enid and Frank were heading home from school when the bus driver made a wrong turn—and drove the bus into the car wash! Brushes started spinning. Tubes were dripping soap all over the place. A hose shot water to wash it all off. Then ZAP! FIZZ! SLOSH! What was that? Had something broken?

Enid looked out the back window—a giant wave of bubbles was coming! In front of them, a truck had stopped moving. They were stuck!

Enid got an idea. She asked the driver to put the bus in reverse and drive backward out of the car wash. The bus pushed through the water and into the sunlight. Water was gushing out of the car wash, and bubbles came floating into the street. What a mess!

Long vowels sound like their names. For example:

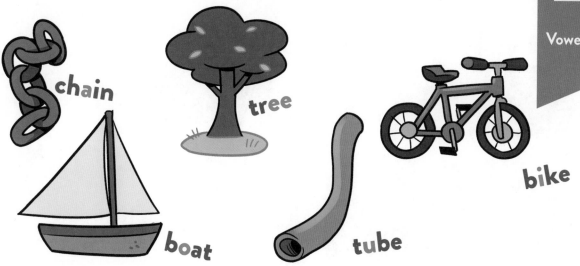

chain

tree

boat

tube

bike

Say each word aloud. Then circle each word with a long vowel sound.

rock

crab

bee

cube

dime

flute

coat

rope

cape

kit

jet

slide

clay

plug

Short vowels sound unlike their names. Write the missing short vowel in each word. Then say each word aloud.

m____p

br____ck

w____b

fr____g

b____ll

f____sh

fl____g

dr____m

br____sh

cl____ck

Read the story on page 258 again. Then write four words from the story that have only short vowel sounds.

_____   _____

_____   _____

Some two-syllable words have both a short vowel *and* a long vowel. Read each word. Then draw a line to connect each word to the correct picture.

Say your name aloud. Does it have short vowel or long vowel sounds? Or both?

Draw a line through the maze to plug in the new bubble maker. Follow a path of only **short vowel** sounds.

Draw a line through the maze to connect the new hose. Follow a path of only **long vowel** sounds.

clank

tick

chime

raffle

screech

START

creak

beep

END

thud

squeak

drip

groan

peep

bang

plop

buzz

whine

LET'S START!

Washable paint

Dish soap

3 small bowls

Spoon

10 drinking straws

Paper

Baking sheet or tray

Light corn syrup

Rubber band

LET'S TINKER!

Say the name of each of your materials aloud. Which ones have short vowel sounds? Which ones have long vowel sounds? **Sort** them into piles by the vowel sounds that you hear.

SHORT VOWEL

LONG VOWEL

LET'S MAKE: BUBBLE VOWELS!

1. Place about 1 teaspoon of paint, 2 teaspoons of water, and 4 drops of dish soap into a bowl.

2. Mix them with a straw.

3. Then **blow** carefully to make bubbles! (Repeat steps 1 through 3 with a new color of paint in a new bowl if you'd like more than one color of bubble paint.)

4. Put a piece of paper inside a baking sheet or tray, to contain any drips.

5. Spoon some bubbles onto your paper.

6. Use a straw to blow the bubbles around and make the shape of each vowel.

LET'S ENGINEER!

It's Tinker Town's BIG bubble-blowing contest! Enid is the current champion, and she must defend her belt. This year, Tinker Town has changed the rules—now you can blow bubbles using more than just one object.

How can Enid blow LOTS of bubbles at one time?

Mix 2 tablespoons of dish soap, 5 tablespoons of water, and 1 teaspoon of light corn syrup in a bowl. **Start** by blowing bubbles with one straw, and then add more. What happens? How can your other materials help? How many bubbles can you blow at once?

PROJECT 1: DONE!
Get your sticker!

Nouns & Pronouns

A **poem** is a type of writing that expresses an emotion or idea and sometimes rhymes.

Read the poem aloud.

If I Could Fly

Look up ahead, I see a bee.
First one, then two—I see three!

Now there are more—four, then five.
Where are they from? Where's the hive?

More bees are here. It's a swarm!
Bees buzzing around just like a storm.

A queen and all her worker bees,
Are making a new hive in the trees.

They are building with wax way up high.
I could see them closer if I could fly!

The poem above uses rhyming words to give the poem rhythm. **Bee** and **three** rhyme. Read the poem again and circle other pairs of words at the end of each line that rhyme.

A **noun** is a person, place, or thing. Look at each picture of a noun from the poem and say the name aloud. Then write each noun on the line.

queen

_____

_____

_____

Regular nouns that end in **s**, **sh**, **ch**, **x**, or **z** become plural when you add **es**. Words that end in other letters become plural when you add **s**.

Write each noun again, adding **s** or **es** to make it plural.

_____

_____

_____

_____

_____

Many nouns become plural by adding **s** or **es**. However, some nouns are **irregular** and do not follow these rules.

Read each noun. Then draw a line to match singular and plural forms.

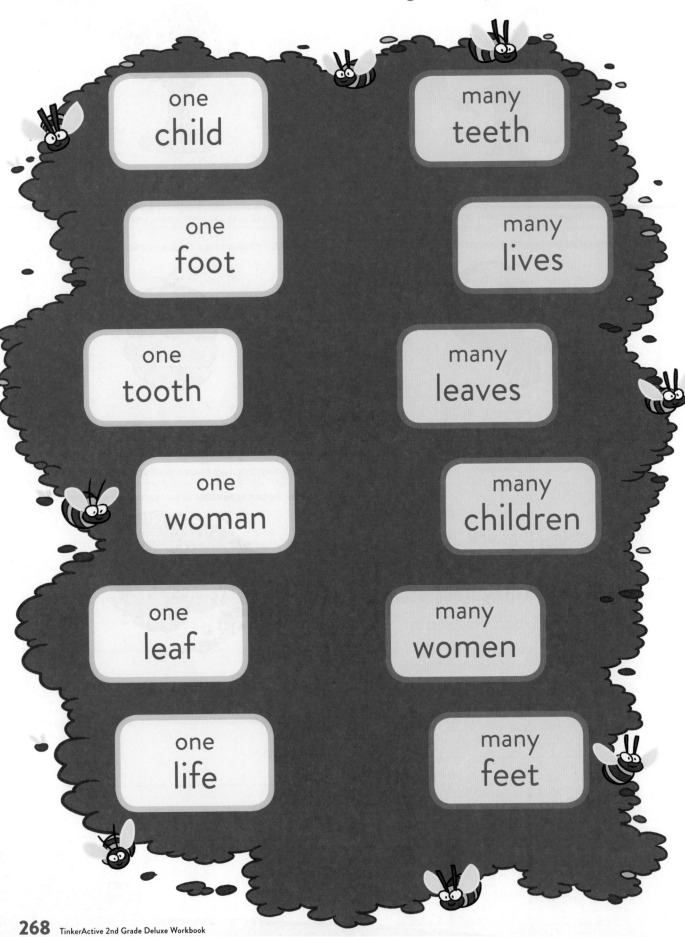

one child	many teeth
one foot	many lives
one tooth	many leaves
one woman	many children
one leaf	many women
one life	many feet

A **collective noun** is a group of people or things.

Draw a line to connect each collective noun to the correct group of people or things.

a herd

a flock

a crew

a class

a deck

a swarm

A **compound word** is when two or more words are joined together to make a new meaning.

Draw a slash between the two nouns that make up each compound word. Think about their meanings. Then circle the picture that matches the compound word.

birdhouse

pancake

starfish

notebook

Go on a hunt around your home to find these compound words or one of your own. Draw a picture of what you find.

A **pronoun** is a word that takes the place of a noun.

The beehive has honey.

It has honey.

It is a pronoun that can take the place of the noun, **beehive.**

Draw a line from each sentence to the bee or bees the pronoun describes.

He is the biggest.

She has orange stripes.

They are sitting on a flower together.

The ladybug is close to **her.**

The worker bee is flying by **itself.**

The red flower is **his.**

LET'S START! GATHER THESE TOOLS AND MATERIALS.

Paper

String

Toilet paper tube

Markers

Paint

Paintbrush

Scissors
(with an adult's help)

Drinking straw

Tape

Pencil

2 or more balls
(of different sizes)

LET'S TINKER!

Tree rhymes with **bee.** What other words do you know that rhyme with **bee**? **Use** your materials to make pictures of the rhymes.

LET'S MAKE: FLOWER FOR A BEE!

1. Color a toilet paper tube using markers or paint.

2. Draw two rings around the middle of the toilet paper tube. They should be about the width of your finger apart.

3. Draw straight lines from both rings to the edge. The space between the lines should be about the width of your finger.

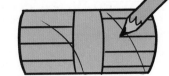

4. Cut each of the lines from the edge to where it touches the ring.

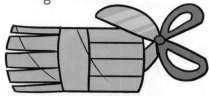

5. Fold each piece of cardboard back to be a petal on the flower.

6. Cut the top 1 inch of a straw in half.

7. Use tape to attach each side of the straw to the flower as a stem.

LET'S ENGINEER!

It's recess time at the Tinker Town school. The MotMots have a ball to play with, and they're not sure what to do with it.

How can they combine "ball" with other activities or objects to have fun?

Write compound words to brainstorm some fun games for the MotMots. **Think** of games you know or make up your own. **Use** your materials to build and play your games.

PROJECT 2: DONE!
Get your sticker!

Read the newspaper article aloud.

TINKER TOWN NEWS

NEW ICE CREAM SHOP IS COOL

Yesterday was an important day for MotMots everywhere. An ice cream shop opened in Tinker Town!

The new store has many flavors: vanilla, chocolate, mint, orange, and even blueberry! There was ice cream in every color. Are you thinking about toppings? There were lots of toppings, too, like sprinkles, cherries, and nuts!

We asked customers in line what they thought of the new store. "It's so COOL!" said one excited little ice cream fan. "I can't wait to come back tomorrow."

Verbs are action words that can tell what happened in the past, present, or future. Rewrite the verb in each sentence in the past tense.

Amelia **rides** to the store.

Amelia __rode__ to the store.

Enid **sees** the sign!

Enid _____ the sign!

Brian **feels** excited.

Brian _____ excited.

Dimitri **sits** at a table.

Dimitri _____ at a table.

Frank **gives** his order.

Frank _____ his order.

Callie **eats** ice cream.

Callie _____ ice cream.

An **adjective** is a word that describes a noun. Adjectives can describe color, shape, size, and more.

Write an adjective to describe each ice cream order.

tall	colorful	red
tiny	chunky	round

Write your own adjective to describe each ice cream order.

An **adverb** is a word that describes a verb, an adjective, or another adverb. Adverbs usually follow a verb in a sentence and often tell when, where, or how something happened.

Circle the adverb that completes the phrase and describes each action.

eating		
happily	sadly	

riding		
quickly	slowly	

eating		
carefully	messily	

banging		
loudly	quietly	

standing		
outside	inside	

sharing		
now	later	

Write your own adverb to describe each action.

eating

_____

talking

_____

tasting

_____

Look at what each MotMot is thinking about. Then write what each one may be thinking. Use the adjectives from the word bank to add details.

cold   fluffy   sweet
giant   chocolaty

Draw the ice cream
you would order! Then
write adjectives to
describe it.

LET'S START!

GATHER THESE TOOLS AND MATERIALS.

 Small paper bag

 Glue

 Tape

 Scissors (with an adult's help)

Foam shaving cream

 Bowl

 Food coloring

 Paintbrush

 Construction paper

 Markers

 5 plastic bottle caps

 Large handful of pom-poms (or cotton balls or balls of foil)

LET'S TINKER!

Make a character out of your paper bag and other materials. It can be a model of you, a MotMot, an animal, or even something made up! **Use** your character to act out verbs. Can you make it dance? Sing? Jump? What else can it do? How many verbs can you act out?

LET'S MAKE: ICE CREAM PAINT!

1. **Add** about 2 tablespoons of glue and ¼ cup of foam shaving cream in a bowl.

2. **Choose** a color and add 5 drops of food coloring. **Mix** with a paintbrush.

3. On a piece of construction paper, **draw** a cone or a bowl with a marker.

4. Use your paint to add "ice cream"!

5. Let it dry overnight.

6. What adjectives would you use to describe your art?

YUMMY!

LET'S ENGINEER!

There's a heat wave in Tinker Town, and the MotMots are working at The Wobbly Cone. The orders are coming so quickly that they got all mixed up! The MotMots need to match each order with the correct customer.

How can they describe each order to the customers to find the correct match?

Use bottle caps as bowls, roll paper into cones, and use pom-poms as scoops of ice cream. Then **build** five of your own mini orders. **Glue** them together and use your other materials to make and add toppings. Then **write** three adjectives that you could use to describe each order on paper. **Describe** each order's color, shape, size, or taste.

PROJECT 3: DONE!
Get your sticker!

Word Building

A **science fiction** story is made up about a world where science plays a big part. There can be spaceships, time travel, or even creatures from other planets! Read the science fiction story aloud.

ROBOT EMERGENCY

Everything was running smoothly at the robot factory. Robot after robot came down the assembly line. So I didn't think that it was a big deal to go and grab a snack. (All I did was make some popcorn.) But when I returned, instead of a shiny row of metal robots, I saw a mess! It was a robot emergency!

On my right I saw a toothless robot. On my left I saw a headless robot. Robots were rolling out of the machine with missing parts—or parts in the wrong places! A robot stumbled by on a leg and an arm.

How fast could I stop this mess? And how would I ever undo it?

While I was frozen in place, a tall and powerful robot unlocked the control panel. He pressed a red button I had never seen before. POP! The robot machine made a loud noise. Then it started making robots even faster than before! Robots of all different shapes, sizes, and colors were shooting out.

I dropped my popcorn and ran for help as fast as I could. Could the robots ever be stopped? I needed backup!

Read the word that describes each robot. Then use stickers from page 389 to add the missing parts back on the robots.

The suffix **-less** means **without**.
Head**less** means **without a head**.

headless　　**armless**　　**legless**

toothless　　**footless**　　**noseless**

Prefixes are special sets of letters that can be added to the start of a word to make a new word. Knowing what a prefix means can help you figure out unknown words. Read the two prefixes below.

re- means **again**

un- means **do the opposite of**

Combine each prefix with the word next to it and write the new word. Then draw a line to match each new word with a robot.

un+wind _unwind_

re+paint _____

re+build _____

un+lock_____

re+fill _____

un+tie _____

Suffixes are special sets of letters that can be added to the end of a word to make a new word. Knowing what a suffix means can help you figure out unknown words. Read the two suffixes below.

-ful means **full of**

-less means **without**

Combine each suffix with the word next to it and write the new word. Then draw a line to match each new word with a robot.

color+ful _____

name+less _____

cheer+ful _____

tooth+less _____

power+ful _____

A **root word** is a word without any prefixes or suffixes.
Underline each root word.

button / re**button** / un**button** / **button**less

repaint

toothless

unzip

powerful

undo

unbuild

colorful

joyful

relock

retie

footless

joyless

Read each word. Then draw a robot to match the description.

headless

joyful

unhappy

helpful

LET'S START!

GATHER THESE TOOLS AND MATERIALS.

Cardboard tubes, small boxes, and small plastic leftover containers

Old magazines

Scissors
(with an adult's help)

Glue

Paper

Foil

Tape

LET'S TINKER!

The prefix **un-** means **do the opposite of; reverse. Use** your materials to explore: What can you stack and unstack? What can you roll and unroll? What else can you do and undo?

Look around your home—can you find anything to lock and unlock, tie and untie, or button and unbutton?

LET'S MAKE: COLLAGE ROBOT!

1. **Cut** out 20 pictures of things from a magazine.

2. **Choose** one to be your robot body and glue it in the middle of a piece of paper.

3. Think about the other parts your robot should have: a head, arms, hands, and fingers? How many legs will your robot have? What about a light, a claw, antennae, or buttons? **Choose** a picture for each part and glue it on the paper.

LET'S ENGINEER!

Tinker Town's fire department wants to start using a robot to find fires and put them out. But they're not sure what the robot should look like or what parts it would need.

How can the MotMots build a robot that would be good at finding and putting out fires?

Design and build your own firefighting robot. What parts will your robot need? A hose for arms? A siren for the mouth? **Take** cardboard tubes, small boxes, or plastic containers and cover them in foil. **Use** tape to hold the foil in place. Then **glue** the parts together to build the body. **Tape** or glue on other materials to add more details. Will your robot be colorful? Powerful? Cheerful? **Describe** it!

PROJECT 4: DONE!
Get your sticker!

Free verse poems have no patterns or rules. They don't even have to rhyme.

Read the poem aloud.

Up, Up, Up!

I'm growing up, up, up.
I was in first grade,
And now I'm in second.
If you'd like to listen, I've learned a lot.
I can do a cartwheel.
Rolling.
   Spinning.
     Jumping.
And I can pack my own lunch.
Cleaning.
   Cutting.
     Counting.
I can even tie my shoes,
All by myself.
What will I be able to do next?
I'm growing up, up, up!

The poem "Up, Up, Up!" uses repeated lines and alliteration to give the poem rhythm.

A **repeated line** is when a phrase or line of the poem is used more than one time.

Write the repeated line from the poem on the previous page.

Alliteration is when the same beginning letter or sound is used in two or more words that are close together.

Read these phrases aloud. Underline the words that have alliteration.

If you'd like to listen, I've learned a lot.

And I can pack my own lunch.
Cleaning.
Cutting.
Counting.

Read the poem aloud.

I can do a cartwheel.
Rolling.
Spinning.
Jumping.

Draw a picture of Callie acting out each word.

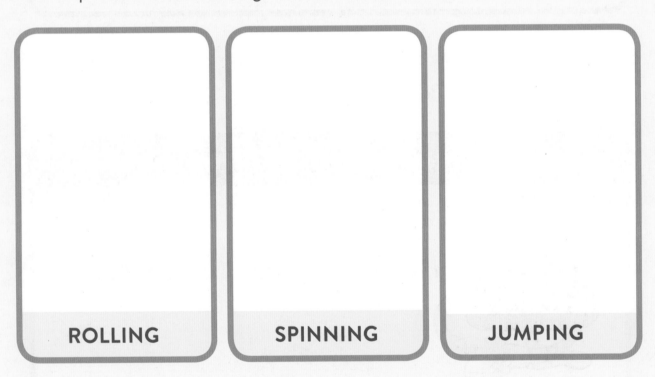

ROLLING	**SPINNING**	**JUMPING**

Read each set of words and act them out. Then follow the directions.

walk   **stomp**   **march**   Circle the action that is the **loudest**.

look   **peek**   **stare**   Circle the action that takes the **longest**.

touch   **tap**   **bang**   Circle the action that is the **softest**.

Read the poem aloud.

And I can pack my own lunch.
Cleaning.
   Cutting.
     Counting.

Look at each picture closely. Draw a line connecting each word to the matching picture.

cleaning   **cutting**   **counting**

**Write about and draw other actions
that you can do to help make snacks or meals.**

Write your own thoughts and feelings about growing up.

I am _____ years old.

I am in _____ grade.

What are you proud that you can do?

_____

_____

_____

_____

_____

_____

What makes you feel happy about growing up?

_____

_____

_____

_____

_____

_____

_____

_____

_____

What do you hope you can do when you get older?

_____

_____

_____

_____

_____

_____

Write your own free verse poem about getting older. This poem doesn't have to use any patterns or rhymes to share your thoughts and feelings. Include information you wrote on the previous page.

Try using repeated lines and alliteration in your poem.

_____

_____

_____

_____

_____

_____

_____

_____

_____

Share your poem with a friend or family member!

LET'S START!

GATHER THESE TOOLS AND MATERIALS.

Crayons

Cardboard

Scissors
(with an adult's help)

Paper cup

20 or more pennies

20 drinking straws

String

Tape

LET'S TINKER!

Arrange your materials by size, and then **describe** the size of each object: Which ones are small, tiny, or itty-bitty? Are any big, huge, or gigantic? What other sizes of materials do you have? What other ways can you sort your materials by size?

LET'S MAKE: ALL ABOUT ME!

1. **Use** a crayon to draw the first letter of your name large on a piece of cardboard.

2. With the help of an adult, **cut** it out.

3. Think of 5 words that start with the same letter as your name. They can be words that describe you or names of things that you like. **Write** these alliteration words on your letter.

4. Use crayons and stickers from page 389 to decorate your letter.

LET'S ENGINEER!

The Tinker Town airport is rebuilding their control tower, and they want to add a helipad so helicopters can land right on top of the building!

How can the MotMots design a tower that can hold the weight of a helicopter?

Use a paper cup with 20 pennies inside to act as your "helicopter." **Design** and build a tower using your materials that can hold the empty cup. Then **add** pennies one at a time—how many pennies can you add before the tower falls? How can you change your design so that it is bigger and stronger?

PROJECT 5: DONE!
Get your sticker!

Working with Unknown Words

Callie's dog, Boxer, started training school last week. Read Boxer's diary and the dictionary definitions aloud.

DATE: APRIL 1

Today is my first day at school. I don't know anyone! I feel very **nervous**. Will I like my teacher? Who will I play with at recess? Will I meet any new friends? I am also feeling very **timid**. I am too shy to make new doggy friends.

DATE: APRIL 2

I made it through my second day at training school! Today I decided to be **brave**. I said "Woof!" to a dog named Bella. She was so nice! We played together at recess. I am feeling **optimistic.** I have hope that I can meet more new doggy friends tomorrow.

DATE: APRIL 3

Today was my third day at school, and it was great. I played with Bella at recess again. I said "Woof!" to more dogs, and I made new doggy friends! I am feeling **relieved.** I am calm and relaxed because I don't feel alone at school.

relieved
adjective – \ ri-ˈlēvd\
experiencing or showing relaxation, especially from anxiety or pent-up emotions

brave
adjective – \ˈbrāv\
having or showing courage and boldness

optimistic
adjective – \ˌäp-tə-ˈmi-stik\
feeling hopeful about the future

nervous
adjective – \ˈnər-vəs\
anxious, apprehensive

timid
adjective – \ˈti-məd\
showing a lack of courage or self-confidence

Read each word that describes how Boxer felt. Then draw a line to connect the word to a matching picture.

brave

nervous

optimistic

relieved

timid

Act out the meanings of
these five feeling words!

Read each sentence aloud, and look at each underlined word. Circle the word below each sentence that means the same thing.

At school we have to eat fast because lunchtime is **brief**.

short   long

I had **chunky** muffins with pieces of fruit inside.

smooth   lumpy

I wanted to be **gutsy**, so I said "Woof!" to more new dogs.

shy   brave

They tasted so **superb** that I ate all five!

awful   great

They were so **puny** that five fit in my paw.

tiny   large

Bella couldn't eat her whole muffin because it was too **massive**.

big   small

A **homograph** is a word that is spelled like another word but that is different in meaning.

Read each sentence. Then circle the picture that shows the correct meaning of the homograph.

Callie's name starts with the **letter** C.

Boxer is writing a **letter** to the teacher.

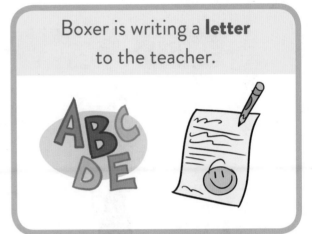

Callie learned to **tie** a knot.

Boxer wore a costume with a fancy **tie**.

Callie put the class pet back in the **pen**.

Boxer got a new **pen** for writing.

The word **duck** is also a homograph. Write a sentence for each meaning.

_____

_____

Write and draw your own diary page. Use a dictionary to help you spell any unknown words.

DATE: _____

_____

_____

_____

_____

_____

_____

_____

You can use feeling words from Boxer's diary. Check the spelling in the dictionary definitions on page 298.

LET'S START! GATHER THESE TOOLS AND MATERIALS.

Book

Dictionary
or online dictionary

Paper
or notebook

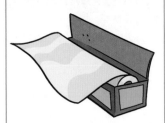
Wax paper

Markers

Yarn or string

Scissors
(with an adult's help)

School glue

Bowl

Ink pad

LET'S TINKER!

Open up a book and find the first word that you don't know. **Look** it up in a dictionary or online dictionary. Then **use** your materials to make a picture of it.

LET'S MAKE: LOOPY LETTERS!

1. Tear off a piece of wax paper about the size of a notebook.

2. Write the first letter of your name on the paper. **Write** it large and take up the whole page.

3. Cut about 20 pieces of yarn, each about the length of your hand.

4. Squeeze some glue into a bowl.

5. Dip each piece of yarn in the glue, one at a time. **Place** the yarn on the letter.

6. Let the letter dry and then peel it off the wax paper.

The word "letter" has more than one meaning. You've made a letter from your name. Can you use your materials to make another kind of letter?

LET'S ENGINEER!

Boxer keeps mixing up Callie's feelings. When she's sad, he thinks it's time to play. When she's happy, he sits in a corner by himself!

How can Callie show Boxer different feelings?

Make five faces that show different feelings. **Press** your thumb into an ink pad and then onto a piece of paper. Then **use** a marker to draw features that make a face: like eyes, a nose, and a mouth. **Write** a feeling word that describes each face. You can **use** a word that you know or a new one that you learned in this project. You can also **look up** a new one in a dictionary or online dictionary.

PROJECT 6: DONE!
Get your sticker!

A **fable** is a short made-up story that often uses talking animals to teach a lesson. There is usually a hero and a villain in the story. Read the fable aloud.

The Lion and the Mouse

One day a mouse was playing in the bright, leafy woods. He raced down tall trees and jumped over logs. He was running so fast that he ran right into the nose of a sleeping lion! The lion woke up and caught the tiny mouse with his giant paw. The mouse shook with fear! "Please let me go! If you help me, someday I will help you," he begged. The lion let out a huge roaring laugh. Someone so tiny could never help him! He got such a good laugh that he decided to be kind and let the mouse go.

Later, the lion was roaming the woods. He was looking for his next snack when SWOOSH! He accidentally stepped into a trap hidden by a hunter. A net lifted him off the ground—he was stuck. "HELP!" he roared at the top of his lungs.

The mouse heard the roaring from far away and ran through the branches as fast as he could. When he got to the lion, he jumped up and started chewing the net. In a few minutes he chewed through the rope and set the lion free! "You laughed at me," the mouse reminded the lion. "You said that a mouse could never help a lion. But now you know! You can't judge what someone can do by how they look. Even someone tiny can be a giant hero."

Read the fable again. Try using different voices for the characters.

Write a ✔ next to why the mouse ran into the lion.

☐ He was running too fast.

☐ He wanted to meet the lion.

☐ He had stepped in a trap.

Circle how the mouse felt when the lion caught him.

Write a word you would use to describe this feeling:

_____

Circle how the lion felt when the mouse promised he would help the lion.

Write a word you would use to describe this feeling:

_____

Write a ✔ next to what the lion did to the mouse.

☐ He kept the mouse.

☐ He let the mouse go.

☐ He asked the mouse to help him someday.

Write a ✔ next to why the lion stepped into a trap.

☐ The trap was made of rope.

☐ The trap was gone.

☐ The trap was hidden.

Write and draw to answer these questions about the story.

WHO were the characters?

_____ _____

HOW did the characters meet?

_____

_____

WHERE was the setting? Add details from the story to your drawing.

WHEN did the lion need help?

WHY do you think the mouse helped the lion?

WHAT do you think would have happened if the mouse had not chewed through the lion's rope? Draw what might have happened below. Then tell a friend or family member the new ending to the story.

Write the numbers 1, 2, 3, and 4 to put the illustrations in order from first to last.

In a fable, there is often a lesson, called a **moral.**

What moral did the lion learn about how he treated the mouse?

_____

_____

_____

Draw a picture of a time that a friend helped you.

Draw a picture of a time that you helped a friend.

Label yourself and your friends
in the drawings.

LET'S START! GATHER THESE TOOLS AND MATERIALS.

Small toy

String

Plastic bottle

Scissors
(with an adult's help)

Cardboard

Glue

Shoebox

Construction paper

Paint

LET'S TINKER!

In the fable, the mouse helped the lion escape from a net. **Find** a toy that you can wrap in string, like the lion in the net. How can you free the toy? Could any of your other materials help?

LET'S MAKE: LIVELY LION!

1. With the help of an adult, **cut** the bottom off a plastic bottle and recycle the top half.

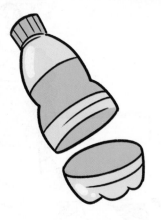

2. Cut a flower shape and tail shape, each about as long as your hand, out of a piece of cardboard.

3. Paint the pieces to be the lion's body, head, and tail.

5. Glue the head on the front of the bottle, and the tail on the back.

4. Add a sticker from page 389 to the flower shape for the lion's face.

LET'S ENGINEER!

Callie is setting up a Fable Table at Tinker Town's art fair. She is going to tell her own fables! She made a few animals, but she doesn't have any settings where she can tell her stories.

How can Callie make settings for her Fable Table?

Make or build your own setting to tell a fable or story. **Decide** where your story will take place—at school, the park, a store, the beach, or someplace else. Then **use** your materials to decorate the inside of your shoebox to look like that setting.

PROJECT 7: DONE!
Get your sticker!

Reading Informational Texts

Read this informational text aloud.

The History of Skyscrapers

Skyscrapers are very tall buildings, including the tallest buildings in the world! Skyscrapers have changed a lot over time. As builders and engineers use new designs and materials, the buildings they make keep getting taller.

In 1857 an inventor took an important step toward building the very first skyscrapers. Elisha Otis designed an elevator that was safe for people to use every day. Before this, people had to use the stairs! Now it made sense to build taller buildings because people could go up and down easily.

The first skyscraper was built in Chicago in 1885—over one hundred years ago. It was only ten stories tall! The city was growing fast, and people needed buildings that were taller but also strong and safe. It was the first building to use a grid made of steel beams, which made it very sturdy.

Many taller skyscrapers continued to be built in the United States, including the Empire State Building and the Sears Tower. Then, in 1998, the tallest building ever built was finished in Malaysia. Ever since then, the tallest skyscrapers have been in other countries around the world.

Using new designs and materials, skyscrapers continue to be built higher and higher. In fact, the meaning of the word "skyscraper" had to change! Most people now say a skyscraper must be over 490 feet tall. That's four times taller than the first skyscraper! However, the current tallest building in the world, the Burj Khalifa, was built in 2010 and is much taller than that: 2,717 feet. But this record won't last for long. New and taller skyscrapers are still being built.

Have you ever seen a skyscraper?

☐ **Yes**   ☐ **No**

A **main idea** is the most important thought or point of a passage or paragraph.

Write a ✔ next to the **main idea** of the passage.

☐ **The first skyscraper was 10 stories tall.**

☐ **Skyscrapers have changed a lot over time.**

☐ **A skyscraper must be over 490 feet tall.**

Draw a circle around the paragraph with this main idea:

The elevator was an important invention that led people to build buildings taller.

Put a ✔ next to the event that happened first.

☐ **The first skyscraper was built in Chicago.**

☐ **The tallest skyscraper in the world was built in Malaysia.**

☐ **Elisha Otis designed the first safe elevator.**

Put a ✔ next to the event that happened last.

☐ **The Burj Khalifa was built.**

☐ **The Empire State Building was built.**

☐ **The Sears Tower was built.**

Answer each question about "The History of Skyscrapers."

Who invented the first safe elevator? _____

Why was this invention important?

_____

_____

Where was the first skyscraper built? _____

When was it built? _____

What is the tallest building in the world right now?

_____

How tall is it?

_____

How tall do you think the tallest skyscraper will be in a hundred years?

_____

What do you think it will look like? Draw and write your answer.

Write one question about something that you still want to know about skyscrapers. Use a question word, like **Who**, **What**, **Where**, **When**, **Why**, or **How**, to begin your sentence.

_____

_____

_____

Tell a friend or family member one new fact you learned about skyscrapers!

Informational texts can share information by using pictures, charts, diagrams, and more. A **timeline** is a chart that shows the order in which events occured. It often includes dates to tell when each event happened.

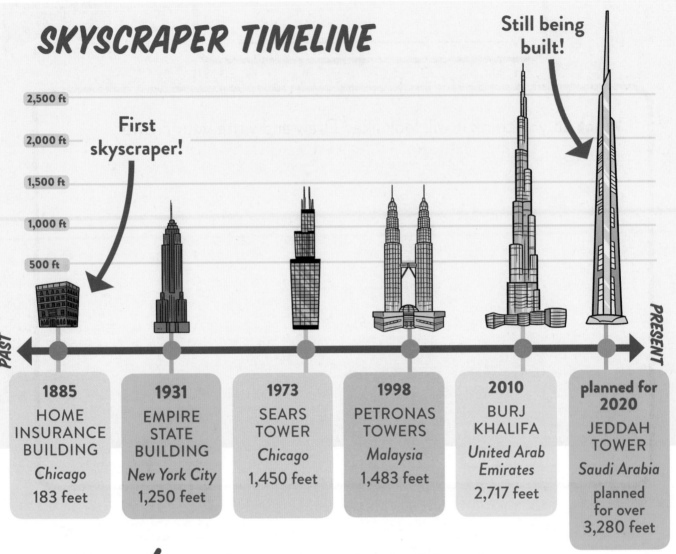

SKYSCRAPER TIMELINE

Still being built!

First skyscraper!

2,500 ft
2,000 ft
1,500 ft
1,000 ft
500 ft

PAST

PRESENT

1885
HOME INSURANCE BUILDING
Chicago
183 feet

1931
EMPIRE STATE BUILDING
New York City
1,250 feet

1973
SEARS TOWER
Chicago
1,450 feet

1998
PETRONAS TOWERS
Malaysia
1,483 feet

2010
BURJ KHALIFA
United Arab Emirates
2,717 feet

planned for 2020
JEDDAH TOWER
Saudi Arabia
planned for over 3,280 feet

Write a ✔ next to how you learned each of these facts: from the text on page 314 or the timeline above.

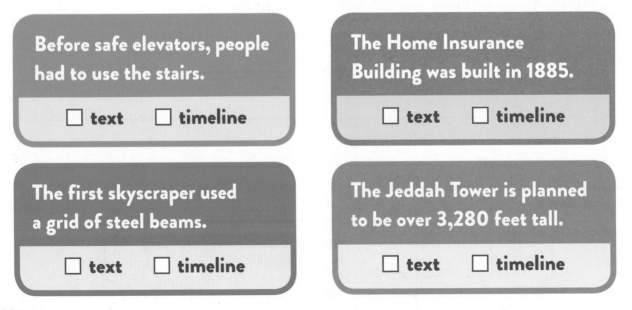

Before safe elevators, people had to use the stairs.
☐ text   ☐ timeline

The Home Insurance Building was built in 1885.
☐ text   ☐ timeline

The first skyscraper used a grid of steel beams.
☐ text   ☐ timeline

The Jeddah Tower is planned to be over 3,280 feet tall.
☐ text   ☐ timeline

Write and draw your own timeline that
shows important events from your life.

**Important Events
in My Life**

PAST

Date: _____

Date: _____

Date: _____

Date: _____

PRESENT

LET'S START!

GATHER THESE TOOLS AND MATERIALS.

4 sheets of thick paper

Scissors (with an adult's help)

Glue stick

Heavy book or object

Markers

Optional: pictures of you at different ages

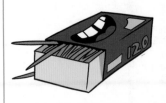
20 or more toothpicks

Clay (or mini marshmallows or grapes)

5 or more rubber bands

LET'S TINKER!

Ask *who, what, where, when, why,* and *how,* to learn more about your materials. Who in your family uses them? What can they be used for? Where are they usually stored? **Ask** other questions using when, why, and how. Can you find a new use for one material by asking questions?

LET'S MAKE: TIMELINE BOOK!

1. Fold 4 sheets of paper in half the long way.

2. Fold each piece in half the other way, and then cut the pages in half on the shorter crease.

3. Arrange the paper V's in a pattern to make mountains and valleys: ∧∨∧∨∧.

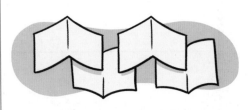

4. Glue the pages together to form an accordion book.

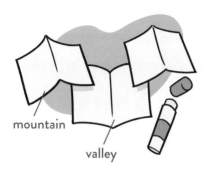

mountain

valley

5. Fold your accordion book and place it under a heavy book or object for a few minutes. This will help it dry flat.

6. Write your name on the cover of your accordion book. Then **number** the pages starting at 1. **Keep writing** until your age!

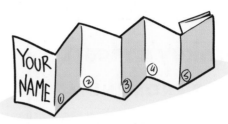

YOUR NAME

7. Glue or draw a picture of you at every age on the matching pages. Then **write** a sentence about your life at that age. Were you a baby? Did you learn to walk? Did you start going to school, or try a new activity?

AGE 5

I PLAYED BASKETBALL!

LET'S ENGINEER!

The skyscrapers in Bungleburg keep wobbling! The builders and engineers of Bungleburg can't seem to keep their skyscrapers standing straight.

How can the MotMots model a stable skyscraper for the Bungleburg engineers?

Design and draw your own skyscraper. Then **use** toothpicks, clay, and rubber bands to build a model. Which design will create the strongest tower? Is it better to use more or fewer toothpicks? Can you build a tower that is taller than a standing up notebook?

PROJECT 8: DONE!
Get your sticker!

Comparing Texts

A **folktale** is a story that has been told over and over. There are often many versions of the same story. Read the two different versions of this folktale aloud.

The Monkey's Heart

A FOLKTALE FROM INDIA

Once upon a time, a monkey lived in a fig tree by a river. One day a hungry crocodile saw the monkey and thought he looked delicious. She wanted to eat his heart! She told her sneaky husband, and he said he'd get the monkey's heart. His wife was confused—the monkey lived in a tree, and the crocodiles lived in the river. How could the monkey be caught?

The next day the sneaky crocodile swam up to the tree and said to the monkey, "On the far side of the river there is a sweet mango tree. I can take you." The monkey liked mangoes, so he hopped on the crocodile's back. In the middle of the river he started to sink. The crocodile snapped, "Sorry, monkey. There is no mango tree. My hungry wife wants to eat your heart!"

Now, the monkey was sneaky, too. "But monkeys don't keep their hearts inside! They would fall out when we climbed trees! I keep my heart in the fig tree," he said. The crocodile took the monkey back to the fig tree to get his heart. The monkey hopped back into the tree and let out a big laugh. "I fooled you, sneaky crocodile! What kind of animal doesn't have a heart inside?"

The Monkey and the Shark

A FOLKTALE FROM AFRICA

There once was a monkey who lived in an apple tree by the ocean. One day the monkey saw a shark in the water below, so he threw some sweet apples down for the shark to eat.

The shark ate the delicious apples. Then he said he'd like to give the monkey a gift, too. He offered the monkey a ride. So the monkey jumped down into the ocean onto the shark's back and went for a ride. In the middle of the trip, the shark said, "I'm sorry, but my king is very sick, so he sent me to get a monkey's heart to heal him."

The monkey was very worried. He thought quickly and said, "Oh dear. I left my heart back at the apple tree!" The shark was confused, so he took the monkey back to the tree. The monkey jumped back into his tree and ran away. No matter what the shark said, he would not come back!

Draw a line to connect each character and event to the correct folktale.

The Monkey's Heart

The Monkey and the Shark

Write and draw to compare these two folktales.

The Monkey's Heart

Draw the characters in this story.

Draw the setting of this story.

What is one way the endings are the same? Draw one similarity.

How do you think the monkey reacted when the crocodile said, "My hungry wife wants to eat your heart"? Act it out.

The Monkey and the Shark

Draw the characters in this story.

Draw the setting of this story.

What is one way that the endings are different? Draw one difference.

How do you think the monkey acted when the shark said, "I'm sorry, but my king is very sick, so he sent me to get a monkey's heart to heal him"? Act it out.

Answer each question.

How does the crocodile think he can outsmart the monkey?

_____

_____

_____

_____

How does the shark think he can outsmart the monkey?

_____

_____

_____

_____

How does the monkey outsmart both the shark **and** the crocodile?

_____

_____

_____

_____

What lesson did the crocodile and the shark learn?

_____

_____

_____

_____

A **Venn diagram** can be used to compare similarities and differences between two stories.

Reread the stories on page 322. Then fill in the diagram.

THE MONKEY'S HEART

BOTH STORIES

THE MONKEY AND THE SHARK

The monkey is the main character.

The monkey started to sink.

The shark says that the king is sick.

Folktales are told over and over—and often the stories change. Try it! Tell a story to a friend. Have them tell another friend and listen. What changes did you hear?

LET'S START! GATHER THESE TOOLS AND MATERIALS.

Construction paper

Scissors
(with an adult's help)

15 drinking straws

Glue

Large piece of foil

Tape

Small rock

LET'S TINKER!

Pick up two of your materials and compare them. What is one way that they are the same? What is one way that they are different? How can you sort your materials based on how they are the same?

LET'S MAKE: MONKEY IN A TREE!

1. **Cut** a sheet of construction paper in half. On one half of the paper, **make** cuts about 3 inches long on both ends.

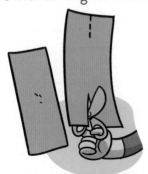

2. **Fold** over the edges of the bottom two pieces, like monkey legs.

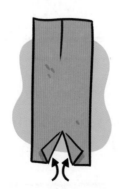

3. **Roll** the top two pieces around a straw, and use glue to keep them rolled. These are the monkey's arms.

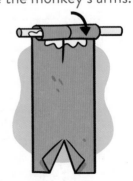

4. **Cut** a small strip of paper and glue it to the back so that it sticks out like a tail.

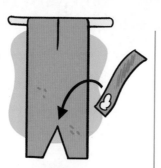

5. Using the other half of the paper, **cut out** 1 large circle and 2 small ones.

6. **Get** another sheet of paper in a different color and cut out 2 large circles.

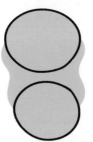

7. **Glue** one large circle onto the middle of the monkey's body.

8. **Glue** the other 4 circles together to make the monkey's face. **Draw** on eyes and a smile.

9. **Hold** up the straw to take your monkey for a swing!

LET'S ENGINEER!

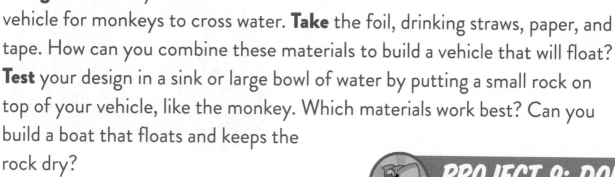

The MotMots read the folktales about the clever monkey. Now they want to help monkeys everywhere ride across the ocean or rivers if they want to get mangoes.

How can the MotMots help the monkeys?

Design and build your own vehicle for monkeys to cross water. **Take** the foil, drinking straws, paper, and tape. How can you combine these materials to build a vehicle that will float? **Test** your design in a sink or large bowl of water by putting a small rock on top of your vehicle, like the monkey. Which materials work best? Can you build a boat that floats and keeps the rock dry?

PROJECT 9: DONE!
Get your sticker!

Fluency

A **script** is the written story for a play, movie, or speech. It contains lines that each character will say and instructions about what the characters should do or act like.

Read the script aloud.

THE LOUD WHISTLE

Zoe is at the park. She is whistling a song. Max walks up to her.

Zoe: Hi, Max! Listen to me whistle!

Zoe puckers her lips and a loud whistle comes out.

Max: Wow! I wish I knew how to do that.

Zoe: I can teach you. First wet your lips. Then pucker them, as if you were making a kissing face. Then blow air through your lips.

Max wets his lips and tries to whistle, but he does not make a sound.

Max: Why isn't it working?

Zoe: I don't know. Try moving your tongue out of the way when you blow.

Max tries again. But he does not make a sound. Xavier walks up.

Max: I just can't whistle. Maybe my mouth isn't small enough. Maybe I'll never be able to whistle at all.

Xavier: Are you trying to whistle? I just learned how. Try this! When you blow air out through your lips, move your mouth and jaw into different positions until you hear a sound.

Max whistles. It's so loud that Zoe and Xavier have to cover their ears!

Max: It worked! Thank you! I'm going to show all my friends.

Max gets up to leave, but Zoe looks confused.

Zoe: What? I couldn't hear what you said. Maybe we should work on whistling quietly next.

Zoe, Max, and Xavier all laugh and whistle a song together.

Create your own ending to the play: What do you think will happen when Max goes to show his friends his new skill? What will Max say and do? What will his friends say and do?

Draw a picture to show what will happen. Then complete the script below.

_____ : _____

_____

_____ : _____

_____

_____ : _____

_____

_____ : _____

_____

Read the play aloud by yourself or with a partner. Try reading it using different voices for the characters.

Read each of the characters' thoughts aloud. Draw a line to connect each thought to the face with the matching emotion.

Whistling is my new favorite thing to do!

I wonder why Max can't whistle?

That loud whistle hurts my ears!

Zoe

Whistling is so cool and I wish I could do it.

I'm so frustrated!

I know I need to keep trying again and again.

Max

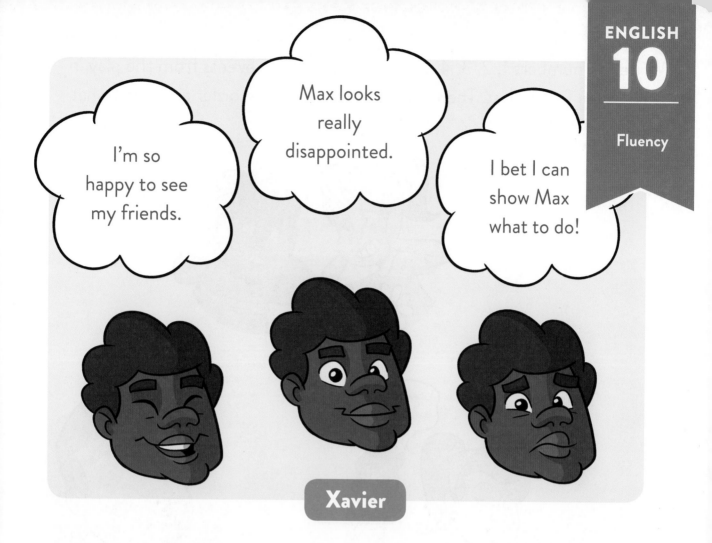

Find a partner to play a game:

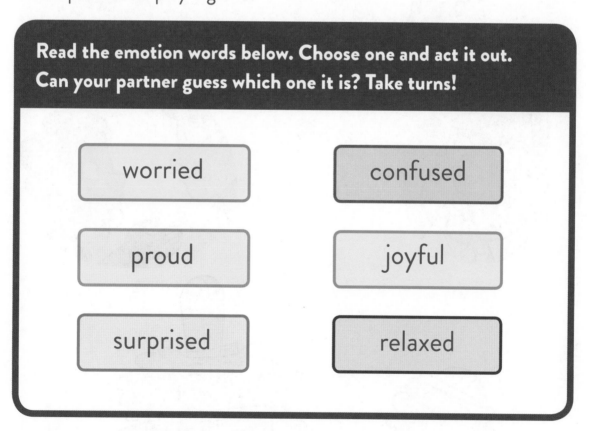

Read the emotion words below. Choose one and act it out. Can your partner guess which one it is? Take turns!

worried	confused
proud	joyful
surprised	relaxed

Write the numbers 1, 2, 3, 4, 5, and 6 to put these events from the play in order from first to last. Then point at each picture in order and retell what happened in the play.

Read the play *The Loud Whistle* again. Think about how Zoe and Xavier tried to teach Max to whistle.

Write about and draw how **you** would teach Max to whistle. (If you can't whistle yet, write about and draw another skill you can teach.)

_____

_____

_____

_____

_____

_____

Share your writing with a friend or family member so someone else can learn, too!

LET'S START! GATHER THESE TOOLS AND MATERIALS.

4–6 pennies

Marbles

Markers

Toilet paper tube

Paper

Scissors
(with an adult's help)

Drinking straw

A few pieces of grass

LET'S TINKER!

Whistling can make a loud sound. **Use** your materials to see what other sounds you can make! What happens when you tap them, bend them, drop them, or shake them? **Describe** the sounds you hear.

LET'S MAKE: PAPER WHISTLE!

1. Draw this shape about the size of your hand onto a piece of paper.

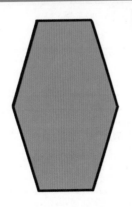

2. Cut it out and fold it in half.

3. Fold over the top edges to make flaps.

4. Cut out a notch.

5. Hold the flaps to your lips and blow!

LET'S ENGINEER!

Dimitri has entered the Tinker Town Whistling Competition. This year the winner will be the MotMot that can whistle in the most ways!

How can Dimitri make a different whistling sound?

Try it yourself! **Wet** your lips and whistle. **Try** flattening the end of a straw and cutting it into a triangle shape. What sounds can you make by blowing into it? Can you whistle by blowing on the side of a piece of grass? Or a leaf? What other materials can you use to make a whistling sound?

PROJECT 10: DONE!
Get your sticker!

Punctuation

The MotMots found a message in a bottle! Read the letter aloud.

To the person who finds this letter,

Ahoy! I'm writing to you from the sea. I sailed away because everyone at home kept calling me a pirate. I got sick of it! They just didn't understand me. My pet parrot stands on my shoulder because he gets lonely. On the way to Bungleburg once, I got sand in my eye. So now I have to wear an eye patch—my mom said so. I also sometimes drop what I am carrying, so I hold a hook in my hand. Why does everyone keep calling me a pirate? Don't they know not to judge a book by its cover? If you are a person who knows that, then I have drawn a map for you. Please keep it a secret!

Your friend,
Redbeard

Look at the map to answer each question. Remember that the names of geographic locations should be capitalized.

Where did Redbeard bury his treasure chest?

_____

Draw a **green** line on the map from Tinker Town to the treasure chest. Travel by water past Bungleburg.

Which sea did you sail on?

_____

Which town is closest to the jewels?

_____

Draw a **blue** line on the map from Tinker Lake to the jewels. Travel by river.

Which town has no buried treasure?

_____

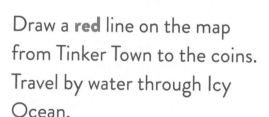

Where did Redbeard bury his coins?

_____

Draw a **red** line on the map from Tinker Town to the coins. Travel by water through Icy Ocean.

Which mountain did you pass?

_____

A **possessive noun** uses an apostrophe to show when something belongs to another person or thing.

The MotMots are going on a treasure hunt, and they are each bringing a piece of gear. Look at each picture and write each possessive noun by adding an **'s** after the end of each MotMot's name.

Amelia **flashlight**

Amelia's flashlight

Callie **map**

Brian **compass**

Dimitri **shovel**

Frank **snacks**

Enid **hat**

Look around your home. Use possessive nouns to describe who things belong to.

A **contraction** is a shorter version of a word or words. An apostrophe is used in place of the missing letter or letters.

Replace the underlined words in each sentence with a contraction.

He's   We're   I'm
Don't   It's   She's   I've

We are going on a treasure hunt! _We're_

I am very excited. _____

He is going to read the map. _____

She is going to dig. _____

Do not forget the sunscreen! _____

It is going to be a long, hot journey. _____

Uh-oh. I have forgotten the snacks. _____

It's Talk-Like-a-Pirate Day in the MotMots' class.

Fill in the missing punctuation for each of these sentences. Use a **period (.)** for telling sentences, a **question mark (?)** to ask a question, and an **exclamation mark (!)** to share a big feeling, like excitement.

Is Talk-Like-a-Pirate Day real___

Yes, it happens every year on September 19 ___

What happens on that holiday___

Everyone talks like a pirate ___

I think it's the best day of the year ___

"Ahoy!" is my favorite thing to say___

I hope I don't have to walk the plank ___

All holidays should be capitalized, like Halloween, Valentine's Day, and Talk-Like-a-Pirate Day!

A **greeting** is the opening of a letter. Common greetings are "Dear Friend," or "Hello!" A **closing** is the ending of a letter. Common closings are "Sincerely," or "Your Friend."

Write a letter to tell a friend about Talk-Like-a-Pirate Day.

Use a comma after the **greeting** here.

_____

_____

_____

_____

_____

_____

_____

_____

_____

_____

_____

_____

                                    _____

                                    _____

Use a comma after the **closing** and write your name below.

LET'S START! GATHER THESE TOOLS AND MATERIALS.

Pencil

Paper

Markers

10 pieces of newspaper

10 small paper bags

Tape

Construction paper

Scissors (with an adult's help)

Glue

Glass or plastic bottle with a lid

LET'S TINKER!

Many words should be capitalized, like people's names, holidays, and geographic locations. The names of products should also be capitalized. **Look** at your materials. Then **brainstorm** and name three of your own products. **Write** the names down, and remember to use capital letters!

LET'S MAKE: 3-D MAP!

1. **Crumple** a few pieces of newspaper into a ball and put them inside a small paper bag.

2. **Fold** over the top and tape it closed.

3. Cut and glue pieces of construction paper to add details to make the paper bag look like your home. **Add** doors, windows, and a roof.

4. Repeat steps 1 through 3 to make other buildings in your town, including your school, a store, and a friend's home.

5. Cut other shapes from construction paper to add more details to your map, like roads, a field, or a pond.

6. Place the buildings and other items where they belong on the floor—some may be close to your home and some may be far.

LET'S ENGINEER!

The MotMots are thinking about when they'll be grown up. They wonder what it will be like! But they don't want to forget who they are today.

How can the MotMots record their favorite things and facts about themselves, and save them for the future?

Make your own message in a bottle. **Wash** and dry the inside of your empty bottle. What can you put inside that shares details about yourself? **Close** the bottle tightly when you are done. **Find** a place to store it until you are graduating third grade. Then **open** it up!

PROJECT 11: DONE!
Get your sticker!

Writing Sentences

A **diagram** uses drawings and designs to share information so that it is easy to read and understand. Read the diagram aloud. Start at the top and follow the arrows.

Most mother frogs lay their **eggs** underwater to keep them wet. Some types of frogs lay over 1,000 eggs at a time.

FROG LIFE CYCLE

Froglets keep growing into **frogs**. Frogs have no tails. They can breathe air and live in the water and on land.

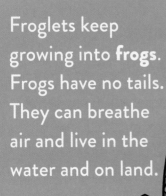

A **tadpole** hatches from each egg. The tadpoles have long tails and live underwater. As they grow, legs and arms develop.

Tadpoles grow into **froglets.** Their gills change into lungs for breathing on land. Their tails shrink and they climb out of the water.

Look closely at each picture to find the difference and circle the one described. Then complete the sentence. Use a **period (.)** to end each sentence.

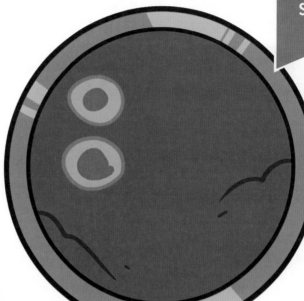

One tadpole is ready to hatch. It will live under the

_____

One tadpole has grown

_____

One froglet is using his legs to climb

_____

_____

_____

Have you ever seen a tadpole? What other animals and their babies have you seen around your home?

Look at each picture and write a sentence about what you observe. Use a capital letter to begin each sentence, and end each sentence with the correct punctuation.

Read each set of facts. Write one compound sentence that includes both facts. Use a comma and a conjunction word, like **and**, **but**, or **so**.

FACTS

Most frogs are carnivorous. They eat other small animals.

Most frogs are carnivorous,
so they eat other small animals.

FACTS

Frogs get water through their skin. They do not drink water.

_____

_____

FACTS

Some types of frogs live in trees. Others live underground.

_____

_____

Read this compound sentence. Then write the two facts as separate sentences.

Frogs do not have ears that you can see, but they can hear well.

FACT # 1 _____

FACT # 2 _____

Write a sentence about what you think each frog will do next.

glass frog

ghost frog

flying frog

leaf frog

Look at the pictures. Then write a sentence in each thought bubble to show what the frogs are thinking. Last, give the story a title and read it aloud.

TITLE:_____

LET'S START!

GATHER THESE TOOLS AND MATERIALS.

3 or more craft sticks

Construction paper

Scissors
(with an adult's help)

Glue

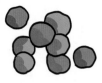

Optional: A few small
round objects
(like pom-poms or buttons)

Index card

Markers or crayons

Paper plate

LET'S TINKER!

Use your materials to make thought bubbles. Then **write** sentences on them to show what you are thinking.

I MISS MY DOG, BOXER.

I LOVE TO EAT BANANAS!

LET'S MAKE: JUMPING FROG!

1. Fold over the top corners of an index card. Then **open** it back up.

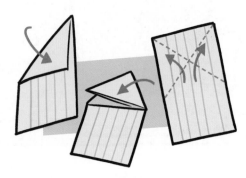

2. Use two fingers to pull in the sides, and press the top triangle flat.

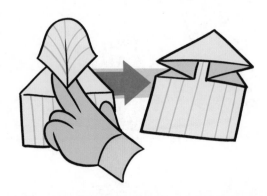

3. Fold the two edges of the triangle up to the top. These make the frog's front legs!

4. Fold in the leftover sides to meet in the middle.

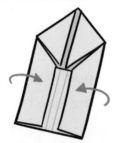

5. Fold the bottom up. Then **fold** the top layer back to form the frog's back legs.

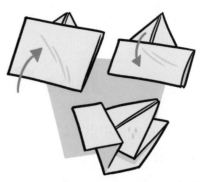

6. Color and add details to your frog. Then **push** down with your finger to watch it jump!

LET'S ENGINEER!

The MotMots are studying the life cycle of frogs, and are thinking about their own life cycles. They've changed a lot since they were baby MotMots!

How can the MotMots make models of their own life cycles?

Use your materials to make a model of your own life cycle. How can you show what you looked like as a baby? What you look like now? And what you might look like when you grow up and when you're old? **Write** a sentence about each part of your life cycle. How have you changed?

PROJECT 12: DONE!
Get your sticker!

Telling a Story

A **biography** is a story about a person's life, written by someone else. Read this biography aloud.

Jane Goodall

Jane Goodall is an English scientist who studied chimpanzees. She became interested in animals when she was very young. She kept a journal with notes and drawings about the animals she saw around her home, like chickens, insects, and worms.

When she was twenty-six years old she went to Tanzania, a country in Africa. She went there to live with chimpanzees so she could study them—something no one had done before! At first, when she tried to watch them, they would run away. But she kept trying. She'd stand far away and watch them eat. After a while, they got used to her being around.

Just like when she was young, Jane kept notes in her journal. She wrote down what the chimpanzees did, where they went, and how they acted. It took a whole year, but the chimpanzees got used to her and let her get closer. After another year they were no longer afraid. She got to know them and gave them all names. She spent time living in the trees with them and even ate their food with them.

From watching the chimpanzees closely, Jane learned things about them that no one else had ever discovered. They had families and relationships. They gave hugs! They used different sounds like a language to talk to each other. They sometimes ate meat, like insects and birds. They used sticks as tools and threw stones as weapons.

Jane became famous for her work studying chimpanzees. Her important discoveries helped scientists all over the world. She used her notes to write many books. Today, she still talks to people about chimpanzees—she teaches others about what chimpanzees need and how people can protect them.

Write a ✔ next to the event that happened **FIRST**.

☐ Jane went to Tanzania.

☐ Jane gave the chimpanzees names.

Write a ✔ next to the event that happened **FIRST**.

☐ Jane made new discoveries about chimpanzees.

☐ The chimpanzees ran away from Jane.

How did Jane use her journal when she was **YOUNG**?

_____

_____

_____

Draw a picture of what you think a page of Jane's journal may have looked like when she was an **ADULT**.

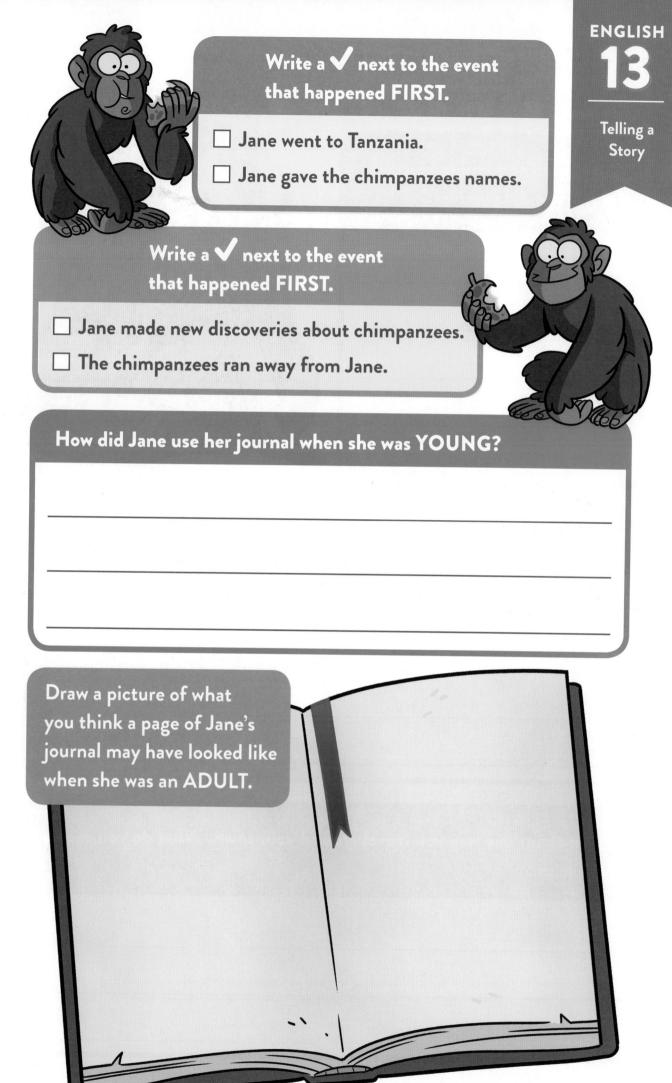

Jane Goodall kept a journal to record notes from her days with the chimpanzees. Write to record your own events and memories.

Write about something you did today. How did you feel?

_____

_____

_____

_____

Write about a place you like to go. How far away is it?

_____

_____

_____

_____

Write about one way you travel around your town. What do you see on your trips?

_____

_____

_____

Write about someone in your family. What do you do together?

_____

_____

_____

_____

Write about something you like to do. What is the best part?

_____

_____

_____

_____

Write about a time you saw a friend. What did you say?

_____

_____

_____

_____

A biography is a story about a person's life, written by someone else. An autobiography is written by an author about his or her own life.

Write and draw your autobiography. Use the events and memories on pages 356–357 to help you.

MY AUTOBIOGRAPHY

Written by: _____

_____

_____

_____

_____

_____

_____

_____

_____

_____

_____

_____

There are many digital tools available to share your writing—computers, tablets, phones, and more. Ask an adult to help you share your story with a friend or family member who is far away.

LET'S START! GATHER THESE TOOLS AND MATERIALS.

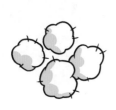
Cotton balls

String

Glue

Pencil

Paper

3 paper bags

Hole punch

Scissors
(with an adult's help)

Old magazines

LET'S TINKER!

When Jane Goodall was young, she wrote notes and drew sketches of the animals she saw around her home. **Use** your materials to make pictures of the animals you see around your home. Do any live inside? Which ones do you see outside? Are there any you wish could live inside with you?

LET'S MAKE: POCKET JOURNAL!

1. Fold the bottom of 3 paper bags over, and glue each in place.

2. Then **fold** each of the 3 bags in half.

3. Take one bag and punch 2 holes along the fold.

4. **Use** that bag as a guide to mark the other 2 bags in the same place with a pencil. Then **punch** holes in both of them.

5. With the help of an adult, **cut** a 2-foot piece of string. **Stack** the 3 folded bags so that all the holes line up, like a book. **Wrap** the string through the holes many times and tie it in the back.

6. Now you can **write** in your journal, and store things in the pockets!

LET'S ENGINEER!

Brian likes to write in a journal like Jane Goodall. He uses it to jot down memories and stories about his life. Today he wants to add some pictures to his journal, but he only has scissors and glue.

How can he make pictures that help him tell his stories?

Choose a story that you want to tell. **Use** the materials to make a collage that tells the story! **Cut** and glue pictures from magazines, newspapers, or photographs. How can you show what you did? And what you said? And how you felt?

PROJECT 13: DONE!
Get your sticker!

Writing Informational Texts

Read the instructions aloud.

How to Tie Your Shoes

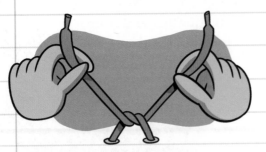

First, cross your laces.

Next, make two big loops.

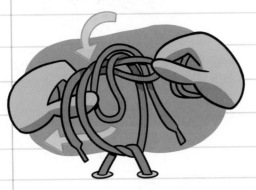

Then, cross the loops and tuck one under the other.

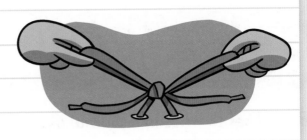

Last, pull the loops tight!

Circle the step that comes first.

What do you think would happen if you skipped this step?

_____

_____

_____

Circle the step that comes last.

What do you think would happen if you skipped this step?

_____

_____

_____

Are there any steps that you think could be skipped? Why or why not?

_____

_____

Read the instructions again. Can you
follow the steps to tie your own shoes?

Write and draw to fill in the missing steps in each set of instructions.

How to Make a Jelly Sandwich

First, get 2 pieces of bread, a jar of jelly, and a spoon.

Next, put a spoonful of jelly on a piece of bread and spread it.

Last, _____

_____

_____

_____

How to Brush Your Teeth

First, squeeze toothpaste onto your toothbrush.

Next, _____

_____

_____

Last, _____

_____

_____

Brainstorm topics that you are an expert on and could teach someone else how to do. Then write and draw them in the chart.

I am an expert on:

Choose one of the topics you are an expert on from page 365. Write your own instructions below. Add drawings to show details.

HOW TO _____

First, _____
_____

Next, _____
_____

Then, _____

_____

Last, _____

_____

Share your instructions with
a friend or family member and
follow the steps together!

LET'S START!

20 craft sticks

10 paper or plastic cups

LET'S TINKER!

Combine and stack your craft sticks and cups to see what you can build. **Share** your design with a friend or family member. **Tell** them the steps you took to build your design. Then **let** them have a turn to build. What steps did they take? **Talk** about your different designs.

LET'S MAKE: CRAFT STICK SNAPPER!

1. Stack 2 craft sticks to make a V shape.

2. Add another craft stick on top, in the middle.

3. Carefully **place** your fourth stick *on top* of the middle stick, but *under* the side sticks.

4. Wiggle the fifth stick *under* the middle stick, but *on top* of the side sticks. (The secret of the snapper is that the sticks are held together with tension—each stick pushes and pulls on the others. This can make it tricky to build your first time. Work with a friend or family member until you get the hang of building it yourself.)

5. Drop your snapper and watch it snap apart!

LET'S ENGINEER!

It's Tinker Town's annual Snapper Contest! Last year, Enid made a V-shaped snapper and won! Now, she must defend her trophy.

How can she build a new unique design for a snapper?

Experiment with the instructions above to design your own craft stick snapper. Can you make one with more sticks? What about fewer? Can you make one that is stronger? Or flies farther? Or one that snaps higher when it drops? What other materials can be added? **Write** or draw instructions for how to make your own snapper design.

PROJECT 14: DONE!
Get your sticker!

Writing Your Opinion

Opinions are someone's thoughts, feelings, or beliefs about something. They are not based on facts, and may not be true. Read each opinion essay aloud.

EMMA

I think that losing teeth is the best! I lost my first tooth yesterday at bedtime, and now I cannot wait to lose more teeth. It fell out while I was reading a book. One minute, I was wiggling it in my mouth, and the next minute, it was in my hand. I jumped out of bed to show my mom. My family was so happy—we had a tooth party! And soon, I'll get an even bigger adult tooth in the same spot.

ALEX

I think that losing teeth is gross. I have lost three teeth so far. All three have fallen out at school while I was eating apples at lunch! Everyone at my lunch table said, "Ew!"—even me. My teacher said I should bring bananas instead.

I do not like the feeling of loose teeth because they move around in my mouth. Also, wiggly teeth make it hard to eat. I hope it is a long time before I lose another tooth.

Circle the face that shows how each character felt about losing a tooth.

EMMA

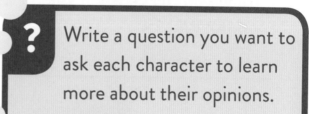

ALEX

? What reasons did the characters give to explain their opinions?

EMMA:

_____

_____

_____

_____

ALEX:

_____

_____

_____

_____

? Write a question you want to ask each character to learn more about their opinions.

EMMA:

_____

_____

_____

_____

ALEX:

_____

_____

_____

Write about and draw your own memories of losing teeth.

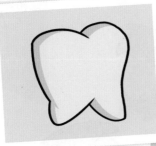

How old were you when
you lost your first tooth? _____

Where were you when it fell out? _____

If you haven't lost a tooth, how old do you
think you will be when you do lose your first
tooth? Why?

_____

_____

Draw a picture of what
happened when you lost
your most recent tooth.

(Or draw what you think
might happen.)

What do you do with your
teeth after they fall out?

(Or draw what you will do.)

_____

_____

How many teeth have you lost in all? _____

Research other people's opinions. Ask friends or family members the questions below and write their thoughts and opinions.

Name: _____

When did you lose your first tooth? _____

What was it like? _____

_____

How did you feel about it? _____

_____

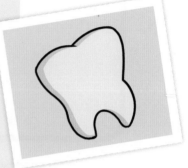

Name: _____

When did you lose your first tooth? _____

What was it like? _____

_____

How did you feel about it? _____

_____

Write about and draw how you feel about losing teeth.

I feel . . . _____

_____

Because . . . _____

_____

_____

Also . . . _____

_____

_____

Another reason I feel
this way is . . .

_____

_____

_____

Write your own opinion essay about losing teeth. Provide reasons for why you think and feel that way. Use the events and memories on page 374 to help you. Include a closing that sums up your opinion.

TITLE: _____

_____

_____

_____

_____

_____

_____

_____

_____

_____

_____

_____

_____

LET'S START!

4 clothespins

Markers

Glue

Construction paper

Scissors
(with an adult's help)

Apple

Knife
(with an adult's help)

Nut butter or honey

Mini marshmallows

White beans (dried)

LET'S TINKER!

Use markers to draw faces and teeth on 4 clothespins. You can also **add** cut paper with glue. Which is your favorite? Which is the funniest? Are any of them scary?

Talk about your opinions with a friend or family member. **Ask** what their opinions are.

LET'S MAKE: TOOTHY SNACK!

1. With the help of an adult, **cut** an apple into slices.

2. Spread nut butter (or honey) on the top of two slices.

3. Line up marshmallows on top of the nut butter on one of the apple slices.

4. Lay the other apple slice on top, with the nut butter facing down like glue.

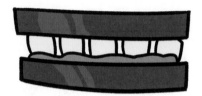

5. Follow the directions again to make another one to share!

LET'S ENGINEER!

Callie loves teeth. She likes chewing with them, counting them, and even losing them. But most of all, she likes getting new ones! Her mouth is always changing as teeth fall out and new ones come in. Callie wants to remember what her smile looks like right now.

How can she make a model of which teeth are in her mouth, and which are not?

Use your beans to make a model of the teeth in your mouth. How can you figure out how many teeth are in your mouth? How can you show which teeth are missing in your model? Can you show which are new larger adult teeth and which are still baby teeth?

PROJECT 15: DONE!
Get your sticker!

ANSWER KEY

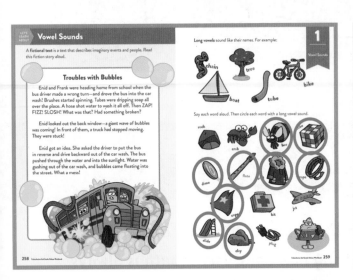

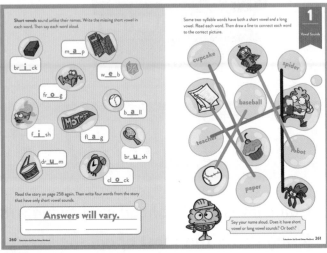

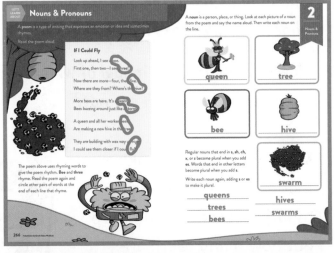

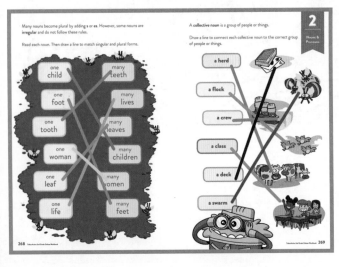

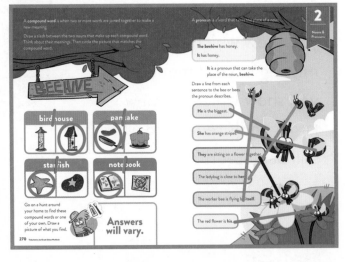

Verbs, Adverbs & Adjectives

3

Read the newspaper article aloud.

TINKER TOWN NEWS
NEW ICE CREAM SHOP IS COOL

Yesterday was an important day for MotMots everywhere. An ice cream shop opened in Tinker Town!

The new store has many flavors: vanilla, chocolate, mint, orange, and even blueberry! There was ice cream in every color. Are you thinking about toppings? There were lots of toppings, too, like sprinkles, cherries, and nuts!

We asked customers in line what they thought of the new store. "It's so COOL!" said one excited little ice cream fan. "I can't wait to come back tomorrow."

Verbs are action words that can tell what happened in the past, present, or future. Rewrite the verb in each sentence in the past tense.

Amelia **rides** to the store.
Amelia **rode** to the store.

Enid **sees** the sign!
Enid **saw** the sign!

Brian **feels** excited.
Brian **felt** excited.

Dimitri **sits** at a table.
Dimitri **sat** at a table.

Frank **gives** his order.
Frank **gave** his order.

Callie **eats** ice cream.
Callie **ate** ice cream.

An **adjective** is a word that describes a noun. Adjectives can describe color, shape, size, and more.

3

Write an adjective to describe each ice cream order.

| tall | colorful | red |
| tiny | chunky | round |

colorful
red
round
chunky
tiny
tall

Write your own adjective to describe each ice cream order.

Answers will vary.

An **adverb** is a word that describes a verb, an adjective, or another adverb. Adverbs usually follow a verb in a sentence and often tell when, where, or how something happened.

Circle the adverb that completes the phrase and describes each action.

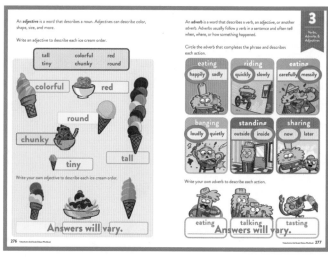

eating — happily / sadly
riding — quickly / slowly
eating — carefully / messily
banging — loudly / quietly
standing — outside / inside
sharing — now / later

Write your own adverb to describe each action.

eating   talking   tasting
Answers will vary.

Look at what each MotMot is thinking about. Then write what each one may be thinking. Use the adjectives from the word bank to add details.

3

| cold | fluffy | sweet |
| giant | chocolaty | |

Answers will vary.

Answers will vary.

Draw the ice cream you would order! Then write adjectives to describe it.

Answers will vary.

Answers will vary.

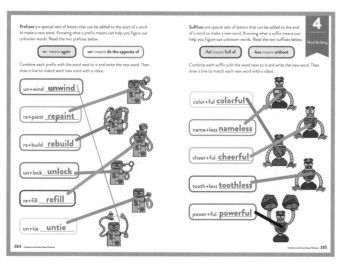

Word Building

4

A **science fiction** story is made up about a world where science plays a big part. There can be spaceships, time travel, or even creatures from other planets! Read the science fiction story aloud.

ROBOT EMERGENCY

Everything was running smoothly at the robot factory. Robot after robot came down the assembly line. So I didn't think that it was a big deal to go and grab a snack. (All I did was make some popcorn.) But when I returned, instead of a shiny row of metal robots, I saw a mess! It was a robot emergency!

On my right I saw a toothless robot. On my left I saw a headless robot. Robots were rolling out of the machine with missing parts—or parts in the wrong places! A robot stumbled by on a leg and an arm.

How fast could I stop this mess? And how would I ever undo it?

While I was frozen in place, a tall and powerful robot unlocked the control panel. He pressed a red button I had never seen before. POP! The robot machine made a loud noise. Then it started making robots even faster than before! Robots of all different shapes, sizes, and colors were shooting out.

I dropped my popcorn and ran for help as fast as I could. Could the robots ever be stopped? I needed backup!

Read the word that describes each robot. Then use stickers from page 389 to add the missing parts back on the robots.

The suffix **-less** means **without**.
Headless means **without a head**.

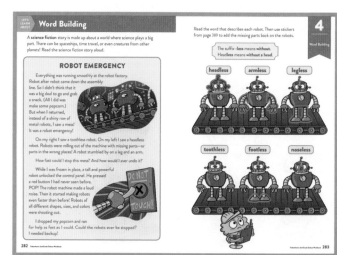

headless   armless   legless
toothless   footless   noseless

Prefixes are special sets of letters that can be added to the start of a word to make a new word. Knowing what a prefix means can help you figure out unknown words. Read the two prefixes below.

re- means **again**   **un-** means **do the opposite of**

Combine each prefix with the word next to it and write the new word. Then draw a line to match each new word with a robot.

un+wind **unwind**
re+paint **repaint**
re+build **rebuild**
un+lock **unlock**
re+fill **refill**
un+tie **untie**

Suffixes are special sets of letters that can be added to the end of a word to make a new word. Knowing what a suffix means can help you figure out unknown words. Read the two suffixes below.

-ful means **full of**   **-less** means **without**

Combine each suffix with the word next to it and write the new word. Then draw a line to match each new word with a robot.

color+ful **colorful**
name+less **nameless**
cheer+ful **cheerful**
tooth+less **toothless**
power+ful **powerful**

4

A **root word** is a word without any prefixes or suffixes. Underline each root word.

button / rebutton / unbutton / buttonless

repaint   toothless   unzip
powerful   undo   unbuild
colorful   joyful   relock
retie   footless   joyless

4

Read each word. Then draw a robot to match the description.

headless	joyful
Answers will vary.	**Answers will vary.**
unhappy	helpful
Answers will vary.	**Answers will vary.**

Word Sounds & Meanings

5

Free verse poems have no patterns or rules. They don't even have to rhyme.

Read the poem aloud.

Up, Up, Up!

I'm growing up, up, up.
I was in first grade,
And now I'm in second.
If you'd like to listen, I've learned a lot.
I can do a cartwheel.
Rolling.
Spinning.
Jumping.
And I can pack my own lunch.
Cleaning.
Cutting.
Counting.
I can even tie my shoes,
All by myself.
What will I be able to do next?
I'm growing up, up, up!

The poem "Up, Up, Up!" uses repeated lines and alliteration to give the poem rhythm.

A **repeated line** is when a phrase or line of the poem is used more than one time.

Write the repeated line from the poem on the previous page.

I'm growing up, up, up.

Alliteration is when the same beginning letter or sound is used in two or more words that are close together.

Read these phrases aloud. Underline the words that have alliteration.

If you'd like to listen, I've learned a lot.

And I can pack my own lunch.
Cleaning.
Cutting.
Counting.

Read the poem aloud.

I can do a cartwheel.
Rolling.
Spinning.
Jumping.

Draw a picture of Callie acting out each word.

| **Answers will vary.** | **Answers will vary.** | **Answers will vary.** |
| ROLLING | SPINNING | JUMPING |

Read each set of words and act them out. Then follow the directions.

walk / stomp / march   Circle the action that is the **loudest**.
look / peek / stare   Circle the action that takes the **longest**.
touch / tap / bang   Circle the action that is the **softest**.

5

Read the poem aloud.

And I can pack my own lunch.
Cleaning.
Cutting.
Counting.

Look at each picture closely. Draw a line connecting each word to the matching picture.

cleaning   cutting   counting

Write about and draw other actions that you can do to help make snacks or meals.

Answers will vary.

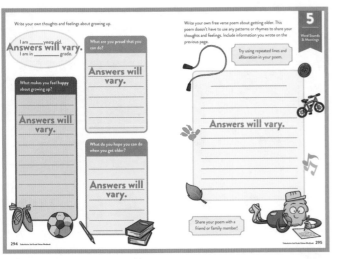

Write your own thoughts and feelings about growing up.

I am _____ years old.
Answers will vary.
I am in _____ grade.

What are you proud that you can do?
Answers will vary.

What makes you feel happy about growing up?
Answers will vary.

What do you hope you can do when you get older?
Answers will vary.

Write your own free verse poem about getting older. This poem doesn't have to use any patterns or rhymes to share your thoughts and feelings. Include information you wrote on the previous page.

Try using repeated lines and alliteration in your poem.

Answers will vary.

Share your poem with a friend or family member!

294   295

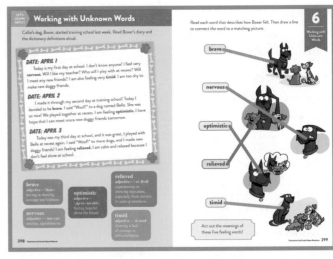

Working with Unknown Words

Callie's dog, Boxer, started training school last week. Read Boxer's diary and the dictionary definitions aloud.

DATE: APRIL 1
Today is my first day at school. I don't know anyone! I feel very **nervous**. Will I like my teacher? Who will I play with at recess? Will I meet any new friends? I am also feeling very **timid**. I am too shy to make new doggy friends.

DATE: APRIL 2
I made it through my second day at training school! Today I decided to be **brave**. I said "Woof!" to a dog named Bella. She was so nice! We played together at recess. I am feeling **optimistic**. I have hope that I can meet more new doggy friends tomorrow.

DATE: APRIL 3
Today was my third day at school, and it was great. I played with Bella at recess again. I said "Woof!" to more dogs, and I made new doggy friends! I am feeling **relieved**. I am calm and relaxed because I don't feel alone at school.

brave adjective – \brāv\ having or showing courage and boldness

optimistic adjective – \äp-tə-'mi-stik\ feeling hopeful about the future

nervous adjective – \'nər-vəs\ anxious, apprehensive

relieved adjective – \ri-'lēvd\ experiencing or showing relaxation, especially from anxiety or pent-up emotions

timid adjective – \'ti-məd\ showing a lack of courage or self-confidence

Read each word that describes how Boxer felt. Then draw a line to connect the word to a matching picture.

brave
nervous
optimistic
relieved
timid

Act out the meanings of these five feeling words!

298   299

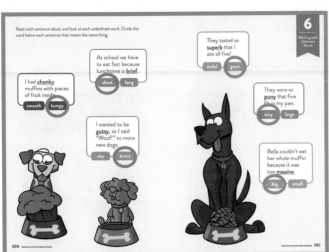

Read each sentence aloud, and look at each underlined word. Circle the word below each sentence that means the same thing.

I had **chunky** muffins with pieces of fruit inside.
smooth / (lumpy)

At school we have to eat fast because lunchtime is **brief**.
(short) / long

I wanted to be **gutsy**, so I said "Woof!" to more new dogs.
shy / (brave)

They tasted so **superb** that I ate all five!
awful / (great)

They were so **puny** that five fit in my paw.
(tiny) / large

Bella couldn't eat her whole muffin because it was too **massive**.
(big) / small

300   301

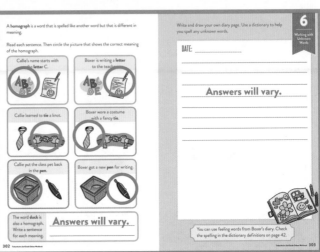

A **homograph** is a word that is spelled like another word but that is different in meaning.

Read each sentence. Then circle the picture that shows the correct meaning of the homograph.

Callie's name starts with the letter C.
Boxer is writing a **letter** to the teacher.

Callie learned to **tie** a knot.
Boxer wore a costume with a fancy **tie**.

Callie put the class pet back in the **pen**.
Boxer got a new **pen** for writing.

The word **duck** is also a homograph. Write a sentence for each meaning.
Answers will vary.

Write and draw your own diary page. Use a dictionary to help you spell any unknown words.

DATE: _____
Answers will vary.

You can use feeling words from Boxer's diary. Check the spelling in the dictionary definitions on page 42.

302   303

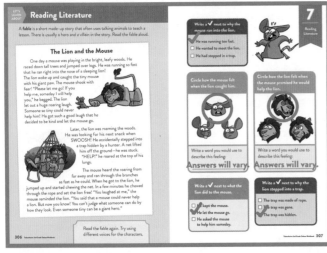

Reading Literature

A **fable** is a short made-up story that often uses talking animals to teach a lesson. There is usually a hero and a villain in the story. Read the fable aloud.

The Lion and the Mouse

One day a mouse was playing in the bright, leafy woods. He raced down tall trees and jumped over logs. He was running so fast that he ran right into the nose of a sleeping lion! The lion woke up and caught the tiny mouse with his giant paw. The mouse shook with fear! "Please let me go! If you help me, someday I will help you," he begged. The lion let out a huge roaring laugh. Someone so tiny could never help him! He got such a good laugh that he decided to be kind and let the mouse go.

Later, the lion was roaming the woods. He was looking for his next snack when SWOOSH! He accidentally stepped into a trap hidden by a hunter. A net lifted him off the ground—he was stuck. "HELP!" he roared at the top of his lungs.

The mouse heard the roaring from far away and ran through the branches as fast as he could. When he got to the lion, he jumped up and started chewing the net. In a few minutes he chewed through the rope and set the lion free! "You laughed at me," the mouse reminded the lion. "You said that a mouse could never help a lion. But now you know! You can't judge someone by how they look. Even someone tiny can be a giant hero."

Read the fable again. Try using different voices for the characters.

Write a ✔ next to why the mouse ran into the lion.
☐ He was running too fast.
☐ He wanted to meet the lion.
☐ He had stepped in a trap.

Circle how the mouse felt when the lion caught him.

Circle how the lion felt when the mouse promised he would help the lion.

Write a word you would use to describe this feeling:
Answers will vary.

Write a word you would use to describe this feeling:
Answers will vary.

Write a ✔ next to what the lion did to the mouse.
☐ He kept the mouse.
☐ He let the mouse go.
☐ He asked the mouse to help him someday.

Write a ✔ next to why the lion stepped into a trap.
☐ The trap was made of rope.
☐ The trap was gone.
☐ The trap was hidden.

306   307

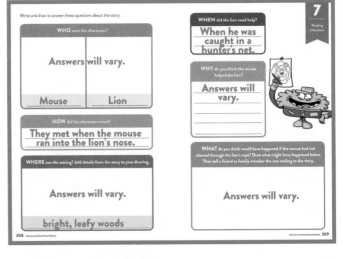

Write and draw to answer these questions about the story.

WHO were the characters?
Answers will vary.
Mouse / Lion

HOW did the characters meet?
They met when the mouse ran into the lion's nose.

WHERE was the setting? Add details from the story to your drawing.
Answers will vary.
bright, leafy woods

WHEN did the lion need help?
When he was caught in a hunter's net.

WHY do you think the mouse helped the lion?
Answers will vary.

WHAT do you think would have happened if the mouse had not chewed through the lion's rope? Draw what might have happened below. Then tell a friend or family member the new ending to the story.
Answers will vary.

308   309

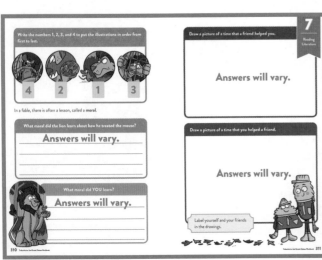

Write the numbers 1, 2, 3, and 4 to put the illustrations in order from first to last.
4   2   1   3

In a fable, there is often a lesson, called a **moral**.

What moral did the lion learn about how he treated the mouse?
Answers will vary.

What moral did YOU learn?
Answers will vary.

Draw a picture of a time that a friend helped you.
Answers will vary.

Draw a picture of a time that you helped a friend.
Answers will vary.

Label yourself and your friends in the drawings.

310   311

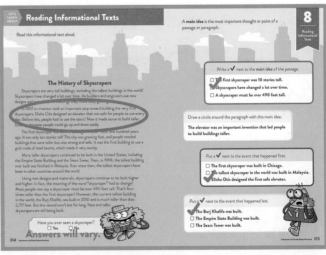

Reading Informational Texts

Read this informational text aloud.

The History of Skyscrapers

Skyscrapers are very tall buildings, including the tallest buildings in the world! Skyscrapers have changed a lot over time. As builders and engineers use new designs and materials, they make skyscrapers taller and safer.

In 1853 an inventor took an important step toward building the very first skyscraper. Elisha Otis designed an elevator that was safe for people to use every day. Before this, people had to use the stairs! Now it made sense to build taller buildings because people could go up and down easily.

The first skyscraper was built in Chicago about one hundred years ago. It was only ten stories tall! The city was growing fast, and people needed buildings that were taller but also strong and safe. It was the first building to use a grid made of steel beams, which made it very sturdy.

Many taller skyscrapers continued to be built in the United States, including the Empire State Building and the Sears Tower. Then, in 1998, the tallest building ever built was finished in Malaysia. Ever since then, the tallest skyscrapers have been in other countries around the world.

Using new designs and materials, skyscrapers continue to be built higher and higher. In fact, the meaning of the word "skyscraper" had to change! Most people now say a skyscraper must be over 490 feet tall. That's four times taller than the first skyscraper! However, the current tallest building in the world, the Burj Khalifa, was built in 2010 and is much taller than that: 2,717 feet. But this record won't last for long. New and taller skyscrapers are still being built.

Have you ever seen a skyscraper?
☐ Yes ☐ No
Answers will vary.

A **main idea** is the most important thought or point of a passage or paragraph.

Write a ✔ next to the main idea of the passage.
☐ The first skyscraper was 10 stories tall.
☑ Skyscrapers have changed a lot over time.
☐ A skyscraper must be over 490 feet tall.

Draw a circle around the paragraph with this main idea:
The elevator was an important invention that led people to build buildings taller.

Put a ✔ next to the event that happened first.
☐ The first skyscraper was built in Chicago.
☐ The tallest skyscraper in the world was built in Malaysia.
☑ Elisha Otis designed the first safe elevator.

Put a ✔ next to the event that happened last.
☑ The Burj Khalifa was built.
☐ The Empire State Building was built.
☐ The Sears Tower was built.

314   315

Answer each question about "The History of Skyscrapers."

Who invented the first safe elevator? **Elisha Otis**

Why was this invention important? **People could go up and down buildings easily so people could build taller buildings.**

Where was the first skyscraper built? **Chicago**

When was it built? **1885**

What is the tallest building in the world right now? **the Burj Khalifa**

How tall is it? **2,717 feet**

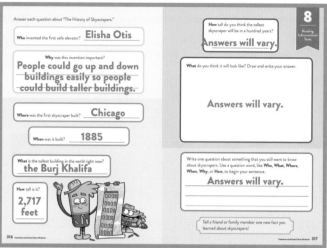

How tall do you think the tallest skyscraper will be in a hundred years? **Answers will vary.**

What do you think it will look like? Draw and write your answer. **Answers will vary.**

Write one question about something that you still want to know about skyscrapers. Use a question word, like Who, What, Where, When, Why, or How, to begin your sentence. **Answers will vary.**

Tell a friend or family member one new fact you learned about skyscrapers!

Informational texts can share information by using pictures, charts, diagrams, and more. A **timeline** is a chart that shows the order in which events occured. It often includes dates to tell when each event happened.

SKYSCRAPER TIMELINE

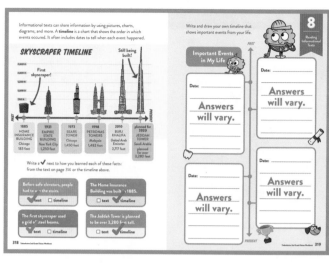

First skyscraper! / Still being built!

| 1885 HOME INSURANCE BUILDING Chicago 183 feet | 1921 EMPIRE STATE BUILDING New York City 1,250 feet | 1973 SEARS TOWER Chicago 1,450 feet | 1998 PETRONAS TOWERS Malaysia 1,483 feet | 2010 BURJ KHALIFA United Arab Emirates 2,717 feet | planned for 2020 JEDDAH TOWER Saudi Arabia planned for over 3,280 feet |

Write a ✔ next to how you learned each of these facts: from the text on page 314 or the timeline above.

Before safe elevators, people had to use the stairs. ✔ text ☐ timeline

The Home Insurance Building was built in 1885. ☐ text ✔ timeline

The First skyscraper used a grid of steel beams. ✔ text ☐ timeline

The Jeddah Tower is planned to be over 3,280 feet tall. ☐ text ✔ timeline

Write and draw your own timeline that shows important events from your life.

Important Events in My Life

Date: **Answers will vary.**

Date: **Answers will vary.**

Date: **Answers will vary.**

Date: **Answers will vary.**

PAST / PRESENT

Comparing Texts

A **folktale** is a story that has been told over and over. There are often many versions of the same story. Read the two different versions of this folktale aloud.

The Monkey's Heart
A FOLKTALE FROM INDIA

Once upon a time, a monkey lived in a fig tree by a river. One day a hungry crocodile saw the monkey and thought he looked delicious. She wanted to eat his heart! She told her sneaky husband, and he said he'd get the monkey's heart. His wife was confused—the monkey lived in a tree, and the crocodiles lived in the river. How could the monkey be caught?

The next day the sneaky crocodile swam up to the tree and said to the monkey, "On the far side of the river there is a sweet mango tree. I can take you." The monkey liked mangoes, so he hopped on the crocodile's back. In the middle of the river the river started to sink. The crocodile snapped, "Sorry, monkey. There is no mango tree. My hungry wife wants to eat your heart!"

Now, the monkey was sneaky, too. "But monkeys don't keep their hearts inside! They would fall out when we climbed trees! I keep my heart in the fig tree," he said. The crocodile took the monkey back to the fig tree to get his heart. The monkey hopped back into the tree and let out a big laugh. "I fooled you, sneaky crocodile! What kind of animal doesn't have a heart inside?"

The Monkey and the Shark
A FOLKTALE FROM AFRICA

There once was a monkey who lived in an apple tree by the ocean. One day the monkey saw a shark in the water below, so he threw some sweet apples down for the shark to eat.

The shark ate the delicious apples. Then he said he'd like to give the monkey a gift, too. He offered the monkey a ride. So the monkey jumped down into the ocean onto the shark's back and went for a ride. In the middle of the trip, the shark said, "I'm sorry, but my king is very sick, so he sent me to get a monkey's heart to heal him."

The monkey was very worried. He thought quickly and said, "Oh dear. I left my heart back at the apple tree!" The shark was confused, so he took the monkey back to the tree. The monkey jumped back into his tree and ran away. No matter what the shark said, he would not come back!

Draw a line to connect each character and event to the correct folktale.

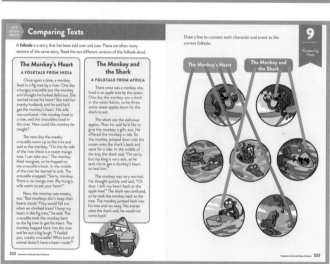

The Monkey's Heart / The Monkey and the Shark

Write and draw to compare these two folktales.

The Monkey's Heart

Draw the characters in this story. **Answers will vary.**

Draw the setting of this story. **Answers will vary.**

What is one way the endings are the same? Draw one similarity. **Answers will vary.**

How do you think the monkey reacted when the crocodile said, "My hungry wife wants to eat your heart?" Act it out.

The Monkey and the Shark

Draw the characters in this story. **Answers will vary.**

Draw the setting of this story. **Answers will vary.**

What is one way that the endings are different? Draw one difference. **Answers will vary.**

How do you think the monkey acted when the shark said, "I'm sorry, but my king is very sick, so he sent me to get a monkey's heart to heal him"? Act it out.

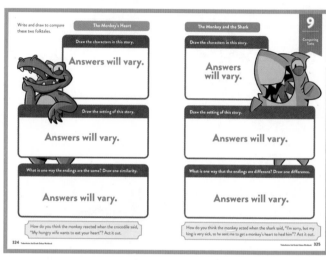

Answer each question.

How does the crocodile think he can outsmart the monkey? **Answers will vary.**

How does the shark think he can outsmart the monkey? **Answers will vary.**

How does the monkey outsmart both the shark *and* the crocodile? **Answers will vary.**

What lesson did the crocodile and the shark learn? **Answers will vary.**

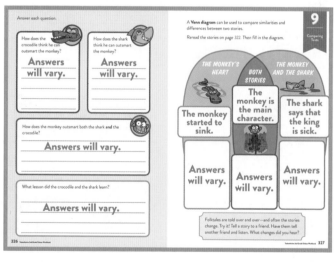

A **Venn diagram** can be used to compare similarities and differences between two stories.

Reread the stories on page 322. Then fill in the diagram.

THE MONKEY'S HEART / **BOTH STORIES** / **THE MONKEY AND THE SHARK**

The monkey is the main character.

The monkey started to sink.

The shark says that the king is sick.

Answers will vary. / **Answers will vary.** / **Answers will vary.**

Folktales are told over and over—and often the stories change. Try it! Tell a story to a friend. Have them tell another friend and listen. What changes did you hear?

Fluency

A **script** is the written form for a play, movie, or speech. It contains lines that each character will say and instructions about what the characters should do or act like.

Read the script aloud.

THE LOUD WHISTLE

Zoe is at the park. She is whistling a song. Max walks up to her.

Zoe: Hi, Max! Listen to me whistle!

Zoe puckers her lips and a loud whistle comes out.

Max: Wow! I wish I knew how to do that.

Zoe: I can teach you. First wet your lips. Then pucker them, as if you were making a kissing face. Then blow air through your lips.

Max wets his lips and tries to whistle, but he does not make a sound.

Max: Why isn't it working?

Zoe: I don't know. Try moving your tongue out of the way when you blow.

Max tries again. But he does not make a sound. Xavier walks up.

Max: I just can't whistle. Maybe my mouth isn't small enough. Maybe I'll never be able to whistle at all.

Xavier: Are you trying to whistle? I just learned how. Try this! When you blow air out through your lips, move your mouth and jaw into different positions until you hear a sound.

Max whistles. It's so loud that Zoe and Xavier have to cover their ears!

Max: It worked! Thank you! I'm going to show all my friends.

Max gets up to leave, but Zoe looks confused.

Zoe: What? I couldn't hear what you said. Maybe we should work on whistling quietly next.

Zoe, Max, and Xavier all laugh and whistle a song together.

Create your own ending to the play: What do you think will happen when Max goes to show his friends this new skill? What will Max say and do? What will his friends say and do?

Draw a picture to show what will happen. Then complete the script below.

Answers will vary.

Read the play aloud by yourself or with a partner. Try reading it using different voices for the characters.

Read each of the characters' thoughts aloud. Draw a line to connect each thought to the face with the matching emotion.

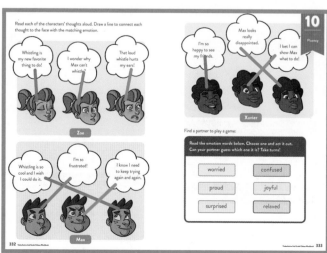

Whistling is my new favorite thing to do!

I wonder why Max can't whistle?

That loud whistle hurts my ears!

Zoe

I'm so happy to see my friends.

Max looks really disappointed.

I bet I can show Max what to do!

Xavier

Whistling is so cool and I wish I could do it.

I'm so frustrated!

I know I need to keep trying again and again.

Max

Find a partner to play a game.

Read the emotion words below. Choose one and act it out. Can your partner guess which one it is? Take turns!

worried / confused / proud / joyful / surprised / relaxed

Write the numbers 1, 2, 3, 4, 5, and 6 to put these events from the play in order from first to last. Then point at each picture in order and retell what happened in the play.

5 / 1 / 4 / 2 / 3

Read the play *The Loud Whistle* again. Think about how Zoe and Xavier tried to teach Max to whistle.

Write about and draw **how** you would teach Max to whistle. (If you can't whistle yet, write about and draw another skill you can teach.)

Answers will vary.

Share your writing with a friend or family member so someone else can learn, too!

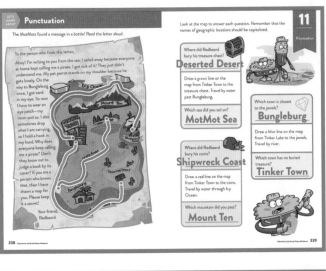

Punctuation — 11

The MotMots found a message in a bottle! Read the letter aloud.

To the person who finds this letter,

Ahoy! I'm writing to you from the sea. I sailed away because everyone at home kept calling me a pirate. I got sick of it! They just didn't understand me. My pet parrot stands on my shoulder because he gets lonely. On the way to Bungleburg once, I got sand in my eye. So now I have to wear an eye patch—my mom said so. I also sometimes drop what I am carrying, so I hold a hook in my hand. Why does everyone keep calling me a pirate? Don't they know not to judge a book by its cover? If you are a person who knows that, then I have drawn a map for you. Please keep it a secret!

Your friend,
Redbeard

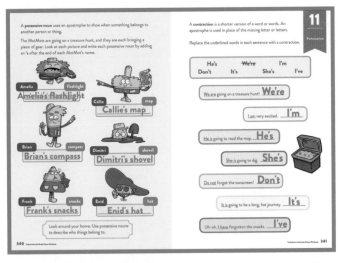

Look at the map to answer each question. Remember that the names of geographic locations should be capitalized. — 11 Punctuation

Where did Redbeard bury his treasure chest? **Deserted Desert**

Draw a green line on the map from Tinker Town to the treasure chest. Travel by water past Bungleburg.

Which sea did you sail on? **MotMot Sea**

Which town is closest to the jewels? **Bungleburg**

Draw a blue line on the map from Tinker Lake to the jewels. Travel by river.

Where did Redbeard bury his coins? **Shipwreck Coast**

Which town has no buried treasure? **Tinker Town**

Draw a red line on the map from Tinker Town to the coins. Travel by water through Icy Ocean.

Which mountain did you pass? **Mount Ten**

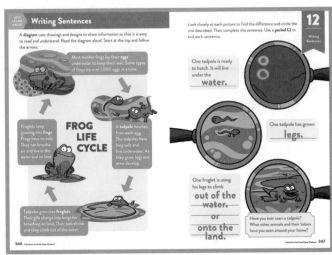

A **possessive noun** uses an apostrophe to show when something belongs to another person or thing. — 11

The MotMots are going on a treasure hunt, and they are each bringing a piece of gear. Look at each picture and write each possessive noun by adding an 's after the end of each MotMot's name.

Amelia / flashlight — **Amelia's flashlight**
Callie / map — **Callie's map**
Brian / compass — **Brian's compass**
Dimitri / shovel — **Dimitri's shovel**
Frank / snacks — **Frank's snacks**
Enid / hat — **Enid's hat**

Look around your home. Use possessive nouns to describe who things belong to.

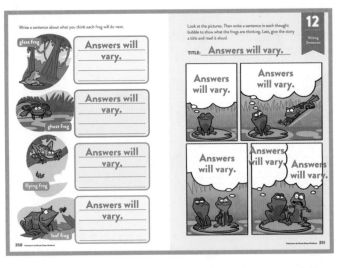

A **contraction** is a shorter version of a word or words. An apostrophe is used in place of the missing letter or letters. — 11 Punctuation

Replace the underlined words in each sentence with a contraction.

He's   We're   I'm   Don't   It's   She's   I've

We are going on a treasure hunt! **We're**
I am very excited. **I'm**
He is going to read the map. **He's**
She is going to dig. **She's**
Do not forget the sunscreen! **Don't**
It is going to be a long, hot journey. **It's**
Uh-oh. I have forgotten the snacks. **I've**

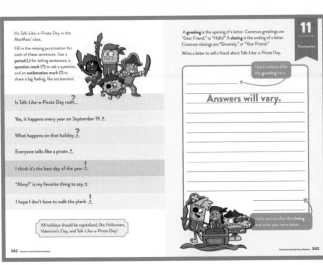

It's Talk-Like-a-Pirate Day in the MotMots' class.

Fill in the missing punctuation for each of these sentences. Use a period (.) for telling sentences, a question mark (?) to ask a question, and an exclamation mark (!) to share a big feeling, like excitement.

Is Talk-Like-a-Pirate Day real?
Yes, it happens every year on September 19.
What happens on that holiday?
Everyone talks like a pirate.
I think it's the best day of the year!
"Ahoy!" is my favorite thing to say.
I hope I don't have to walk the plank!

All holidays should be capitalized, like Halloween, Valentine's Day, and Talk-Like-a-Pirate Day!

A **greeting** is the opening of a letter. Common greetings are "Dear Friend," or "Hello!" A **closing** is the ending of a letter. Common closings are "Sincerely," or "Your Friend." — 11 Punctuation

Write a letter to tell a friend about Talk-Like-a-Pirate Day.

Use a comma after the greeting here.

Answers will vary.

Use a comma after the closing and write your name below.

Writing Sentences — 12

A **diagram** uses drawings and designs to share information so that it is easy to read and understand. Read the diagram aloud. Start at the top and follow the arrows.

Most mother frogs lay their **eggs** underwater to keep them wet. Some types of frogs lay over 1,000 eggs at a time.

A **tadpole** hatches from each egg. The tadpoles have long tails and live underwater. As they grow, legs and arms develop.

Tadpoles grow into **froglets**. Their gills change into lungs for breathing on land. Their tails shrink and they climb out of the water.

Froglets keep growing into **frogs**. Frogs have no tails. They can breathe air and live in the water and on land.

FROG LIFE CYCLE

Look closely at each picture to find the difference and circle the one described. Then complete the sentence. Use a **period (.)** to end each sentence. — 12 Writing Sentences

One tadpole is ready to hatch. It will live under the **water.**
One tadpole has grown **legs.**
One froglet is using his legs to climb **out of the water.** or **onto the land.**

Have you ever seen a tadpole? What other animals and their babies have you seen around your home?

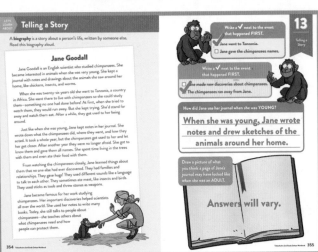

Look at each picture and write a sentence about what you observe. Use a capital letter to begin each sentence, and end each sentence with the correct punctuation.

Answers will vary. (×4)

Read each set of facts. Write one compound sentence that includes both facts. Use a comma and a conjunction word, like and, but, or so. — 12 Writing Sentences

FACTS: Most frogs are carnivorous. They eat other small animals.
Most frogs are carnivorous, so they eat other animals.

FACTS: Frogs get water through their skin. They do not drink water.
Frogs get water through their skin, so they do not drink water.

FACTS: Some types of frogs live in trees. Others live underground.
Some types of frogs live in trees, but others live underground.

Read this compound sentence. Then write the two facts as separate sentences.
Frogs do not have ears that you can see, but they can hear well.
Frogs do not have ears that you can see. They can hear well.

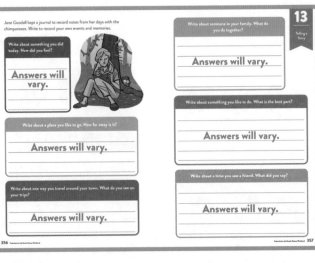

Write a sentence about what you think each frog will do next.

glass frog — **Answers will vary.**
ghost frog — **Answers will vary.**
flying frog — **Answers will vary.**
leaf frog — **Answers will vary.**

Look at the pictures. Then write a sentence in each thought bubble to show what the frogs are thinking. Last, give the story a title and read it aloud. — 12 Writing Sentences

TITLE: **Answers will vary.**

Answers will vary. (×4)

Telling a Story — 13

A **biography** is a story about a person's life, written by someone else. Read this biography aloud.

Jane Goodall

Jane Goodall is an English scientist who studied chimpanzees. She became interested in animals when she was very young. She kept a journal with notes and drawings about the animals she saw around her home, like chickens, insects, and worms.

When she was twenty-six years old she went to Tanzania, a country in Africa. She went there to live with chimpanzees so she could study them—something no one had done before! At first, when she tried to watch them, they would run away. But she kept trying. She'd stand far away and watch them eat. After a while, they got used to her being around.

Just like when she was young, Jane kept notes in her journal. She wrote down what the chimpanzees did, where they went, and how they acted. It took a whole year, but the chimpanzees got used to her and let her get closer. After another year they were no longer afraid. She got to know them and gave them all names. She spent time living in the trees with them and even ate their food with them.

From watching the chimpanzees closely, Jane learned things about them that no one else had ever discovered. They had families and relationships. They gave hugs! They used different sounds like a language to talk to each other. They sometimes ate meat, like insects and birds. They used sticks as tools and threw stones as weapons.

Jane became famous for her work studying chimpanzees. Her important discoveries helped scientists all over the world. She used her notes to write many books. Today, she still talks to people about chimpanzees—she teaches others about what chimpanzees need and how people can protect them.

Write a ✓ next to the event that happened FIRST. — 13 Telling a Story
✓ Jane went to Tanzania.
☐ Jane gave the chimpanzees names.

Write a ✓ next to the event that happened FIRST.
☐ Jane made new discoveries about chimpanzees.
✓ The chimpanzees ran away from Jane.

How did Jane use her journal when she was YOUNG?
When she was young, Jane wrote notes and drew sketches of the animals around her home.

Draw a picture of what you think a page of Jane's journal may have looked like when she was an ADULT.
Answers will vary.

Jane Goodall kept a journal to record notes from her days with the chimpanzees. Write to record your own events and memories.

Write about something you did today. How did you feel?
Answers will vary.

Write about a place you like to go. How far away is it?
Answers will vary.

Write about one way you travel around your town. What do you see on your trips?
Answers will vary.

Write about someone in your family. What do you do together? — 13 Telling a Story
Answers will vary.

Write about something you like to do. What is the best part?
Answers will vary.

Write about a time you saw a friend. What did you say?
Answers will vary.

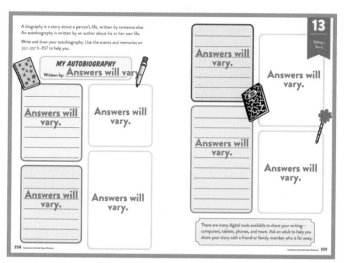

A biography is a story of a person's life, written by someone else. An autobiography is written by an author about his or her own life.

Write and draw your autobiography. Use the events and memories on 357-357 6–357 to help you.

MY AUTOBIOGRAPHY
Written by: Answers will vary.

Answers will vary.

Answers will vary.

Answers will vary.

Answers will vary.

Answers will vary.

Answers will vary.

Answers will vary.

Answers will vary.

Answers will vary.

There are many digital tools available to share your writing—computers, tablets, phones, and more. Ask an adult to help you share your story with a friend or family member who is far away.

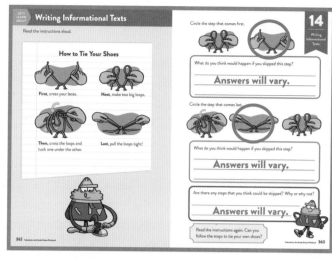

Writing Informational Texts

Read the instructions aloud.

How to Tie Your Shoes

First, cross your laces.

Next, make two big loops.

Then, cross the loops and tuck one under the other.

Last, pull the loops tight!

Circle the step that comes first.

What do you think would happen if you skipped this step?

Answers will vary.

Circle the step that comes last.

What do you think would happen if you skipped this step?

Answers will vary.

Are there any steps that you think could be skipped? Why or why not?

Answers will vary.

Read the instructions again. Can you follow the steps to tie your own shoes?

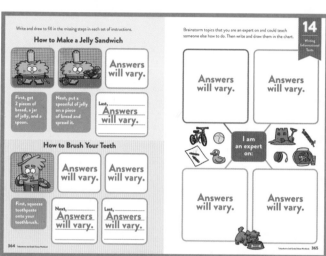

Write and draw to fill in the missing steps in each set of instructions.

How to Make a Jelly Sandwich

First, get 2 pieces of bread, a jar of jelly, and a spoon.

Next, put a spoonful of jelly on a piece of bread and spread it.

Answers will vary.

Last, Answers will vary.

How to Brush Your Teeth

First, squeeze toothpaste onto your toothbrush.

Answers will vary.

Answers will vary.

Next, Answers will vary.

Last, Answers will vary.

Brainstorm topics that you are an expert on and could teach someone else how to do. Then write and draw them in the chart.

Answers will vary.

Answers will vary.

I am an expert on:

Answers will vary.

Answers will vary.

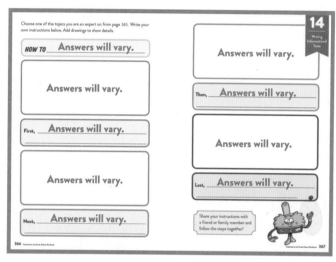

Choose one of the topics you are an expert on from page 365. Write your own instructions below. Add drawings to show details.

HOW TO Answers will vary.

First, Answers will vary.

Next, Answers will vary.

Then, Answers will vary.

Answers will vary.

Last, Answers will vary.

Share your instructions with a friend or family member and follow the steps together!

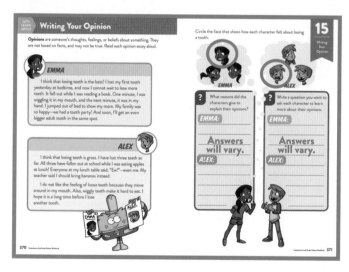

Writing Your Opinion

Opinions are someone's thoughts, feelings, or beliefs about something. They are not based on facts, and may not be true. Read each opinion essay aloud.

EMMA

I think that losing teeth is the best! I lost my first tooth yesterday at bedtime, and now I cannot wait to lose more teeth. It fell out while I was reading a book. One minute, I was wiggling it in my mouth, and the next minute, it was in my hand. I jumped out of bed to show my mom. My family was so happy—we had a tooth party! And soon, I'll get an even bigger adult tooth in the same spot.

ALEX

I think that losing teeth is gross. I have lost three teeth so far. All three have fallen out at school while I was eating apples at lunch! Everyone at my lunch table said, "Ew!"—even me. My teacher said I should bring bananas instead.

I do not like the feeling of loose teeth because they move around in my mouth. Also, wiggly teeth make it hard to eat. I hope it is a long time before I lose another tooth.

Circle the face that shows how each character felt about losing a tooth.

EMMA

ALEX

What reasons did the characters give to explain their opinions?

EMMA:
Answers will vary.
ALEX:
Answers will vary.

Write a question you want to ask each character to learn more about their opinions.

EMMA:
Answers will vary.
ALEX:
Answers will vary.

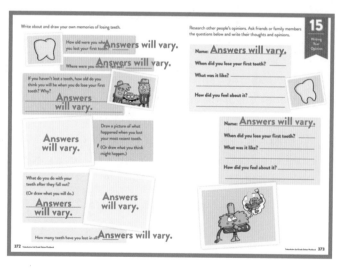

Write about and draw your own memories of losing teeth.

How old were you when you lost your first tooth? Answers will vary.

Where were you? Answers will vary.

If you haven't lost a tooth, how old do you think you will be when you lose your first tooth? Why? Answers will vary.

Answers will vary.

Draw a picture of what happened when you lost your most recent tooth. (Or draw what you think might happen.)

What do you do with your teeth after they fall out? (Or draw what you will do.) Answers will vary.

How many teeth have you lost in all? Answers will vary.

Research other people's opinions. Ask friends or family members the questions below and write their thoughts and opinions.

Name: Answers will vary.

When did you lose your first tooth?

What was it like?

How did you feel about it?

Name: Answers will vary.

When did you lose your first tooth?

What was it like?

How did you feel about it?

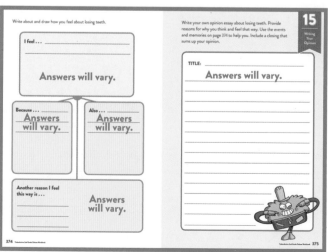

Write about and draw how you feel about losing teeth.

I feel . . .
Answers will vary.

Because . . .
Answers will vary.

Also . . .
Answers will vary.

Another reason I feel this way is . . .
Answers will vary.

Write your own opinion essay about losing teeth. Provide reasons for why you think and feel that way. Use the events and memories on page 374 to help you. Include a closing that sums up your opinion.

TITLE:
Answers will vary.

Odd Dot
120 Broadway
New York, NY 10271
OddDot.com

ISBN: 978-1-250-76055-5

WRITERS   Enil Sidat and Megan Butler

ILLUSTRATORS   Les McClaine, Tae Won Yu, and Chad Thomas

EDUCATIONAL CONSULTANT   Lindsay Frevert

CHARACTER DESIGNER   Anna-Maria Jung

COVER ILLUSTRATOR   Anna-Maria Jung

BACK COVER ILLUSTRATOR   Chad Thomas

INTERIOR DESIGNER   Tae Won Yu, Colleen AF Venable, and Tim Hall

COVER DESIGNERS   Carolyn Bahar, Colleen AF Venable, and Tae Won Yu

EDITOR   Daniel Nayeri and Nathalie Le Du

DISCLAIMER
The publisher and authors disclaim responsibility for any loss, injury, or damages that may result from a reader engaging in the activities described in this book.

TinkerActive is a trademark of Odd Dot
Printed in China by Hung Hing Off-set Printing Co. Ltd., Heshan City, Guangdong Province
First edition, 2020

10 9 8 7 6 5 4 3 2 1